D1175701

How to Marry Super Rich

Beloved Infidel

The Rest of the Story

College of One

Confessions of a Hollywood Columnist

The Garden of Allah

A State of Heat

How to Marry Super Rich: Or Love, Money and the Morning After

SHEILAH GRAHAM

Grosset & Dunlap

PUBLISHERS
NEW YORK

Foreword

No MATTER what they say, girls—and about 25 percent of the boys—want to marry rich. Girls are brainwashed in the nursery. Boys who are lazy dream of being supported through life by a rich woman, regardless of her looks or temperament. They may change their minds when they observe the hell of a loveless rich marriage, although as Madame Jolie Gabor told her three daughters, "It's just as easy for a woman to love a rich man as a poor one—easier." Frank Perry, the well-known film director, was sixteen when his grandfather asked him, "Would you like to marry a rich girl?" "I guess so," replied Frank. "Here's how you do it," said Grandpa. "Don't date poor girls."

What does a woman—or a man—have that others do not, to close the deal? You can sleep with a man for twenty years and you are lucky to get the bus fare. If you dig in a coal mine you are likely to come up with coal. If you go to Coney Island you get a Nathan's hot dog. You must go where the rich are—Palm Beach, Newport, Dallas, St. Moritz, Marbella, Cannes, or Kuwait —if you can stand the smell of oil. A tip. Those aging oil kids prefer young blondes.

Don't go on a cruise. A boat used to be a hunting ground

for women on the prowl. Today there are too many females on boats looking for a rich husband. But for a man, searching for a rich lady to wed and support him, an ocean liner can be a gateway to Paradise.

It is easier today to pin down a millionaire. There are more of them of both sexes. And if you are not compatible it doesn't have to last forever. In this casual age a divorce is easy to obtain, plus a seven-figure settlement. Is the risk worth the gamble? Does the end justify the means? Immoral? Amoral? It can't be. Look at the charming ladies and lads who have achieved the dream—to marry rich.

The following chapters will explain how certain notable and respected ladies and gentlemen made it to the top of the financial tree, by cleverness, cunning, and charm. Go thou and do likewise.

Contents

List of Illustrations

1. *A Worldly Woman —*
Dru Mallory Heinz

"I'M HAVING a few people in for cocktails this evening. Can you come?"

"I can't, I'm not dressed and I have a ghastly toothache," replied Dru Mallory from the studio couch in her New York apartment. The red-haired beauty had recently abandoned a small career in Hollywood films (1945–1951) for New York City, where she believed she would have a better chance to fulfill her destiny as the greatest hostess in the world. For that, it might be necessary to marry a rich man.

The telephone caller gave good parties. She always had several unattached wealthy men around. "All right, I'll come," said Dru, who in truth did not need much persuading. Parties and giving parties had always been her passion, although in her early days as a hostess the guests had brought their own food and liquor. She had called them "picnics" to remove possible embarrassment.

At the cocktail party in New York, Dru Mallory, not too successful in films and on the fringe of Los Angeles–Pasadena society, a woman who never discussed her origins, met multi-millionaire Henry (Jack) Heinz II, the "57 Varieties" man.

Handsome Jack had recently been divorced by his second wife. He was footloose and fancy-free, and he fancied the lovely creature who was smiling so confidently at him. It was as though she swallowed millionaires for breakfast, lunch, and dinner. There was no conversational fumbling, no shyness, and at the same time, no aggressive assault on one of the nicest, richest, unchained bachelors in the U.S.A.

Dru was a widow at the time, but she was not wearing weeds. She was clothed in her one expensive cocktail dress—you never know whom you will find across a crowded room. Her only jewelry, a string of simulated pearls. On Dru they looked real.

"Haven't I met you somewhere before?" said Jack, taking in the flaming hair, creamy complexion, exquisite figure, and full, ripe beauty. It sounded like the usual opening line, but they *had* met, she told him, in South Africa, several years before her Hollywood gamble, when she was still married to Dale Maher, who worked at the U.S. embassy in Cape Town.

"Of course," cried Mr. Heinz gallantly. He had always been noted for the charm that concealed the fib. How could he have forgotten such a gorgeous creature? But he had. She was one of many lovely ladies he met continually at the embassy parties and such around the world.

"Will you have lunch with me?" asked Jack, who was used to being courted by the female sex. But this girl didn't seem to care. "Let's see," her beautiful brow wrinkling, trying to remember. "I have a date for tomorrow and the next day. But"—brightening—"the day after will be fine."

Several lunches and dinners later, she told Jack she had a rather pressing date in France—"to marry a Frenchman." He was a count and they had known each other for some time. He had telephoned asking her to come to Paris and marry him. She wasn't sure, but she left soon after for France.

It was true, Dru's friends told Jack. The marriage to the count had been expected. This, of course, made Jack realize at once that he was in love with Dru, and forty million Frenchmen would not take her from him—not a count, or a king, for that matter. Besides, in his world of money, he was regarded as royalty.

Jack followed Dru to Paris. When he asked her to marry him and return to New York, she took the proposal calmly. She smiled when he said, "I've always had a crush on you." They were married in August, 1953.

Dru told him as much about her life as she thought would interest him. There were some things she would not discuss. She didn't talk much about Hollywood, although that part of her life was well known, and she did not have to insist she was Irish because her ancestry was written all over her lovely wild Irish face. She resembled Greer Garson when she first came to Hollywood.

An early newspaper profile of Dru gives her name as the former Drue English, born in Norfolk, England, with four centuries of Irish heritage. But the third Mrs. Heinz never talks about her family. She might have grown on a bush for all anyone knows about her beginnings. As for the years in Hollywood, Mr. Heinz discourages interviewers who ask questions on the subject. Neither of them is ashamed of it, but it is the past. They would both rather talk about the present and the future.

I met Dru a few times in Hollywood, both of us sitting on bar stools in Romanoff's or at the homes of mutual friends. She lived in a crummy old Spanish house on Schuyler Road, above the Strip. Her early Spanish bathtub was huge, reminding one of the Roman receptacles in the British Museum. The decor was on the very bright side. Lots of purple. The living room looked like a well-kept bordello. But don't get me or Dru wrong. She has always been what we call respectable. There was a balcony off her bedroom on which she spent a great deal of her time, listening to the night sounds—the birds, the crickets, and the distant traffic. The balcony was her favorite rendezvous for romance. She loved to lie on her back looking at the sky. She was fey and unexpected. At the house of a friend I saw her lie down suddenly on the carpet, look up, and exclaim, "Isn't this ceiling wonderful!" She remained on the floor for several minutes while the guests and conversation swirled around her.

She was a striking-looking woman—and still is—with the instinct of all great hostesses for running an interesting salon. She could bring all kinds of fascinating people together on a collision course, which made for excitement. She broke the monotony of the Beverly Hills parties.

As a rule there were more men than women in the Mallory living room. But she always paid more attention to her women guests. Smart. Women, especially in America, can make or break you socially. Her sights were set on the successful in all areas, with a special fondness for authors. Budd Schulberg was a constant visitor. She would have liked Hemingway, but he did not go to parties.

Dru's very British accent was a handicap for her film career—that and also the fact that she was too spontaneous in real life to be a good actress for the screen. She gave her performances in the living room, which made her popular with people, but not with the camera, which limited her acting career. In between the parties she managed to obtain small parts in a few films. There was nothing much in the columns or trade papers about her roles—she never took them too seriously—but there was a great deal about the parties she gave and those to which she was invited.

Dru, described recently by a former boyfriend as a "swinging kid," always added something to a group. She was amusing and natural, drank very little—she did not need alcohol to be the life of every gathering. It was all done effortlessly. She never carried her portfolio. You couldn't see or hear the effort, as you don't when watching a great dancer.

In Hollywood, Dru rarely talked about Mr. Maher from whom I assume she derived her professional name of Mallory—or perhaps it was a family name. I wouldn't have the nerve to ask her. You only knew that he was in the U.S. foreign service. His existence in her circles was shadowy, and you didn't ask questions because she obviously did not want to talk about him.

There were rumors of a romance with hotel billionaire Conrad Hilton. "At her annual Thanksgiving party I always had the feeling I was eating Connie's turkey," said the same male friend. Hilton and Dru were seen together at various restaurants and functions, but he was not a visible visitor to Schuyler Road. I'm sure that if he had bought the house for her, as gossiped, it would have been a mansion on a grander scale.

There was also talk of an exciting romance with one of the rich Rowan brothers of Pasadena. But Dru has always been an independent person and I doubt whether she would accept many favors from a man unless she was married to him. She merely adored entertaining and making people happy, at first on a thin financial scale, but since her marriage to Jack Heinz, grandiose is a pale word to describe her soirees and the people who come to them.

In England they are members of what a disgruntled non-invitee described as the "Snowdrop set." Lord Snowdon and his wife, Princess Margaret, are among the Heinz's closest friends. The Heinzes were invited to the royal wedding in May, 1960. A month later Jack donated £70,000 to London's Tate Gallery. In December of the same year they sponsored the Spoleto Festival Ball for the third time. The Snowdons attend most of the Heinz parties, no matter where, how, or when. In 1970, at the annual Heinz summer party following the fashionable Ascot races, Snowdon was reported in the British columns as having splashed wine over the queen's horse trainer, the late Peter Cazalet.

According to the stories circulated widely in print and the fashionable drawing rooms, Tony tried to cut in on the then sixty-four-year-old Cazalet, who was dancing with the chic Countess of Westmorland. Peter reportedly said coldly, "This is not America." Whereupon the queen's brother-in-law tossed a glassful of chablis in his face. The British, as you know, are *so* imperturbable, and Cazalet and the countess continued to dance.

When they came level again with Snowdon he hurled the contents of another glass—red wine this time. Cazalet's son Victor obliquely confirmed the rumors to the reporters, stating, "My father behaved like a perfect gentleman." No comment from Tony from Kensington Palace.

It is rather significant that although invited by the Heinzes to the same event in 1971, this time held in the London Zoo, the Snowdons did not attend. It was decided it would be safer for them to be in Scotland, where hastily scrambled duty had called the princess.

The triplex penthouse at Fifty-second Street near the East River, bought from Henry and Clare Luce in 1959, has been the setting for many Heinz parties. Dru could not wait for the reconstruction and refurbishing to be finished, and in December of that year she tossed one of her more bizarre soirees. Important guests arrived to find scaffolding and paint cans all over the place and to be greeted by two monkeys, one dressed as a builder, the other as a house painter.

A recent big party on Fifty-second Street was in honor of their chum Lady Hartwell, previously known as Lady Pamela Berry, whose husband, Michael, owns the most prosperous newspaper in England, the *Daily Telegraph*. Pam is the daughter of the first Earl of Birkenhead, the famous British barrister. So you can see that her credentials are in order.

Dru considered the party so socially important that she lost weight for the event, causing society reporter Suzy to write that Dru Heinz had been absolutely lissome lately, and for the occasion was wearing Ungaro's "most beautiful black creation, nipped in at the waist and pleated from the thighs down." You have to be thin for pleats from the thigh down, otherwise the rear end stretches for miles. Lady Pam was aware of the preparations in her honor and came to the party—to quote Suzy again—"all in navy blue moiré, with a green moiré pleated ruffle running down the front and around the hem."

Other high-ranking guests included Lady Jean Rankin, daughter of the Scottish Earl of Stair (she is also lady-in-waiting to Queen Elizabeth); the Countess of Dudley; Lady Victoria Percy, daughter of the Duke and Duchess of Northumberland; the Earl of Snowdon; and such high-placed commoners as Mrs. David Bruce (her husband is the former American ambassador to the Court of Saint James), Mrs. Vincent Astor ("trimmed in feathers"); the Arthur Schlesingers, Jr.; Lee Radziwill; and Alan J. Lerner.

Parties, parties. A small party (only seventy-five guests) in June, 1959, at their house in Hayes Place off Berkeley Square in London: cocktails in the courtyard followed by dinner inside, and back to the courtyard for dancing till dawn. A sample of the hoity-toity guest list: the Duke and Duchess of Sutherland, the Duke and Duchess of Bedford, the Duke and Duchess of Argyll, Sir Charles Clore, John Profumo—before the Christine Keeler caper— the Marquess and Marchioness of Blandford—at that time Tina, once the wife of Ari Onassis and now Mrs. Stavros Niarchos—Lord and Lady Mancroft, Air Chief Marshall Sir William and Lady Elliot, Henrietta Tiarks, now the Marchioness of Tavistock, and, for a sprinkling of the arts, designer and photographer Cecil Beaton and designer Oliver

Messel. Actualy, Cecil and Oliver are almost as much British society as anyone else named. Theater designer Messel, is, as you may know, uncle to Queen Elizabeth's sister, Princess Margaret. Tony Armstrong Jones had not yet married Margaret; that was to come in May of the following year. Tony's date for the party was the Chinese actress Miss Jacqui Chan, whom he was courting at the time.

But Dru is not the only party-lover in the family. In 1959, a busy year for the Heinzes, Jack chartered a special train to convey 250 people from London to Wigan in Lancashire, to celebrate the opening of his new $18 million factory. The day trip set him back £5,000 for food and liquor and the morning newspapers for every guest. It's little touches like this that separate the charming millionaires from the gross ones.

In May of 1961, Jack brought the Pittsburgh Symphony Orchestra to London, hired a specially designed barge and was aboard while they gave concerts from the boat floating up and down the river Thames.

At the end of October '63, Mrs. Heinz, by this time known by her friends as Madcap Dru, decided to use picturesque Greenwich Village as the setting for an evening of fun. She led a large group of her own special four hundred to cram Le Bijou, the tiny French restaurant on West Fourth Street, and then marched them to Trude Heller's discothèque for a riotous session of the twist. (Le Bijou is no more, but Trude Heller's is still going strong in Florida.)

Most winters in the New York penthouse or in the London house, Dru has given a pajama party. All guests, male and female, wear pajamas—not the ordinary pajama of course; these come from Dior, Balmain, Givenchy, Yves St. Laurent, and so on. It is *de rigueur* for the ladies to arrive in fur coats over the pajamas, which they shed—not the pajamas, let me add hastily, the coats—as soon as the private elevator deposits them at the penthouse. The men cover the sleepwear with overcoats, removed when they enter.

In Sewickley, near Pittsburgh, Dru and Jack gave a party for millionaires only—how I would have liked to be at that one! Twenty millionaires arrived in their own planes—among them the Paul Mellons and the David Rockefellers. This was early in the marriage. Dru rarely goes to Pittsburgh now, and she is

missed. She was a shot in the arm for Pittsburgh society. Jack
still goes there, of course. The family multi-million-dollar business was founded in Pittsburgh by Jack's grandfather, the late
Henry John Heinz, who started with a pickling and preserving
corporation.

But on with the dance, and with Dru joy is never unconfined.
In June of 1968—Jack was then sixty—they gave a fancy dress
party for three hundred Ascot-goers. The American ambassador
to the Court of Saint James, Walter Annenberg and his wife,
known as Lively Lee, were there, also the Bedfords, the Duke
of Marlborough, the Duke and Duchess of Devonshire, billionaire Paul Getty, Margaret, Duchess of Argyll, Princess Joan Aly
Khan, and the Maharaja and Maharani of Jaipur.

Dru has not yet given up hope that her husband will one
day be appointed American ambassador to the Court of Saint
James—she insists "London only." He probably will be. You
cannot evade Dru's positive approach to everything she wants
in life.

For the Heinz triple-A guest list only the very best food is
served—caviar, fresh Scotch salmon, roast beef, and so on, with
the best champagne and wines. Dru's personal eating tastes re-
flect her humble British beginnings—steak and kidney pudding,
Scotch broth, cheese. "Most of all I love lemon-curd tarts. We
can't get them in America, so for every cup of tea in England
I eat two lemon-curd tarts."

I could go on forever about the parties, but it would be unfair
to Dru and Jack to give the impression that the only thing they
do is give parties. They devote a great deal of time to philan-
thropy. Dru is interested in the arts. Her early claim to culture
was that as an art student in Paris she had met Matisse.

In 1957 Dru became a member of the Art Co-operative in
London for young unknown artists. She bought many paintings
from the group. But she also admires the famous artists and in
the same year paid $10,000 for a Chagall landscape and about
half that for each of two Boudins, plus a still life by Derain.
Which proves that Dru is also a good business lady. They are all
worth at least ten times as much today.

Long ago, in 1947, Jack gave 1,200,000 cans of Heinz products
as a Christmas present to British hospitals. The mammoth gift
was gratefully received. Britain was still suffering from shortages

of food caused by World War II. If legal in the United States, he might have been honored with a knighthood, which would make Jack a Sir and Dru a Lady Heinz.

During the war, a great deal of the Heinz factory output went into supplying canned, processed, and dehydrated foods for the U.S. military. In July, 1949, Jack received the French Legion of Honor medal for his work in international economic relations. In the same year the Foreign Traders Association gave him its annual award for outstanding service in furtherance of world peace. In 1952, Heinz was elected president of Community Chests and Councils of America.

From the beginning of the Spoleto Festivals in Italy, both Heinzes have given money, time, and super organization to support the cultural event—theater parties, balls, luncheons, dinners, film premieres. In 1967, Dru took over the entire theater of the *Hallelujah Baby* Broadway musical for a night, with its audience paying heavily for the privilege.

A small thing, but it highlights the thoughtfulness of Mr. Heinz toward his employees: everyone who worked for him, no matter where in the world, had time off for English afternoon tea. "Real tea," said Jack. "I will never use tea bags." This was some time ago, and I hear that the wretched but simpler tea bag has taken over.

Heinz Hall in Pittsburgh, built by Jack, is the setting for concerts, light opera, ballet, and plays. As a rich man he feels he should encourage culture. But he still finds time to personally select beautiful gowns, furs, and jewels for his wife.

As a rich woman, Dru (who started her adult life in a small apartment in a back street) now has six luxury homes to call her own. The New York penthouse overlooking the East River is decorated in bright greens and golds (no purples!), with the walls highlighted with expensive paintings, from early Florentine masterpieces to her latest Picasso acquisition. She has bought so many works of art since her marriage to Jack that recently she reluctantly sold some at the Parke-Bernet Galleries.

The house in Hay's Place in London is the ultimate in elegance and extravagance. It's the deluxe town house of them all. Just two bedrooms (one for the Italian couple who look after the house) and, for entertaining, a large living room—with, of course, the usual mod cons (modern conveniences), as they say in England. The frontage, which is badly painted in two colors, so the uninitiated will believe it belongs to poor folk, is only forty by thirty feet and is mainly garage, behind which is the flagstone courtyard, highlighted with tubs of blue hydrangeas. If Dru were to sell the house today with its antique furniture and paintings, she could get more than a million dollars for it. But she won't sell—unless it is to move one day to the American embassy's Winfield House in Regents Park—the lavish estate that was donated to the U.S. Government by Barbara Hutton.

There are also homes in Bermuda, Nassau, the south of France, and a stately British home, Binfield Lodge in Berkshire, some thirty miles from London. The Queen Anne house, circa 1690, has seventy-one acres, and features a lake, swimming pool, hard tennis court, apple orchards, and paddocks for the horses. There are twelve bedrooms, six bathrooms, five reception rooms. Binfield Lodge has its own lodge, with two cottages for the overflow of guests. Alas, I can never be invited there by Dru. The Heines have just sold the estate for $375,000. The Nassau home is on a small island, reached by private bridge with a railroad that belongs to this lucky couple.

Jack would like to buy a chalet in St. Moritz. He skis, but Dru does not go in for winter sports. In fact, I don't know of any sports in which she partakes. Actually, she is more of an indoor girl than out. Watching the horses run is something else, and you will find Dru at all the fashionable courses in America and Europe. I can't imagine Ascot, both Derbys, or Longchamps, near Paris, minus the lovely Mrs. Heinz the Third.

There might have been another home when heiress Josephine Hartford Bryce separated from her last husband. Dru made an offer for one of the two houses in Jamaica owned by Mrs. Bryce—one in the town and Xanadu, the house on the ocean ("In Xanadu did Kubla Khan/A stately pleasure-dome decree") —but Mr. Bryce did the decreeing this time. Dru begged to buy it, but Mrs. Bryce had built it for her husband and all Dru's persuasiveness could not purchase the house. Josephine is a generous gal, and when they parted, she gave the place to Mr. Bryce, who loves the sea.

But the Bryces are a separate chapter. This one belongs to Dru and her prize husband, who is so attractive he would be almost as sought-after, complimented, and admired if he had only one million dollars. No one has added up his total wealth, but I would estimate it at somewhere between $300 million and $500 million.

He has increased the capital since 1941, when, at the age of thirty-two, H.H. the Second became president of the H. J. Heinz Company—his father had died in February of that year. The second Henry (Jack) had been working as a salesman from the London office under a different name. He had also been a director for several years under his own name. He is enthralled with the business, arrives early to work and leaves late. It was his idea that every Heinz telephone, all over the world, would have a 57 in the number. He is the best salesman the company ever had.

Jack's first wife, Joan Diehl, a San Francisco debutante whom he married in June 1935, had made her debut in Pittsburgh, where her family was living at the time. She was presented at the royal court of England in 1932. They were divorced in Florida in 1942. Five years later, Jack married Joan Ewing Jenney at the home of her parents in Mount Kisco, New York—I believe that Jack still has a home there. There was a son from this marriage—Henry John Heinz III, who is a member of the Heinz corporation, but is equally interested in politics. In November, 1971, at the age of thirty-four, young Heinz won the Republican seat in Congress for the Eighteenth Congressional District in northern Pittsburgh. Who knows, one day Dru may have her own quarters in the White House. John and his wife have a son, Andre, nicknamed Rusty. What, no H. J. Heinz IV? Dru has a married daughter from her first marriage. There are some grandchildren.

Dru Mallory a grandmother? Hard to believe. She is just as glamorous as Marlene Dietrich, much younger, and more outgoing and warmer. As warm as she was in the days of poverty and struggle when she did the cooking for her guests when they failed to bring the food. In fact she had always prepared food in advance, unlike some hostesses who are never seen until they announce, "Dinner is served." Besides, Dru didn't want to miss any of the conversation. "It is maddening to be in the kitchen, sweating over a hot stove and hearing laughter from the living room and not to know what is going on."

In the course of her social marathon, Dru has had to drop

some of the people she knew at the beginning. If you kept in touch with every friend you ever made, you would be chained to the telephone. One of the dropped told me of attending a party at the Café de Paris in London given in the early summer by the Earl of Warwick for his daughter. "The room was stifling, with all the people crowded at the bar, which ran almost the length of the room. I was with a maharaja and his wife, and we were jammed into a hot corner. I said, 'I'll get you something to drink,' and struggled to the bar and bumped into Dru, whom I had known in her early days." According to my informant, Dru said, "What are *you* doing here?" "I was asked," replied the lady sharply.

I'm not sure it was quite like that. The emphasis was probably on the word *doing*, because I have yet to hear of Dru being rude to anyone, especially to a woman in public. In any case, Dru has also had to take her lumps.

When a man who had known her when, saw her at a fashionable party in New York, he asked in astonishment, "What is *she* doing here?" "Her husband," he was told, "is one of the richest men in America."

What is the secret of this amazing woman? How did she climb the long ladder to her present enviable position? Well, in addition to her warmth and perception, she is also a great maneuverer. But, unlike less successful women, she knows *when* to maneuver. She also understands the true values of life and love. She has always had a restless spirit and a keen analytical mind. She has a good sense of humor and can laugh at herself. Dru will help friends in need, loan them money and pay their hospital bills. She is organized but subtle. She puts her light in an oblique setting. She has never mentioned what she has, and what she has is intelligence, charm, and *guts*. Also money.

A woman like Dru knows how to handle her sex—not too much, not too little. After marriage, poor girls who marry rich men can be as cold as they like, but not Dru, from the look of sexiness on her face. The Drus of this world know how to do the right thing by instinct. They are usually spectacular and make sure they are noticed. Above all, Dru is her own woman, a worldly woman.

2. The Kansas City Cattle Heiress? — Mrs. C. V. Whitney

ONCE UPON A TIME there was a blond, blue-eyed girl called Mary Lou Schroeder. She worked as a disc jockey in Kansas City. Like many blond, blue-eyed girls, Mary Lou was popular with the boys. At the age of twenty-one, she decided that Kansas City was too small and unexciting for her, and so the pretty, corn-fed blond went to try her luck in New York City.

Again she was popular with the boys. Very popular. It seemed that all the playboys of the East were after Mary Lou to make a dishonest woman of her. She laughed at them all, and sometimes she kissed them and sometimes she didn't.

She lived sort of catch as catch can, modeling, doing a job here and there, and always legitimate. If she liked you, you were in. If not, all the money in the world could not break down the door.

Mary Lou wanted to be an actress, but she had never acted and was too poor to take lessons in drama—and not talented enough to win a scholarship to one of the schools of acting. A crystal ball could have revealed that she did not need acting lessons or a scholarship to star in Hollywood movies and marry a rich producer. Meanwhile she was careful with the savings she had brought from Kansas City, and at the beginning lived in a one-room walk-up on West Fifty-eighth Street. Later she found two rooms, under the El tracks on Third Avenue—the same apartment Bobo (Mrs. Winthrop) Rockefeller had used a few years previously.

Mary Lou was soon absorbed into the New York City night-life. She made the rounds with all the young eligibles, including Prince Aly Khan, of course, and some not so eligible. You could see her every night, either at El Morocco, the Stork Club, "21" Club, and so on. The rich young men were like bees after the sweet honey, but none of them offered honorable matrimony.

So the poor little girl from Kansas City continued to pinch and scrape in the daytime, while after dark she was treated to the best that the exciting city could offer. In her prayers at night she thanked God for the doggie bag, the contents of which she ate for breakfast-lunch the next day. But more usually she fortified herself with several cups of coffee, to sustain her until the evening feasts.

The forced fasting transformed her chubby shape into the sort of figure that is the aim of every would-be fashionable woman. She might have continued in this unsatisfactory state for years, but early luck was coming her way in the shape of a sharp young New York press agent, Ted Howard. He was introduced to the pretty model one night at El Morocco. He immediately spotted Mary Lou's potential.

Ted had press-agented the tragic Joanne Connelley (who appears later in this book) into the top debutante spot of her year. He decided to do the same for Mary Lou. After kissing her good-night, the Howard brain went to work. He invented a new background for her, a rich one. All of a sudden there was a spate of column items that a Kansas City cattle heiress was spending the season in town—our little radio station girl no less.

When Ted put Mary Lou on a horse and whacked it and the photographers into the exclusive portals of El Morocco, she was written about in every newspaper in the city—all eight of them.

Not quite as Lady Godiva, although her long blond tresses fell frontally and back to her waist.

From chubby cheeks to gaunt hollowness and pencil slimness, Mary Lou looked the prototype of Alfred Hitchcock's film dreams, a Grace Kelly (who didn't do too badly herself). Mary Lou didn't have a dime to her name, but she was now the most popular jet-set lady in New York.

In the nightly rounds she had seen Frank Hosford, a young traction heir from the Midwest. His nickname was Fink-a-Dink, a pleasant joke because of his stout figure and good nature. Ted decided it was time for his protégée to marry a rich man. Looking over the list with some colleagues, they decided unanimously that Fink-a-Dink, who was lonely and already dazzled by her, should be the lucky bridegroom. He was introduced to Mary Lou and joy oh joy, they immediately fell in love with each other.

And so it came to pass that Mary Lou Schroeder eloped with Frank Hosford, now described as an insurance company executive, from Phoenix, Arizona. Frank installed his wife and her younger sister—Mary Lou has always been good to her family—in a twenty-eight-room mansion in Greenwich, Connecticut, where he went into the used-car business. His relatives, who were social, were upset by the marriage. They had disapproved of Mary Lou and did not regard the girl from Kansas City as a suitable wife for Frank. All that nightclubbing with so many playboys, and so little cash of her own.

Nonetheless, Mary Lou and Frank were happy in the big Greenwich house, which featured a paneled library, a carved oak circular staircase, a fuchsia rug in the dining room, an enormous hallway, and a huge living room with small furniture. The new Mrs. Hosford, a big girl, evidently liked space.

Frank's fortune was estimated at between $4 million and $5 million, but according to a Hosford relative, Mary Lou and her husband evidently went through most of it at a fast pace. He enjoyed highballs but every now and then would go on the wagon, such as the time after he fell down in the drawing room and woke up with a black eye. After a blackout on a New Year's Eve, Frank went off the liquor permanently.

With cash on the low side, they had a hard time paying the bills. A cousin of Frank's was there when they had called for a man to fill up the gas tank in his car. He refused, demanding cash first. Mary Lou sweet-talked him into filling up.

How long ago and how incredible this must all seem to Miss Plump of Kansas City, who has been Mrs. Cornelius (Sonny) Vanderbilt Whitney since January 24, 1958, an hour after his Nevada divorce from the former Eleanor Searle. I remember the reams of stuff in the New York newspapers about the divorce. Eleanor had been married to Whitney for sixteen years. They had a child and she was not going to give up easily, even though Sonny had announced, on August 1, 1957, that he was divorcing her to marry Mary Lou.

The court awarded Eleanor $3,500 a month alimony, plus $500 monthly support for their son, Cornelius Searle Whitney, age thirteen. A default judgment was handed down after Eleanor's lawyers disagreed with Sonny's complaint of mental cruelty. Eleanor said she had never agreed to a divorce and would not abide by it. In making his decision, Judge Merwin Brown took into consideration that Sonny had already given her shares in his Hudson Bay Mining and Smelting Company valued at $225,000, several real estate mortgages, and jewels valued at around a quarter of a million dollars. But Sonny was in such a hurry to marry again, he agreed to give Eleanor an additional settlement of $3 million.

At his marriage to Mary Lou in the Indian Room of the El Ranch-O-Tel Hotel, in Nevada, Sonny wore a black business suit with a gray tie. She was radiant in a white velvet dress with a turquoise-blue coat—it was a cold January—and a white orchid corsage from the groom. After the champagne reception, they left for a honeymoon–business trip to a place called Flin Flon—really!—in Manitoba, where his Hudson Bay Mining Company was located.

He was fifty-eight, Mary Lou, thirty-one. Sonny's first wife, Marie Norton, was now married to Averell Harriman, who was then governor of New York. His second wife was the former Gladys Hopkins, with whom he had a daughter, Gail. Number three, Eleanor, had been a receptionist at Pan American World Airways, of which Sonny was he board chairman, when they married in 1941. There were two children from the first marriage, Harry Payne and Nancy Whitney, Searle with Eleanor, and there would be a daughter, Cornelia, with Mary Lou, who already had four children from her marriage with Mr. Hosford.

How does a woman with four growing-up kids marry such an attractive multimillionaire? In Mary Lou's case, the secret was proximity. Circumstances brought her close to the man who was susceptible to her considerable charms.

There are two versions of how Cinderella Mary Lou Schroeder Hosford won her Whitney. One was that when Sonny was planning his program of four patriotic film blockbusters, his press agent announced that Sonny was searching for a dignified, fresh-faced woman who would personify the farmland of America in the first film of the quartet, *The Missouri Traveler*.

The Hosfords were then living in Arizona. Mary Lou, who had a local radio show, was friendly with the woman who ran the Little Theatre in Phoenix, and she contacted Mr. Whitney in Hollywood and told him about Mary Lou. According to this version, it was hard to persuade Mary Lou to leave her husband and children in Arizona and fly to Hollywood to make the test. But she managed to tear herself away. To Whitney, who was still married to Eleanor, it was love at first sight. When he was asked later to name the best investment he had ever made, he replied, "The two dollars I paid for the license to marry Mary Lou."

The other version of how Mary Lou met Sonny was that he was having lunch at the Backstage Club in Phoenix with a polo-playing friend, when he saw Mary Lou at a nearby table and was immediately struck by that love-at-first-sight feeling which knows no rhyme or reason, and he signed her on the spot to test to be his leading lady. At the time of the marriage, Mary Lou told the reporters that she fell in love with Mr. Whitney because "he's the greatest American I have met in my entire life. . . . He wants to make the United States a better country for our children to live in." How they met or why they fell in love doesn't really matter. The fact that she married him, and they are still married, does.

But first they each had to get a divorce. Frank Hosford loved his wife and the sudden breakup of his marriage broke Fink-a-Dink's heart. But Frank was a kind man and he must have realized what the marriage to Whitney would do for Mary Lou and their children, and he surrendered without a struggle. She sued on grounds of excesses, outrages, cruel and inhuman treatment. All that is known of him today is that he is living quietly in California. And he is still on the wagon.

Sonny and Mary Lou lived for a while in the swanky Bel Air suburb of Beverly Hills. I interviewed her there in the spring.

"Oh yes, I am still continuing with my career," she assured me. Clever! A girl should not give up her career as soon as she says "I do." She should slide out of the job without undue haste, or he might think that's what she married him for—to give up the drudgery.

"I'm not a homewrecker," she asserted. "But our marriages were on the rocks anyway. And I didn't like the move from Greenwich to Arizona. But," she added disarmingly, "at heart I am a hausfrau. My first duty is to my husband and my children. I will make only one film a year and that will be for Sonny." This was fortunate, because no one else was rushing to sign her. I saw her movie, and she looked genteel and healthy, but was not a great actress.

It was not long before Mary Lou devoted *all* her time to her home, or rather homes, and her family. But she was not a hausfrau. When you have a husband who inherited $30 million, which he mushroomed into $200 million, you don't have to wash up or cook; although Mary Lou learned in Kansas City how to be a great cook and has written some books on the subject. Even as a poor girl working in local radio, and plump as she was then, Mary Lou always knew how to cook. She is better in the kitchen than the chefs she employs. You don't hear *her* screaming for Women's Lib. She is too busy being a woman. There are nine homes to look after. A nasty someone told me, "Mary Lou has nine houses, but no homes." Aren't some people jealous? Each Whitney home has a kitchen especially designed for Mary Lou's cooking feats.

The New York City residence is at 834 Fifth Avenue; ten years ago they built a $1 million farm, Whitney House, in Kentucky. Apart from the horses, the big feature is the atrium and the huge swimming pool. Cady Hills is the glorified cottage in Saratoga left to Sonny by his father. The Florida home is in

Saint Augustine. The estate in the Adirondacks covers one hundred thousand acres. The Long Island Oyster Bay home sweet home, set in fifty-three acres, is in white brick, Tudor style, with fourteen rooms, a wing for the servants, plus stables and two large greenhouses. There are twenty rooms in the farm in Lexington. The Whitneys spend exactly three weeks in August at the Cady Hills four-story home just for the racing season.

Whitney Park, the Swedish-style chalet in the middle of those Adirondacks acres, is registered as the family lumber corporation. Mary Lou was so taken with Flin Flon, Manitoba, that her loving husband bought a house there for her. There are three homes in Spain—Marbella, Majorca, and Trujillo. They were recently persuaded to buy some land in the Portuguese Algarve by Viscount Rossiere, who is poor but well connected and sells real estate on the side.

Mrs. Whitney would very much like her husband to be named the U.S. ambassador to Spain, and it nearly came off. These poor girls who marry rich men *always* want an ambassadorship for their husbands. It is the crowning achievement, to be treated like a queen. Unfortunately, the departing ambassador has the right to veto the man coming in. A man who has had more than one wife is not considered right for a Catholic country. Also, Mary Lou's background was perhaps not aristocratic enough for the *haute* society of Spain. A pity, because Mary Lou, all five foot three and a half inches of her, looks more well born than some of the dumpy duchesses of old Europe.

Mary Lou has more going for her than her face and figure. She is bright—she has left nothing to chance in maintaining her position as Mrs. Cornelius Vanderbilt Whitney. She has done everything to improve herself. She now speaks fluent Spanish and French. She had instruction from a calligraphist to improve her handwriting. She even changed the sound of her voice, from a rather high-pitched and somewhat grating midwestern sound to a pleasant, well-modulated tone.

A woman who has climbed into society is allowed one relapse. And Mary Lou reportedly had hers a few summers ago at a grand ball in Saratoga. She seemed to think that Sonny was dancing too closely to a pretty opera singer. Her heart breaking because she thought she was losing her Grand Prize, but managing to smile through pursed lips, Mary Lou tapped Sonny on his back and asked, wasn't it time for "their" dance?

The publicity photographs rarely show Mary Lou smiling. "She's all prunes and prisms," says an otherwise kind Hosford relative, adding, "Have you noticed how close together her eyes are?" I hadn't noticed, but it is true that in all the photographs at this and that ball, Mary Lou mostly has her mouth pursed in a tight, filled-in *O*.

She has beautiful skin, which never sees the sun. Outdoors, when it is bright, she wears a wide-brimmed hat. She is a natural blonde, but as so often happens, the color in middle age needs a little help. She should worry, with such a rich, devoted husband always busy with so many varied interests, which include his presidency of C. V. Whitney Farms, one of the biggest stables in the world, and his chairmanship of the board of the Hudson Bay Mining and Smelting Company. He is also chairman of Marine Studios, Inc., which owns Marineland, the Palos Verdes aquarium in southern California. Plus his commitment to Pan American Airways, *and* a good percentage of the *Gone With the Wind* movie, which long ago grossed more than $150 million. His cousin, Jock Whitney, sold out, but Sonny held on, and every time this fabulous film is rereleased it means more millions for Cornelius V. and what used to be called MGM Films.

The industrious billionaire is the grandson of William C. Whitney, who made his fortune in oil and utilities and who served as secretary of the navy under President Cleveland. Sonny's mother, Gertrude, the famed "Grande Dame," was a daughter of the rich, rich, rich Cornelius Vanderbilt.

Sonny, like some other rich sons, was not content to rest on his father's reputation. With the help of a mining engineer, he salvaged $1 million from a venture his father had written off as a loss. Papa then gave him permission to spend $600,000 to develop a new mine in Canada, and additional sums in 1927 to enlarge Pan American Airways.

With all the wealth and business and social position of her husband, it is strange that Mary Lou was not accepted socially in Palm Beach until three years after the marriage. Another girl who made it big, Mrs. Winston (Cee Zee) Guest, gave a dinner party for the C. V. Whitneys at her home there in February, 1961. The other society hostesses soon followed.

At the Palm Beach Flamingo Ball early in 1965, Mary Lou wore the diamond-and-ruby tiara that had belonged to Empress Elizabeth of Austria in the royal days before World War I. Mary Lou is always draped in jewels and Sarmi gowns for the big balls of which she is either chairman, on the committee, or a guest.

The jewelry heaped on her fair neck and fingers by the doting Sonny has tempted the smartest thieves in the world. In the summer of 1965 the Whitneys reported that gems valued at $781,800 had been stolen from the Cady Hills summer house. They had delayed reporting the loss "in the hope that the jewels had been mislaid." The robbery included a small turquoise— Mary Lou's favorite color—owl pin, "the first gift Sonny ever gave me." She had discovered the theft while dressing for a supper dance they were giving for the Philadelphia Symphony Orchestra at the Saratoga Performing Arts Center. She had imagined the jewels were still in the case that always accompanies her from house to house, where it was promptly put under some blankets in a closet in her bedroom. There were still a few trinkets valued at $175,000 left in the box. Wiping away her tears, Mary Lou wore them with her pink-and-silver Sarmi and went bravely to the ball.

The night of the Big Robbery, all the servants had been given permission to be away from the house—the cook, valet, kitchenmaid, chambermaid, parlormaid, all except the laundress, who was asleep. Among the missing gems was the huge Whitney diamond-and-sapphire pin weighing 37.64 carats, and valued at $500,000. Thank God, Empress Elizabeth of Austria's tiara was not among the missing gems. It was in the Whitney vault at the bank. Everything was covered by insurance, but the little turquoise owl could never be replaced in her heart, not even by the copy Sonny had made. While Mary Lou adores her jewels, she says she is just as fond of the ribbon she wears to tie back her hair from her ears. Well, almost as fond.

Among the secrets of a happy marriage are interests in common. Sonny and his wife both enjoy painting, and they recently had a joint exhibition-sale of their work in the Findlay Galleries. Two of them, one his, one hers, were given to the Syracuse University Museum. They have been painting and drawing for years and had exhibited first in Palm Beach.

The present number-one lady in American society gives the impression of being haughty and snobbish. She is not. When she recently bumped into press agent, Ted Howard, she stopped to kiss him and to talk about the old days.

"She was friendly, just like she used to be," said Ted. But there is a big difference. Mary Lou is no longer in the night-clubs. Her behavior is impeccable. Not only does Sonny never have cause to worry about her, but she is just as careful of his reputation as she is of her own. He is twenty-seven years older than she is, but still has that glint in his eye when he looks at his wife.

Mrs. Whitney does not hide the fact that she did not make a formal entry into society. When she was asked, "Which year did you come out?" she replied, "I didn't, but my sister did"—under the Whitney wing. Her daughter M'lou made her debut several years ago at The Debutante's Cotillion in New York City. Last year her daughter Heather trod the same charismic path.

Mary Lou Schroeder of Kansas City has gone as high as she can go in her sphere. Her parties are the most sought after, and she makes news all over the world. Recently I listened to two society women talking about her. Said one, "I guess she's come a long way." To which the other replied, "No, *all* the way."

3. On Her Toes—The Marchioness of Londonderry

WHAT DOES IT TAKE to marry one of the most eligible titles in Britain? Brains? Style? Patience? Dancer Doreen Wells possesses all three. She was thirty-five when she exchanged her ballet shoes for the two-hundred-year-old coronet of Alexander, Marquess of Londonderry. It was Doreen's first marriage. His lordship's second. There were two ceremonies—the first in March, 1972, at the Durham City Register Office, then a fancier affair at Wynyard Park, County Durham, the family estate of the ninth marquess. His two daughters attended both nuptials and presented Doreen with a horseshoe "for luck." Their son Frederick Aubrey, was born near the end of the same year.

Doreen met Alexander while dancing with the Royal Ballet on tour in Newcastle, not far from Wynyard Park. Doreen was a prima ballerina, but only on the road. In London she played secondary roles, until recently when she took to her toes again in the lead role of *Romeo and Juliet* at London's Covent Garden. She was treated with ultimum respect—a title *can* make a difference—although most of her intimates claim she is still the same unaffected girl whose father was a cabinet maker in Wal-thamstow in the East End of London.

A few disgruntled former friends claim that Doreen has be-come somewhat snobbish and has dropped the people who knew her when she was just a good dancer in the ballet, but without the drive and ambition that creates superstars of the caliber of Fonteyn, Ulanova, Markova, and Plisetskaya. But you know how jealous your acquaintances can be when you sud-denly become successful in your professional and/or private life. And if, after reaching the heights socially, you were to keep in touch with all of your earlier friends, you would never have time to do anything but sit by the telephone answering calls from the old crowd who wish to be included with the new.

Brown-haired, dark-eyed Doreen led a discreet life before her marriage. She enjoyed parties but did not allow them to inter-fere with her work. She has always had a cool head, and good taste in clothes—even with the simple blue jeans and sweaters that she still wears at home in London or County Durham.

While far from being a go-go girl, she was a normally sexual woman and I imagine that, having reached the age of thirty-five, she was "with it" in that department. Are there any thirty-plus spinsters today who have not had at least one love affair? Doreen has always been well adjusted to life and love. There were some romances before the marriage to Alexander. She had a fling with David Neild, a handsome man who was adviser to the Sultan of Oman—Oman, then under the protectorship of Great Britain, is one of the seven Trucial Independent States.

Mr. Neild met Miss Wells when he returned to London, and they fell in love. The association lasted several years. There was also a rich man whom she knew while she was living in the house in First Street, Chelsea (so called because the first cricket match ever played in London was in that area—it was country-side then). She had visited Paris to see him before he died.

While Doreen knew her way around, she has always exuded a freshness, simplicity, and quiet charm which, allied to a pretty face and figure, set her apart from most of the other aspiring ballerinas.

The marquess, as her friends before him, found her easy to be with. He is not as stuffy as his title might indicate. He flaunts long, dark hair, loves jazz and pop music, and politically leans to the Left, which does not make him popular with his fellow peers.

Doreen, who was gregarious between ballets, enjoyed visiting her friends and downing a drink or two. Some girls say, "Oh, I don't usually drink but I'll have just one," and then swallow the whole bottleful. Doreen says, "Yes, I like a drink." Especially champagne, lots of it. But no one has ever seen her take the one too many. She has a strong head to match her dancing feet, although she looks as though a puff of wind could blow her away. If she had a rehearsal the next day, she would excuse herself early and take herself home in a taxi. Her favorite food was, and still is, bangers and mash—sausages and mashed potatoes, but now she also eats steaks, salads, and health foods. The slender marchioness is a big eater. Some women get fat if they look at potatoes, but not our dainty little dancer. As a child, bangers and mash, the staple diet for poor people, was her favorite food, and what you love in childhood you often continue to like when you are grown up and can afford something more expensive.

Doreen's simplicity was the magnet for the marquess, who is a secure man, some months younger than his present wife. When you have possessed a famous title and enormous wealth from the age of eighteen, you could become autocratic and difficult. But not Alexander, perhaps because he lives in the creative world of the arts where titles mean less than talent, and money is supposedly despised.

He adores his in-laws, cockney accent and all, especially his mum-in-law. Last Christmas Doreen's parents, with their other children, were guests of the Londonderrys at the castlelike home in Durham County. They stayed over for New Year's and, I'm told, a rollicking time was had by all.

The marquess did not bother to invite the neighboring nabobs, who were not at all disappointed. They regard the marquess as a hippie—a dreadful noun in northern county society. His grandmother would have been shocked, or maybe not. Her close friend had been an ex-working-class man, Ramsay MacDonald, who was prime minister when the Labour Party was in power. In Edwardian days the late marchioness was the most important political hostess. Her spectacular balls at Londonderry House attracted the cream of the politicians and high society, including King Edward VII and Queen Alexandra, with a slight sprinkling of the most famous writers and painters. The present marchioness and her mate prefer less exalted personages and would rather spend an evening pub-crawling than attend or give the finest ball of the season.

When the house next door to Doreen's in First Street came onto the market, she persuaded her noble husband to buy it and turn the two houses into one. Neither is large—two floors and a basement each. After the first gasp of curiosity, the neighbors have paid little attention to the titled pair who lead a life that is more simple than their own.

Once a week you might see the marquess stashing the soiled linen into the baby's pushcart, and trundling it down the street to the laundry. Or, if he is busy, the chore is handled by Lady Sophia or Lady Cosima Vane-Tempest-Stewart, the two daughters from his previous marriage. Or the marchioness will take it. They employ a daily cleaning woman but prefer to do the cooking themselves.

Until she returned to her career, Doreen looked after the baby herself. She is just as diligent with her stepdaughters, and they adore her and their half brother. The girls are good babysitters. A male neighbor came to Doreen's assistance when he saw her struggling to lift the baby carriage, containing the young Viscount Castlereagh, up the outside steps into the house. She accepted the help with a smile and thanked him, although she has not seen him to talk to again.

The baby viscount was almost robbed of his title and the riches that go with it. Before the end of Alexander's first marriage, his wife Nicolette, who married him when she was seventeen years old, gave birth to a son who automatically became Viscount Castlereagh. The marriage had been foundering, and the marquess sued her, claiming that the boy was not his. Blood tests proved him right. After the divorce, Nicolette married Georgie Fame, the pop singer. The son bears his name. They have a second child.

Doreen is a fine wife and mother. To ensure the good health of her baby, she retired from the ballet for thirteen months.

"But," she stated, "my husband wishes me to continue my career as a dancer." Three and a half months after the birth of Viscount Frederick Aubrey Castlereagh, she returned to Covent Garden to play a slave girl in *Aida*.

While Doreen has never hidden her humble birth, she has never pursued publicity, and nowadays she is somewhat bored with the questions about her early life in Walthamstow and the fact that her father was a carpenter. But she willingly posed for photographs holding her baby son to promote her four-minute role in *Aida*. You'd have thought she was the star to judge by the reams of stuff in the newspapers—one headline: "Marchioness Goes Back to Slavery." It is not slavery if you like what you are doing, even if, as Doreen confessed, "it is nice to be back, but it is very tiring, and I move rather more slowly."

It is my belief that when and if the marchioness has another child, she will abandon her career, with its strenuous hours of rehearsal, to spend all her time with her family. Why wear yourself out in the strenuous life of a dancer when there are more important delights in your life?

And yet as a child, Doreen's ambition was to be a great ballerina. She began training at the age of seven. She was always graceful and petite, loved to dance, and her parents found the money for the lessons. But to be the greatest, you must be willing to murder your competition. Doreen was always too placid to reach the top by treading on the other toes. She is also kind. The daughter of the owner of a pub near Piccadilly frequented by the Londonderrys confided that she too would like to be a ballerina. Doreen immediately sent her several pairs of ballet shoes.

At an early age it was predicted that Doreen would become a star. She was so conscientious and disciplined, and pretty, it seemed a foregone conclusion. But she never quite made it with the big ones, although when Margot Fonteyn's ambassador husband, Roberto Arias, was shot in Panama, and she planed to him, Doreen was invited to take over her leading role on tour with Rudolf Nureyev until Miss Fonteyn returned. Having danced with Nureyev, what else is there for a nonambitious dancer to achieve?

In one ballet, *La Bayadère,* shortly before she married the marquess, Doreen wore the Londonderry tiara. This gave her great pleasure. Nowadays the tiara is mostly in the family vault with the rest of the Londonderry jewels.

Londonderry House is now a hotel and any Tom, Dick, or Arab—it is always full of Middle East oil millionaires—can rent a room or a suite and stare across the road at the always fascinating Hyde Park and listen to the continual traffic sounds, a poor substitute for the clop-clop of the horses and the greased wheels of the carriages in the time of the old marchioness.

But you don't have to feel sorry for the present title holder. The million-and-a-half-dollars received for the mansion went into the purchase of a handsome villa in Tuscany, near Florence, in Italy, where you can still hear the clop-clop of the horses, dragging the carriages for the tourists. The marquess recently sold his 1,440-acre farm, the Long Newton estate in Durham.

Doreen has said that she would not worry if circumstances forced her to return to Walthamstow (ha! ha!). Luckily there is no chance of that. The marquess and his wife adore each other and their son, who will one day inherit the title and properties that now belong to his father. They are happy with their life-style. "It's like a dream," says Doreen.

Of course, even when you enjoy living like a hippie, it must be comforting to know that you can step out of the rags anytime you choose to live like a lord. Even poor hippies, as they grow older, become more conventional and comfort-loving.

I am adding my own horseshoe for good luck to Doreen. She deserves it for waiting until an age when most spinsters get panicky to marry the *right* man. No one can be more right than the good-looking, liberal, rich Alexander Charles Robert Vane-Tempest-Stewart, the ninth Marquess of Londonderry.

4. *The Reluctant Heiress—Nancy Oakes*

NANCY OAKES IS a rich girl who married three men with little or no money. Nancy is not as weathy as Doris Duke or Barbara Hutton, although next to Barbara she is the poorest little rich girl I know. She was born with a gold mine in her mouth, and thank goodness her childhood was happy—she was described as a fine child—because the rest of her life, except in the early stages of unmarried and legal love, has been one miserable happening after another. She is a compulsive complainer and she has cause to complain.

The unhappiness began with the bizarre murder of her father, multimillionaire Sir Harry Oakes, in 1943, when Nancy was eighteen years old. She has been plagued by illness, at odds with her two children and three husbands, all of whom, Nancy informed me, tried to extract her money, with some success. She is a mixture of caution, impulsiveness, stinginess, generosity, nice and not so nice. She is reserved, gregarious, and lonely. She can talk on the phone for two hours nonstop from Mexico City to London. She has three homes, in Nassau, Mexico City, and London, but when she is in the British capital she prefers to rent a suite at Claridge's, the hotel for ex-kings and queens. I tried to call her there when she was last in London, and it took me ninety minutes to get through. I daren't hang up because she would have started another call and I had to confirm our lunch date. The telephone operator finally took pity on me and interrupted her monologue to explain how long I had been waiting.

We lunched at Burke's Club in Mayfair, and she told me about her last husband and her troubles, mostly her children. Her seventeen-year-old son had disappeared from her mews house in which he was living. No forwarding address. "I don't ever want to see him again," she told me vehemently, but before the meal was over she said, rather slyly, "I know where he is, I tracked him down, but"—raising her voice—"I will never see him again." Of course she did.

After our lunch we went shopping at the nearby Asprey's glamor store in Bond Street. It was in the fall, and Nancy bought Christmas presents for her surviving brother and other members of her family. They knew her well at the shop. Talk about deferential!

Afterward she wanted me to stroll down the street with her. But I had had enough and, inventing the excuse that I had an appointment, I fled into the nearest taxi, leaving Nancy looking disconsolately after me. I knew she was lonely, but I had to get away to forget the continuous complaining chatter that started as soon as we left the shop. Inside she had forgotten all her troubles and her face was bright with the joy of giving. If only she could be shopping all the time!

She has had some big battles with her daughter, who is twenty-two, but she loves both her children and will always rescue them with her money, after telling everyone over and over that she will not. She has stood by her husbands while she was still in love with them, but when the inevitable separations and divorces, with the demands for large settlements, arise, she fights like a tigress to hang on to her fortune, or to cut down the amount they want.

Perhaps we would never have heard of Nancy Oakes but for

the murder of her father, who was reportedly worth $200,000,-000 when the murderer, who has never been caught, bludgeoned him to death in his bed at the home in Nassau, covered the body with feathers, then set it all on fire.

Nancy's whole adult life has been shaped by the murder of her father and the subsequent arrest of her first husband, Count Alfred de Marigny—his father was reported to be a German butcher—who was accused of the crime, but later acquitted.

Sir Harry's widow, Lady Eunice Oakes, from Sydney, Australia, has said, "Ill fortune pursued the family since Nancy's first marriage," which took place shortly before the murder. Both of them wept at the inquest on Sir Harry. They had lost the man who had been as protective of the family as his surname indicates. Oakes had been a gold prospector who went to Canada from Maine, what they call a "down easter." When he discovered the gold, he and his family became Canadian citizens, subject to Canadian death duties, but when he died he was a citizen of Nassau. The United States, Canadian, and British governments tussled for his millions.

Nancy's parents had disapproved of the marriage to Marigny and did everything in their power to prevent it. Sir Harry threatened to disinherit Nancy if she went against his wishes, but you can never stop a young woman in love. Two days after her eighteenth birthday, when she became legally of age and could touch her trust fund, the heiress eloped with Alfred. They spent the honeymoon in Bar Harbor, Maine, and Mexico, where Nancy became ill with typhoid fever and was pregnant before she had fully recovered. Back in the Bahamas, she underwent a series of operations to cure a mouth infection, a residue of the typhoid. Lady Oakes gave Marigny $16,000 to pay the hospital bills. But when Alfred took a room in the hospital next to his wife's, Sir Harry bellowed, "Kick him out!" He again threatened to disinherit his daughter, but at his death she received her rightful share.

The count was previously married to Ruth Fahnestock, the heiress to a financial empire, who reported that Alfred had spent $100,000 of her money, and within a month of his marriage to Nancy he spent $14,000 of hers. But the new countess was very loyal to her husband, and wrote to her parents, "I want no more to do with the family until Freddie"—her nickname for Alfred—"is accepted by you."

He seemed the logical suspect for the murder of his father-in-law. Especially as he had been heard to say on several occasions that he would kill him. You know how it is, when you hate someone you say "I'll kill him!" but you usually don't.

Sir Harold Christie, a business friend of Sir Harry's, was staying with him in the Nassau home when he was murdered. At first he was the number one suspect. Since his bedroom was next door to the murdered man's, he should have heard some noise and gone in to help. But apparently he was a sound sleeper and heard nothing.

When Marigny was acquitted, he was ordered by the court to leave the Bahamas and return to his native land, Mauritius, a British island in the Indian Ocean. "I will not desert him," cried Nancy, who chartered a yacht, and, instead of Mauritius, they sailed to Cuba.

Nancy has always been highly strung and impulsive. As a schoolgirl in New York City, she met two young men-about-town at the soda fountain in Schrafft's on Madison Avenue. One was a rich boy from the Argentine, and after downing their soft drinks, they went out on the town. It was all very innocent and giggly, as one of the two gentlemen told me. But it might have been dangerous for the tense heiress. When she was nineteen and still under the strain of her husband's trial, she collapsed because she could not get a plane reservation from Nassau to Miami to visit her mother in Palm Beach.

Alfred was divorced by the wealthy Ruth Fahnestock in 1940. His marriage to Nancy was annulled in 1949 on the basis that the divorce from his first wife, Lucie Alice Cahen—Alfred had married her in 1937—had not been valid.

Nancy complained that Alfred had tried in every way to get money from her. The same old story from the heiresses who marry poor men. After the annulment he ran a marriage agency in Los Angeles. During their marriage they had stayed at a hotel in Beverly Hills where Nancy had been robbed of $10,000 worth of jewels. They had been happy then, as they still were after the death of Sir Harry, when money was in short supply as the various countries tied up his fortune while they wrangled over the death duties.

A year after her father's murder, Nancy had been reduced to auctioning off their household goods. The washtubs brought ten dollars apiece. The dining table twenty-five dollars. No wife could have been more devoted to her mate. In 1945, when there were reports of a divorce from Marigny, Nancy said, "Nonsense!" In the same year they separated, and Alfred went alone to Canada, working his way there as a seaman on a ship. Later Alfred became a salesman for aluminum frames for doors and windows. He had gained nothing from his rich marriages.

Five years later, Nancy married Baron Ernest von Hoynigen-Huene. His title was solid. His finances were not. It was a candlelight ceremony in Saint Mary's Anglican Church in Nassau. The baron had been living with his family in the basement of a hotel in Oberammergau, Germany. Nancy, who was always generous to her husbands while she loved them, built the baron's parents a house in the town of the Passion Play.

In between the marriages and divorces, there were several romances. She had been in love with Alexis Lichine of the wine family in France. Here was one man who was not after her money. But when Alexis married Arlene Dahl—they each believed the other was well fixed for finance—they discovered they were not.

Nancy's mother, to whom she is attached, disapproved of the romance with Lichine, and perhaps this is the reason Nancy did not marry him, although his friends say that the real reason was that Alexis didn't want to. Nancy can be a darling girl, but is also moody and demanding, as most rich women are. When she invited me to spend Christmas with her in the Mexico City mansion, which has a swimming pool in the living room, I said to myself, never. I like her but wouldn't be able to take her insecurities at close quarters.

Years ago, just after World War II, after Nancy was separated from Marigny, she was in love with a Danish Royal Air Force officer, Flight Lieutenant Joergen Edsberg. They planned to marry after each divorced their spouses. But on April 22,

1946, Joergen was killed in a plane crash. Nancy immediately went to Denmark to put flowers on his grave, which had been kept open for her.

For several years, Nancy's great love was Richard Greene, the now-rich Robin Hood of the early TV series. She would have married him, but he was worried about his career as Robin. He was sure his women fans would not approve of the match.

In 1957 Nancy was trying to divorce Hoynigen-Huene. The rumor printed at the time was that she would marry Michael Parker, who was a friend of Queen Elizabeth's husband, Prince Philip, and a personal secretary to His Royal Highness. In 1958, Michael canceled plans to return to London from New York so he could be with Nancy, who was in hospital to undergo a sinus operation. Earlier in the year the widespread gossip about Nancy and her Lieutenant Commander Parker was strongly denied by both. Said Nancy, "My personal life has taken such a beating and battering that I feel as if I have been run over by a steamroller." However, in 1959, Nancy and Michael were spotted on holiday in Scandinavia. Her two children and Michael Parker's two spent Christmas that year together in Switzerland.

By heiress standards, Nancy's three marriages were of fair duration. The first, to Marigny, lasted seven years, although they separated after two years. Baron Ernst had nine years, from '52 to the divorce in '61. The third marriage, to Patrick Tritton, began on March 1, 1962. It lasted more than a decade. Pat is the son of an old friend of mine, Judith Hurt Tritton—she is now Mrs. Hugh Armstrong.

Before I left England for America in the mid-thirties, Judy and I were bosom buddies, skiing together, swimming together, taking houses in the country together, skating together, and partying together. You can imagine my surprise when after being introduced to Nancy at a dinner about two years ago in London, she said, "My mother-in-law is a friend of yours." Nancy, as usual, was giving the dinner. I had been brought along by a mutual male friend. She had asked to have me placed on her right.

We talked about Judith and Patrick, whom I had seen in his mother's arms soon after his birth. "I like her very much," said

Nancy. "But Pat and I are now separated and of course she must be on his side." Knowing Judy, I doubt whether she would be for her son if he were in the wrong.

"I haven't seen Pat for months," continued Nancy somberly. "I expect he's hunting in his beloved Mexican mountains." She had met the attractive, Eton- and Cambridge-educated Mr. Tritton in Mexico City, where he worked for the British Chamber of Commerce. They were married at the British Embassy and honeymooned in England and the Continent. No member of the Oakes family attended the marriage.

Soon after, the honeymoon was over—literally and figuratively—and Nancy, using her maiden name, registered as a student at Bennington College. Now they are divorcing and a close friend of Nancy's, who once wanted to marry her, told me last year, "I saw Nancy today and she said that Pat is demanding payment for every day of the ten years of their marriage." The per diem added up to a fortune. "She said he claimed this was severance pay for the work he'd performed for her."

How can a couple who once loved each other be so cruel when it is all over? It seems the more the love, the more the hatred, although Nancy has long ago forgotten her grievances against her first husband, Marigny, and sees him occasionally.

At one time Nancy was enamored of Dr. Stephen Ward, the central figure in the Christine Keeler–John Profumo case. He had hoped to marry Nancy—his money troubles would then have been over—but when she ditched him, he became embittered and began the association with call girls that led in the end to his suicide. If Stephen had married Nancy, there might not have been the scandal that threw out Prime Minister Macmillan.

Was Lady Eunice Oakes right when she implied that the family had been a happy one until Nancy's first marriage disrupted the Oakes harmony? Perhaps it was a case of too much money. Sir Harry's annual income was around $3 million. He had made his fortune from the Canadian Lake Shore Gold Mines. He was a generous man. After he was knighted in 1939, he donated $200,000 to the Saint George's Hospital, which, in his old age, was a home away from home for the ailing Sir Winston Churchill.

By living in Nassau, Sir Harry saved $5,000 a day in taxes. In Canada, which had been considered his domicile, he would have had to pay 75 percent of his income in taxes. He had homes in Bar Harbor, Palm Beach, and Nassau. Some friends said that his annual income was not $3 million but $20 million. Sir Harry owned fourteen square miles of Nassau. He paid $1 million for the Colonade Hotel there in the days when hotel buying was cheap.

The story of how Sir Harry discovered gold is interesting, if true. He had been prospecting for fifteen years and was making a final attempt. He boarded a train in Canada but was thrown off for not having the fare. He slept on the siding and awakened in the morning covered with gold dust. With his discovery of the Lake Shore mine, Oakes became one of the richest men in the world. Sir Harry himself had dug the first shaft. 'Tis said that years later he made a point of finding that stern train conductor and gave him a reward.

Sir Harry's marriage to the former Eunice McIntyre had been happy. They were married in Sydney, Australia. She had some money of her own, and that started him off. The Oakes had five children, three boys and two girls. Sydney died in a car crash. William Pitt lived to succeed to his father's title, but expired soon after of acute alcoholism. Harry Philip was born in 1932 and is still alive. Nancy arrived in 1925, her sister Shirley in 1929. Shirley was more organized than Nancy. She went to Yale Law School and married Alan Butler, who founded Butler's Bank in Nassau.

William Pitt Oakes was thirteen years old when his father was murdered, and when he died seventeen years ago, he was separated from his wife, also named Eunice—who had been a Miss Bailly—a beautiful, flaming-haired, startlingly white-faced British beauty, described as usual as a model and small-part actress. Her second husband, Robert Gardiner, is much richer than William Pitt, who was not poor, having received $10 million plus a trust fund as his share of Sir Harry's estate.

The younger Eunice and Nancy keep in touch. When Eunice married Gardiner, owner of Gardiner's Island, Long Island— it has been in the family for centuries—plus hundreds and hundreds of acres in the expensive areas of the nearby resorts of

Southampton and East Hampton, Nancy was among the guests.

Rich Robert and not-so-rich Eunice were married thirteen years ago in a spectacular wedding at Saint Thomas Church on Fifth Avenue, New York City. They wed in a hurry, but not because Eunice was pregnant, let me add hastily. The marriage has not been blessed with children, and now it is too late; Eunice is forty-six.

It has been an unusual marriage. While Mr. Gardiner delights in draping Eunice with jewels, and saying "Don't they look lovely on her," she says they still belong to him. (As many of Elizabeth Taylor's jewels still belong to Richard Burton.)

Robert recently paid $625,000 for a house in Palm Beach because "it went with my French furniture." Eunice has two separate homes of her own, an apartment in Winthrop House fronting the ocean at Worth Avenue in Palm Beach, and a cottage in the Algarve. She paid $58,000 two years ago for the Florida apartment and recently could have sold it for $120,000. "I decided to keep it," she told me. "You never know what can happen in life, and my homes are my security." Uneasy lies the head that today is wed to an attractive rich man.

In general, the lady vultures are always waiting for a sign to grab a rich man. In the good old bad old days, once a girl got married she could relax. But not today. He is yours now, but will you have him tomorrow? Eunice, who spent last summer in the Algarve minus her husband, is worried about losing her beauty, and was heard to say, "What will I do then?" Like the squirrel, she is saving her nuts for the possible winter.

Sister-in-law Nancy is fifty-nine years old. But will her luck change with her half century? A great deal of what happens to you is luck, although some unfortunates, rich and poor, seem to attract misfortune, as Nancy has during her adult life. At one time, when she was ill in Nassau, she lost some teeth and hair. The tussle with typhoid left her with a deterioration of the jawbone, which caused the damage to the teeth. She is constantly in and out of hospitals. It is sad, because *au fond* Nancy is a very nice person, always ready to help her friends and sympathetic to their problems when she is not obsessed with her own.

When Nancy was staying recently at Claridge's in London, a friend asked her, "Why aren't you using your own home here?"

She thought for a moment, then said, "Just say I'm having a very expensive breakdown!" She doesn't smoke because of her sinus problems and drinks wine only.

She is accident-prone. She eats a T-bone steak and breaks a tooth. A stone on the sidewalk, and Nancy will be sure to trip over it—that sort of thing. But she is well organized in some areas, manages her money capably except with escorts and husbands, and she makes sure when traveling to take with her everything she might want. Soon after World War II, she arrived in Capri complete with a water-purifying machine and crates and crates of toilet paper. (During the war, toilet paper was in extremely short supply, and when I was on the newly built first *Queen Elizabeth*, which had been turned into a troop transport, the theme song for officers and men was "There ain't no toilet paper in the largest ship in the world.")

Recently Nancy has been having passport problems. The luckless lady is in danger of becoming stateless. She is no longer considered American. But as long as she is married to Patrick Tritton she could have a British passport, although the government in Nassau will not give her one. Canada, after the trouble with Sir Harry Oakes's estate, will not give her one either.

And so the troubles mount, and as a woman on her own she sometimes finds it hard to cope. All her adult life she has had to pay emotionally every foot of the way. In all the partnerships, she had to be the strong one, although her nature is shy and retiring.

A friend of mine who lives in San Francisco told me not long ago, "I've just passed the most extraordinary day of my life with the three most timid women in the world. I had breakfast with Greta Garbo, lunch with Doris Duke, and dinner with Nancy Oakes."

Trying to make some sense of her life, Nancy last year hired a ghost to help write her memoirs. But dredging the past made her ill, and the ghost has vanished.

Would any woman like to change places with the rich Miss Oakes?

5. "There Was a Ford in Her Future"—Cristina

MILAN: summer of 1960: Friday, late at night. Maria Cristina Vettore Austin dabbed at her tears and telephoned her faithful friend, Alessandro Mossotti. "I'm so lonely," she wept. "I can't stay in Milan any longer. I'm going away." Alessandro, a journalist-photographer, had seen Maria Cristina through many bouts of depression before. Always the same theme of loneliness. But this time there was a note of desperation in her high-pitched Italian voice.

Cristina Austin had friends and acquaintances in Milan, to which she had returned after the death of her British husband, Captain William Austin. With her tall slender figure, tawny hair, and tanned good looks, she became a member of the international jet set—winters in St. Moritz, summers in the South of France, staying with her rich friends. She was vivacious and amusing, two attributes essential for a girl who wants to be popular in the chic world of money. It was only when she returned to her home—an apartment in Milan near her younger brother—that she could shed the swinger image and be herself, a serious, introspective girl, lonely and longing to marry a man who would give her emotional and material security. She was too intelligent to feel close to the high-stepping ladies of Milan and the rich playboys who, like Cristina, attended every party in hopes of finding the magic wand that makes dreams come true. She had met Alessandro at the usual cocktail party. He was not handsome or rich—he owned a small magazine strictly for the intelligentsia. They were immediately *simpatico*, and he became a sort of father confessor to the beautiful unhappy lady. They saw each other three or four times a week.

Before her marriage to Captain Austin, Cristina had worked as a model, saleslady, and assistant to "Biki," owner of the best dress shop in Milan. Biki had been sorry for the girl, who, Alessandro informed me, was the daughter of a poor farmer near Venice. There was something special about the girl, a brightness, a longing for the good things of life. Biki had taken her to live in her own home, where she met members of the European and American jet set.

Cristina had no money at all, except what she earned at Biki's. But now she had her own attractive three-room apartment in a fashionable part of Milan. There was no longer the necessity to work. Captain Austin, it was reported, had left her comparatively well off. No one in Milan had ever seen the captain, who, according to one account, had come to Italy with the British invasion forces. Another report had Cristina meeting him in England or Scotland. Others said he was a fairly rich Canadian who suffered ill health and who took his bride to live with him, first in Montreal, then in the Bahamas, where he died not long after the marriage.

He left Cristina a house, which she sold, some money, and some jewels. She had always been elegantly dressed—Biki had allowed her to wear the model-size clothes—but now she could afford to pay for them, at a good discount; remember, she was an Italian bargainer, and still is. She was invited to some of the good parties and accepted in good society because of her reserved, ladylike ways. Then why did she frequently sob her heart out and say she was lonely?

Saturday. Early morning. Alessandro had a journalistic appointment, but he canceled it and drove to Cristina's apartment.

He found her lying on the bed with its rose silk headboard and gold-colored decoration in the center. "She was still crying," Alessandro revealed to me last summer, in Milan. "She told me, 'I've decided to go to São Paulo [in Brazil] where I have a good friend.' Not a lover," Signor Mossotti assured me, "just a very good friend." Feminine women, of whom Cristina is the most, often have one or two special men friends whose only desire is to help the little lady when she is in trouble or depressed. "She asked me to take her to the airport, where she would fly to Paris and change planes for Brazil."

Fortunately for Cristina's future, there was a two-hour delay between planes. She had time to telephone Mrs. Rosemary Kanzler, a rich member of the international set, whom she had met in the South of France. "You can go to Brazil tomorrow," said Rosemary, "but come to my party tonight at Maxim's. You'll meet some fascinating people."

She changed at Rosemary's home, nothing flashy, a simple long dress—she has always dressed simply. The party was for Princess Grace Kelly and her husband, Prince Rainier. Henry Ford II, the auto billionaire, was seated at the right of Princess Grace. Her thoughtful hostess put Cristina on Henry's right. It was one of those love-at-first-sight thunderbolts. After the introduction and the usual pleasantries, Mr. Ford did not speak to Grace throughout the evening. He concentrated on Cristina. The pretty American princess was furious, to the point of complaining to Mrs. Kanzler. After all, she was the guest of honor.

Henry escorted Cristina home to Mrs. Kanzler's—Rosemary, an aunt by marriage to the Ford family, had married one rich man after another, all of whom left her an enormous fortune when they expired.

The forty-two-year-old chairman of the Ford empire was at Rosemary's home early the next morning, and Cristina did not go to Brazil. Instead, she was persuaded by Mr. Ford to go to New York. She was never lonely again, but five years were to elapse before the farmer's daughter was able to marry the super-millionaire, who was still married to his first wife, the former Anne O'Donnell, who was rich in her own right as the daughter of a rich industrialist.

The five years of waiting were not easy for Cristina. She had everything she had ever wanted, an elegantly furnished apartment at 530 Park Avenue in New York, beautiful jewels, expensive fur coats, and some discreet visits from Henry, but she had been raised by nuns in a convent and it was a sin to be in love with a man if you were not his wife.

In the first three years of the clandestine courtship, a tight security hid her incredible secret from the press and world at large. The couple were not seen in public together until 1963, after Anne Ford had announced her separation from Henry. There had been some blind items in the gossip columns about a mysterious Italian lady, but it was not until Henry was no longer living officially with his wife that Cristina's name was coupled with his in print.

While somewhat more open about their association, they still tried to avoid the press, but when Henry, after paying $500,000 for a yacht built for him in Holland, named it the *Santa Maria*, the journalists and photographers hunted Maria Cristina from city to city and country to country. "It's terrible for me in America," she said, in a moment of exasperation, "but it's worse for me in Europe." When Henry, who is not a good sailor and had never wanted a yacht before meeting Cristina, sailed into Portofino in 1963, it was assumed that he had come to visit Cristina, who was hiding out somewhere in the lush city. "Oh, no," he insisted, "there's a storm coming up and I was told by radio to come into port." Naturally he spent the evening with Cristina, who was so shaken up by the media that she announced after Henry's departure that she was going to the Engadine in Switzerland to rest or she would have a nervous breakdown.

It was worse when Henry and his party, which included Cristina, arrived at the Newport, Rhode Island, harbor. Henry refused to comment and they retired below decks. Later, when Cristina ventured on land, she was cornered by a sharp reporter who asked, "Now that Mrs. Ford has announced a separation, are you and Henry planning to marry?" I am sure she was longing to say yes, but in fact she was not absolutely sure herself. At one time when she was in her very worst state of depression, she believed that Anne, who was a Catholic, would never divorce Henry. Henry did not believe she would either—he had become a Catholic on his marriage to her—he was nineteen, she seventeen. And to assuage Cristina's disappointment he offered to buy her a stupendous present. "What would I want," she asked a friend, miserably, "when all I want is Henry?"

But in the summer of 1964 Mrs. Ford finally consented to the divorce, which required all sorts of religious and legal documents, plus a settlement of $16 million, the contents of the family home at Grosse Pointe Farms—"stripped clean," a friend stated—and, of course, several Ford-made limousines, and the custody of son Edsel, who was fifteen. Daughters Charlotte and Anne were respectively twenty-one and nineteen, and they liked their stepmother-to-be, who seemed to have more in common with them than their very social mother.

The marriage was to have taken place on December 17, 1964, but was postponed to February, 1965, because of a sudden operation for Cristina. I had a scoop on the story, but I didn't get it until Saturday midday. I gave it to my newspaper, the *New York Post*, but for some unexplained reason they did not run it. You can imagine the numbness of this girl who had waited so long to become Henry's wife when the doctor told her she had a perforated ulcer and must be operated on at once. She entered the hospital under a different name and Henry used a different name when he visited her.

Before the marriage, I was invited to the opera with Cristina and a mutual friend. We picked her up at the Regency Hotel on Park Avenue in a Lincoln Continental, the luxury car made by Ford, and she was pleasant but not too chatty, not a word about Mr. Ford. I am sure that she had been warned that I was a newspaperwoman. When we dropped her back at the Regency where Mr. Ford maintained a penthouse, I made the mistake of stroking the long sable coat she was wearing. "Don't do that," she said, sharply, then, more affably, "You never stroke fur, you shake it out." I have not forgotten. My own furs are now shaken thoroughly when I take them off.

Cristina is a careful girl. When you have been born poor, you either spend recklessly when you have the money, or the early habit of frugality remains with you. In New York she shops at Macy's and Bloomingdale's. In Milan she goes to a hangout for young people where you pay a few lire (600 to the dollar) for a fruit-juice drink. While her favorite dressmaker for formal dress is Dior, she is just as happy in a $50 Peck & Peck sport out-fit. Her favorite food is still *pasta e fagioli*, the Italian peasant soup crammed with small beans and spaghetti—it is also the favorite dish for Sophia Loren, another girl who was made rich by the man she married. Henry's favorite dish, if you are curious, is onion soup.

"We like nothing better," said Cristina recently, "than to sit in front of a television set with a bowl of our favorite soup on a tray, me barefoot in my dressing gown, Henry in shirtsleeves." The former swinger in the international set has changed considerably in recent years. She still likes parties, but not as often. "If you go out every night, it becomes a bore." Now it is an event.

Unlike most of the rich people in this book, the Henry Fords do not have homes all over the place. There is a twenty-room mansion in Grosse Pointe Farms, a lodge in Canada, the yacht, and a private jet. But when they are in New York, they stay at the Regency or the Carlyle. In Milan they book a suite at the Hotel Principe-Savoy, in Rome the Excelsior or the Grand, the Shoreham in Washington, and the Palace Hotel in St. Moritz.

Like most Italian women, Cristina is unpunctual, and this habit could have cost her the marriage to Henry who said, somewhat wryly, "Cristina kept me waiting for an hour and a quarter for the ceremony." She had flown to New York from Washington early on the morning of her wedding day to pick up something and to return by early evening for the marriage at 8 P.M. You have to be very organized and/or cool to do this sort of thing on your wedding day.

It was raining hard and foggy in New York, and when it came time to return, the airline official informed her that visibility was too low for a takeoff. "But you must," she implored, "I shall be desperate if you don't." "Lady," said the official, "bad weather. We can't leave." "Please," cried Cristina, "we must go, even in a tempest, we must get there." Two hours passed before it was safe to fly, while Cristina was at bursting point.

"Henry was waiting for me on the fourth floor of the Shoreham Hotel," Cristina reminisces. "Henry said, 'I had to wait a long time for you.' [He might also have been referring to the five years of patient waiting.] The judge was upset. He had a party that evening. He put us quickly in front of the mantelpiece. It was all over in a minute. The public relations man [for Ford] put a glass of champagne in my hand and said, 'Congratulations!' I said, 'Are we really married?' It was all so fast. I could not believe that we were actually married."

The ceremony was nothing like Henry's nuptials with Anne. Five hundred people had attended the reception. Not more than ten were at the second ceremony, and these included his two daughters, Charlotte and Anne, who had been in on the secret. The judge who married them was unaware of his famous name until just before the ceremony. There were no photographs at the wedding, and if Henry knew what the bride wore, he obviously didn't remember. "She was very beautiful, and that was enough." According to a newspaper report the day after the wedding, Cristina wore a simple beige dress, Henry was in a dark business suit. The announcement was made in a brief two-paragraph statement by the Ford family attorney—that the marriage had taken place, the couple had left for Europe and would live in Grosse Pointe Farms, a Detroit suburb, on their return.

The day after the wedding, they flew to New York in their private jet, and then by commercial plane to London. They told the press assembled at Heathrow Airport that they thought they had been discovered by a reporter at the airport in New York, "but," Cristina grinned, "he was waiting for Elizabeth and Richard Burton!"

It still seemed like a dream to Cristina, the marriage, the honeymoon in London and St. Moritz, where they both love to ski. Milan was a must, where her mother was and still is living, also to meet all the relatives and friends. She had left Milan five years previously, a lonely, weeping woman, hoping to find a new life in Brazil. It was the most triumphant homecoming that anyone could wish for.

The subsequent years have been happy. Cristina, friendly and natural, is usually smiling in her photographs. In former days, when she didn't like a person, she showed it. "Now I have learned to smile, even when I don't feel like it." Henry is more easygoing than his wife, who has that Italian temperament. He usually falls in with her wishes. An example: they were in their suite at the Palace Hotel in St. Moritz when Henry jumped up, exclaiming, "I'll get in some skiing before lunch." "Bambino," said Cristina—her nickname for the auto magnate who employs 350,000 workers around the world (it means "little boy" in Italian)—"it isn't possible. Lunch is almost ready." He looked disappointed, but acquiesced without an argument. He does not care too much for Venice, but on the honeymoon Cristina wanted to go there to show off her prize. "We won't have time," Henry grumbled, "I want to get to Rome to see my tailor." "Bambino, we *must* have time for Venice." They went to Venice.

But don't get the idea that the present Mrs. Ford is bossy. She is always feminine and makes her demands in a soft, smiling way. Recent photographs usually show them hand in hand. They are happy because she uses the velvet glove in their marriage. All successful wives do—poor and rich. Cristina builds up her husband's ego, where her predecessor perhaps put her husband down. European women are trained for this role. Mention Women's Lib to the average Italian woman and she wouldn't know what you are talking about.

"I'm fascinated by this man," Cristina says. "He loves the simple life, and likes to walk barefoot"—as she does. He loves her, he says, because of her simplicity. She flies with him on his business trips—recently they were in Australia. But because his enormous job keeps him so busy, Cristina has gone to some parties without him, with his blessing. She has often been at the White House for dinner, with another Henry—Kissinger. Mr. Ford was not photographed with her when she chaired Sol Hurok's party for charity to celebrate his sixty years as a world-renowned impresario. She danced with the octogenarian, smiling and listening to him attentively.

It has not always been delight and joy for the favored couple. Shortly after the marriage, Mr. Ford received the news that he had been excommunicated from the Catholic Church. "We were flabbergasted," says Cristina, "and my religious mother nearly died of heart failure."

There has been another cause of distress for Cristina. A couple of years ago, when her friend Mossotti was in New York, he visited her in her Regency penthouse and again found her in tears.

"Look," she said, showing him a page in an Italian newspaper that contained uncorroborated remarks about her early life. "But to make it worse," Cristina wept, "someone sent this story to Henry. How can people be so nasty? In any case, Henry knows all about me."

Henry trusts his wife one hundred percent and the damaging article was tossed aside with a laugh. He has been in public life long enough to know that people can be jealous of those with wealth and happiness. The articles—I believe there was another one—soured Cristina for several months on her native land. She stopped sending money. She had worked hard for Italian charitable causes.

On the honeymoon, Mr. Ford, at her suggestion, donated the cash to build a kindergarten in the village where she was born. She had been chairman for this and that Italian charity. She told Alessandro that she was crying, not because the article had been sent to her husband, but that people would be so mean as to send it to him.

Cristina never talks about her early life, or her marriage to Austin. Except to say that her parents were poor and that she lived with the captain in Canada, England, and the Caribbean. She has two married sisters and the brother who lives in Milan. She is very loving and helpful to her family, whom she visits as often as she can. On a recent visit to Milan, Henry had work to do and could not accompany her. But he telephoned her from Detroit three times a day to say he loved her and how was she getting along. He phoned her just as frequently before the marriage. He is so glad he married her that when Rosemary Kanzler married again, Henry, who does not fling his money around, gave her the wedding—he paid for everything—as his gift.

Apart from Cristina's down-to-earthness, another reason why Henry loves her is the fact that *she* does not fling his money around. "Because you have the money is no reason to waste it," she says. "And if you did"—jocularly—"you wouldn't have it for long. But"—complacently—"it *is* nice to know you have it." At a recent party she was wearing a diamond and emerald necklace with matching earrings, but it is a rare occasion when Cristina is glittering with gems. Her favorite jewel is the large pear-shaped engagement ring from her husband.

Actually, she looks her best at informal occasions—a tight

blouse or sweater to emphasize her small but shapely top, and the high-waisted bottom-tight pants of the day. Henry was slightly displeased with his wife at President Johnson's White House dinner for Princess Margaret and Lord Snowdon. Cristina's low-cut gown revealed much of her physical charms, and he told her so. For a while her neckline was more high tide, but the line had receded again on a recent cover of a fashion magazine.

If you examine Cristina's features one by one, you would conclude that her face is not conventionally beautiful. Her nose is on the large side, as is her mouth, but the complexion is glorious —it always seems tanned, although she does not go in for outdoor sports too much. Her smile is infectious. The gray eyes wide and candid. The hair shining and free.

Cristina has revealed that she did not care for life in Grosse Pointe Farms at the beginning of the marriage, but she has made the adjustment, and is now happy there. Her favorite sport is bicycling, and she has made pedaling fashionable in Henry's hometown. Otherwise, except for the skiing, she is more of a sports spectator. She takes good care of herself—her age has varied in the reports, but I would guess she is in her mid-forties, while looking younger.

Mrs. Ford defers to her husband in everything except the running of their house. She never interferes with his business, and she makes sure he does not interfere with hers. She likes to cook and does at the lodge in Canada. She would like to do more at Grosse Pointe, but, she says, "As soon as I poke my nose into the kitchen, Luigi"—the Italian chef—"frowns at me and I leave quickly." Ever since that dinner for Princess Margaret, she has asked Henry's advice on her clothes. If he can't come with her, she telephones and describes the gown or the shoes. She puts it all so persuasively that he would feel a brute to disagree with her choices.

They do not entertain much. "But when I do, I do it properly," says Cristina. "The best of everything, food, silver, candles, flowers, the whole works." But mostly, like many average American couples, they prefer to dine alone and spend the evening watching television, or he peruses his stamp collection, and early to bed. Henry has always gone to bed early to report for his work at eight in the morning. Cristina, after those late nights before the marriage, used to sleep until noon. Not now. What is satisfactory for Henry is ditto for Cristina.

It was not too late for Cristina to have children with Henry— she was in her late thirties when they married, but there are none, and there were no children from the marriage with Captain Austin. She was asked recently if she was sorry there were no bambinos playing around the Ford hearth, and she replied candidly, "Sometimes. Especially when I see Henry's grandchildren. But"—smiling broadly—"I don't need children. I am so happy and have so much to live for with Henry, my own bambino, my own little boy." She admits she sounds corny, "but it is true." It may not have been quite so true for Cristina in the beginning. But it is now.

6. *Poor Little Rich Girl— Barbara Hutton*

THE SONG "I Found a Million-Dollar Baby in a Five-and-Ten Cent Store" was a hit in the early thirties, but you could not buy the sheet or the record in any of the Woolworth stores. The message was too true. A titled fortune hunter, Prince Alexis Mdivani, had found such a million-dollar baby in the Woolworth family—roly-poly Barbara Hutton.

"If I'd only known how pretty I was when I was twenty, my life would have been happier," sighs Miss Hutton today. She *was* beautiful, like the much younger Dina Merrill, her cousin. Neither of them ever needed a face-lift, but to my certain knowledge, Dina has had two. Barbara isn't telling.

When the blond, pretty, but still-plump Miss Hutton was twenty-one, she underwent some operations that were never quite explained. I heard a rumor at the time that Barbara was having some of her poundage removed. Many rich women have undergone this operation, but again, Barbara isn't telling. She was beautifully thin after the surgery, but never again was she to enjoy good health.

Barbara has always been known as the poor little rich girl, in spite of, or because of, her fortune—estimated today at more than $100 million. What a sad life she has had. In and out of hospitals, in and out of marriages.

Seven times a bride, now at sixty-one she is alone, except for a few dedicated employees and a few friends. For the rest, when you are as rich as Barbara you are never sure whether you are loved for your money or yourself. This is the handicap for rich men and women, they can never be sure.

So much has happened to Miss Hutton, it is difficult to know where to begin. Perhaps I should first list Barbara's husbands. Then you can judge their motives—did they love her or did they marry her for her money? At the age of twenty she married Prince Alexis Mdivani. He was ten years her senior and had been married previously to American heiress Louise Van Alen. A mere twenty-four hours after the divorce from Alexis, Barbara was clutched to bed and board by Count Kurt von Haugwitz-Reventlow, seventeen years her senior.

Less than two years later, Barbara separated from the count, but it took another seven years for the divorce. After two years, the ever-optimistic countess became Mrs. Cary Grant. Cary won the golden ring in 1942. In 1945 he went the way of all Miss Hutton's husbands—out. But Barbara had not given up her search for the perfect mate. Later in the same year in Paris, so-called sportsman Freddie McEvoy, a British push-button man for the way to a rich woman's heart—and fortune—introduced her to Prince Igor Troubetzkoy. They were married on March 3 in 1947. Four years later the prince was in the ashcan of broken marriages.

Porfirio Rubirosa had been married three times previously before he took Barbara for his fourth bride on December 30, 1953. Seventy-two days later, they announced a separation. The international playboy was to cost Barbara approximately $2 million. On the day of the wedding, the ailing bride gasped, "I feel as if someone has hit me over the head." It wasn't her head that had been hit, it was her healthy bank account. By mutual agreement, Rubirosa divorced Barbara in his native Ciudad Trujillo, after her assurance that she would not contest the suit. She seemed eager to oblige.

In the same year of the divorce from Rubi, Baron von Cramm, the German tennis ace, courted the heiress with all the delicacy, sensitivity, and charm of an exquisite European. Barbara married the tall, handsome baron in the winter of 1955. The rumors of trouble in the marriage started as early as the spring of 1956. They divorced in 1960, after each promised that no details of the whys and wherefores should be released.

She was fifty-two years old and afraid of a lonely old age when she married Prince Doan Vinh, forty-eight, at her home in Cuernavaca. By Christmas, 1969, the ailing bride was being carried from her bed to her dining room to eat the holiday turkey alone in her New York home. As of going to the printers, Barbara is still married, but separated from the prince. She has vowed she will never marry again. I'm inclined to believe her this time, although her name was recently linked with a new love, Angel Turuel, a Spanish matador. She will divorce the prince should she desire an eighth marriage. But perhaps she has learned the lesson that when a young man courts a rich aging lady, he is usually after her bankroll. And if Prince Doan were to pass away first, it would save this bruised woman the anguish of all but one of her previous divorces.

Prince Mdivani, Count Reventlow, superstar Cary Grant, Prince Troubetzkoy, Rubirosa, von Cramm, Prince Doan Vinh. Seven husbands, six divorces, and one current separation.

What went wrong, and how much did the multi-marriages cost the multimillionairess? If we start at the very beginning, we might discover why Barbara Hutton earned the title "poor little rich girl." She was born in November, 1912, daughter of Edna Woolworth Hutton, and granddaughter of Frank Woolworth, who opened his first five-and-ten-cent store in June, 1879, in Lancaster, Pennsylvania. In 1905 the Woolworth chain was worth $10 million. By 1939 the five and ten cents added up to $319 million.

Barbara's early years were marred by misfortune. Her father, Frank Woolworth, had moved to Fifth Avenue, New York, in 1901. Her mother died when she was five. (There were rumors —unsubstantiated—that she had committed suicide.) Miss Hutton then lived with her Woolworth grandparents, whom she loved. She was only seven when her grandfather died. Five years later her grandmother passed away. Each death meant more millions of dollars and more grief for the heiress.

When you are twelve years old, money doesn't mean much, and to the wicked witch in fairy-godmother clothing Barbara should have said give me happiness instead of more money. But while Barbara has admitted that her wealth has given her little joy, she has also confessed that it is good to have so much money. You can do as you please, live where you like, and help others.

When Barbara was thirteen, her father asked that her annual living allowance be increased from $12,000 to $35,000. When she was fifteen, he requested a raise to $60,000, plus $250,000 to re-model the family home.

After her father remarried, Barbara decided she would live on her own. Not long after, her father died. She was still under age, and her executors went to court to ask for adequate living expenses for the million-dollar baby.

The adolescent girl wanted a penthouse. A New York judge decided that to buy a penthouse for a girl of Miss Hutton's enormous future wealth would cost $463,000, and so decreed. "I want my own private railroad car," the blond, blue-eyed teen-ager demanded. In those years of the late twenties—before the Wall Street crash—*everyone* whom Babs knew had their own private railroad car. For this the nice judge allowed another $120,000 from the bulging estate, plus another $36,000 annually to operate and maintain it.

"She is an assertive child," understated one of her relatives at the time. "After spending so much time with her grandfather, she is bound to be as demanding as he was." Barbara had hated her private schools and the bodyguards who accompanied her everywhere to foil possible kidnappers. Now she was free to do as she pleased.

Miss Hutton's debut in 1930 was a spectacular $60,000 supper-dance at the Ritz-Carlton in New York, for which silver birch and eucalyptus trees had been brought from California. The affair filled the society columns for weeks. I vaguely remember some photographs at the time and thought what a pity such a lovely rich girl should be so plump.

In the same year Barbara was presented to King George V and Queen Mary at Buckingham Palace. The three Prince of

Wales feathers wobbled on her shingled head as she made her curtsy, as did her legs from the overweight torso. Her white dress with its train was expensive, but nothing looks elegant on a girl who is carrying fifty pounds too much.

In 1933, when she was not quite twenty-one—at twenty-one she would come into an inheritance of $42 million—Barbara's family (her Woolworth, Hutton, and Donahue relations were keeping an eye on her) decided that a trip around the world would remove some of the restlessness from the rich prize package. No one could have foreseen the disastrous marriage to Prince Mdivani.

She had met him in America when he was married to Miss Van Alen. Barbara was fifteen, an age at which little girls begin to admire mature men. The ocean liner dropped anchor in Siam, and who should be there to meet her at the dock, yes, the dark, handsome Prince Mdivani of Russia. She was delighted when he offered to show her all the sights and she fell in love with him. It was like a fairy tale, the pretty American heiress and the impoverished handsome Georgian prince.

Barbara's aunt announced the engagement and they were married that year in Paris. "All American men I know are businessmen," Barbara stated at the time. "Once they marry a girl they wrap themselves up in work. It's going to be fun being a princess." Mdivani's right to call himself a prince was in question. There were stories that he was a Mohammedan from Egypt took place in the Russian cathedral in Paris, with both wearing and had become a Christian to marry Barbara. The marriage crowns—the custom for Russian nobility.

A Japanese newspaper report stated: "She admired his expertise in wise spending and in gaining access to the choicest circles." Poor little rich girl! When she returned alone to New York in November—Prince Alexis was in Egypt—it was stated in the press that Barbara, by downing coffee only, had gone from 145 pounds in weight to 102 pounds. Today her daily diet reportedly consists of twenty Coca-Colas, milk, and medication.

Mdivani had decided on their honeymoon that his bride must lose some of the unattractive weight. Whoever heard of a fat fairy princess? To please him she began the diet, losing forty pounds in the first year, at the end of which Barbara was saying,

"I didn't realize that the worst thing I could possibly do was to marry a titled foreigner. I didn't know Alexis had planned to marry me ever since he had first known me." When they married, Alexis received a dowry of a million dollars. The final settlement gave him another $2 million.

In August, 1935, not long after the divorce proceedings had started in Reno (this was before the quickie divorces in Mexico), Mdivani was killed in one of the many racing cars his adoring wife had given him. He died speeding along the road from Palamos, Spain, to Perpignan, France. He had been living on his wife's trust fund for him. You would have thought that now Miss Hutton would have remembered the advice of her grandfather, to beware of fortune-hunting titled Europeans who made a business of marrying American heiresses.

He would have hated them more if he had known that his granddaughter would surrender her precious heritage as a United States citizen after she married Danish-German Count Kurt Reventlow in the Reno home of Dr. A. J. Bart Hood, in a five-minute Presbyterian ceremony. Actually, the count was more German than Danish. A Prussian by ancestry, he had fought with the Germans in World War I.

Kurt was a sharp one. He had met and courted Barbara in London while she was planning the divorce from Mdivani. He followed her from London to Reno, where he rushed her through the marriage ceremony before she had time to think. How much thinking can a young woman do in twenty-four hours?

After the honeymoon with the count, the gullible girl stated, "I am now completely happy. My search for true love is ended." The renouncement of her American citizenship made her unpopular with the U.S. public and press. Something was rotten in Denmark. Barbara's lawyers hastily announced that the reason for the change in nationality was not that she loved America less and Denmark more, but that her taxes in the United States were too costly, which of course did nothing to make her more popular. "Why are people so hostile?" she demanded. "Just because one has a little money." And despairingly: "There are so many hostile people everywhere."

American Communists would use as a reason for revolution

the fact that this rich woman who had never worked a day in her protected life preferred foreign men as husbands, and, they demanded, why should this spoiled brat have so much money to waste while they and their families were subsisting on starvation wages for which they toiled so hard? After Barbara renounced her U.S. citizenship, shopgirls picketed the Woolworth stores for higher pay.

As Countess Reventlow, Barbara spent a great deal of time—and money—in London, which she preferred to the colder Denmark. She used $4.5 million to build the largest house in Regents Park. The decor at Winfield House was canary-yellow and blue, including the livery for the footmen.

After the divorce from Kurt, Barbara decided the mansion was too big and had too many unhappy memories. She asked the United States government to take it as a gift and use it as a home from home for the U.S. ambassadors to Britain. The costly gift was at first refused, but later reconsidered and accepted. Winfield House, with its precious paintings and furnishings, has given comfort and pleasure to "our man in London," most of whom, from the first occupant, W. A. Aldrich, to John (Jock) Hay Whitney to the recent occupant, Walter Annenberg, have added costly items to what was intended as a present from Barbara to her second husband. Alas for Kurt, they parted soon after they moved in.

The divorce was not the usual "we are still friendly" affair. It was fought bitterly by both parties, the count wanting a large slice of her money and Barbara determined to cut the $5 million she stated he was asking for her freedom.

According to printed reports from Barbara at the time, her mate informed her that if he did not receive the $5 million, he would give her "three years of hell with headlines." In 1941 the King of Denmark (he died recently) finally issued a decree that the wrangling must stop, and a divorce was granted. They fought over the education of their son, Lance. Barbara wanted him in American schools and universities. The Dane deemed France and Switzerland the right scholastic countries for his son and heir—his wife's heir, that is. The fight over the custody of their son, who died in 1972 in a private plane crash, took even longer than the seven years of fighting for the divorce. She hired a bodyguard to keep Reventlow from young Lance. His death left her without a child to inherit her fortune. Next of kin are two first cousins and two second cousins.

The count did not get as much as he had hoped for—only a measly $1.5 million settlement. He had already received the usual $1 million dowry at the time of the marriage. Two and a half million dollars. Not bad for a poor Prussian of minor nobility for a few years of marriage, during most of which Barbara had been trying to get rid of him.

Explaining her alliance with Reventlow, Barbara said, "I was young and impressionable and he was the handsomest man I'd ever seen. When we were introduced I couldn't take my eyes off him"—of which the dollar-loving German-Dane was well aware.

Reventlow died in 1965, leaving the money he had received from Barbara to Lance, with a smaller sum going to a British niece. Lance's first wife, Jill St. John, the actress, has not revealed the financial details of her divorce settlement, paid for, I would bet, by her mother-in-law. Barbara had attended Jill's marriage to her son. She did not appear for his subsequent marriage to Cheryl Holdridge, a starlet in Hollywood films and a former Walt Disney "Mouseketeer," who, when Lance died, received the million-dollar fund settled on him by his mother, plus the money he inherited from his father, plus the jewels given to her by her mother-in-law, who bought them back recently for $1,200,000.

In the last years of his life, Lance was not friendly with his mother, who was ill and too absorbed with her marital mishaps to give him much attention. But she was heartbroken when he died. I'm sure she loved him, but from the time he was a man they were unable to communicate. It was another tragedy for Barbara. What shall it profit a mother to have all the material things she wants and lose the affection of her son, an only child? Why don't these rich women have more children? It could make their old age less lonely.

Miss Hutton said it was fate that made her decide to live in Beverly Hills. She bought a beautiful house and gave some exclusive dinner parties, to which some of the superstars were invited. The guest list was triple A. Invitations to her intimate little dinners—fourteen to sixteen guests—were eagerly sought. And no one had to persuade Cary Grant, then a young thirty-seven, to come to dinner at Barbara's house. Of course she fell in love with him.

A year after the divorce from the count, Cary and Barbara were married. They had met briefly in Europe two years before, and while Barbara was trying to regain her U.S. citizenship, the British Cary had become a citzen, in June, 1942. They were married July 8, 1942, at the home of his agent in Lake Arrowhead in the picturesque San Bernadino mountains. It was a six-minute Lutheran ceremony. Shortly before the elopement, Cary signed a paper renouncing all claim to her fortune.

Cary was thirty-eight, Barbara thirty. She wore a navy silk skirt and blouse and carried the pink roses that Cary presented to her. Mr. Grant, always a conservative dresser, wore a blue-gray suit and black tie. He was understandably nervous. Not so Barbara. This time she was sure it was forever. To begin with, Cary was not after her money. He was well off and into his long years as a superstar.

Cary was far from being as rich as Barbara, but even then he was making deals to own his own films, after the short periods when they belonged to the studios. His price per picture was $300,000. In those days it was worth a million of our devalued dollars and Cary carefully stashed it away. He lived frugally—and still does—and it was as though an earthquake had struck California when, in late 1939, Mr. Grant sent his *Gunga Din* salary of $300,000 to help war charities in his native England, which needed money as much as men. Several other British actors went back to fight for the homeland, among them David Niven, Lawrence Olivier, and Richard Greene.

Cary was not an easy man to live with, according to his four wives. Barbara's lawyer, the famed late Jerry Giesler, filed the divorce suit in July, 1945, charging "cruelty without provocation" causing "grievous mental distress, suffering, and anguish." How can a man who is so charming in his films and in public cause all that in his personal life? Like most actors, Cary has always been insecure. His chief insecurity is money. He has always been afraid that he will end up as poor as when he began life as Archie Leach (his real name).

I was sorry for him when his mother died early last year. Cary adored her and had tried to bring her from Bristol to live with him in Hollywood. But the old lady wouldn't budge. He made several trips to her every year, took all of his wives—in turn—to visit her. He flew there when she died in an expensive nursing home, at the ripe age of ninety-two. Cary paid all the bills.

During Cary's marriage to Barbara, a Hollywood wit labeled them "Cash and Cary." But this was unfair. Barbara was to say later that Cary was the only one of her husbands who had not cost her money. When they divorced in 1945, she was able to say, "He's a dear. We're still good friends but he just isn't interested in anything but his career." What did she expect? That he would retire and live off her millions? The others did, but not Cary. Barbara wore her favorite black during the Los Angeles divorce hearing, on August 30, 1945. Her slip was showing, literally and figuratively, under her black moiré silk suit.

Lucky—financially, that is—with Mr. Grant, unlucky with her next husband. Less than two years later she signed her name Princess Igor Troubetzkoy. He was four years her senior. Igor met her in Paris during 1946. Each of Barbara's weddings diminished in splendor. Igor, thirty-five, and not married before, had to be content with a ten-minute ceremony on March 3, 1947, at the town registry in the small Swiss town of Chur, seventy-two miles from Zurich. They celebrated with coffee and cake at a local pastry shop.

Between her marriages to Mr. Grant and Prince Troubetzkoy, Miss Hutton bought a magnificent fifteen-room hideaway in the Casbah, Tangier, because "I've always wanted to live like an Arab!" What, and be one of a dozen or more wives? Not bloody likely. In any case she recently put up the FOR SALE sign —for $2 million.

When the glow with Igor subsided, Barbara described him as "the meanest man in the world." The marriage cost her the usual million-dollar advance payment, and reduced her weight to ninety-two pounds. According to reports emanating from Barbara's court, Prince Igor wanted a further settlement for the divorce, but she was determined to thwart him. If this sort of thing kept up she might be reduced to semipoverty. Mixed with her gentleness and weakness where men are concerned, there is also some of Granddad's tough fighting spirit.

But Troubetzkoy had the determination of his aristocratic Lithuanian forbears. After Barbara filed the first of her attempts to divorce him in Cuernavaca, he retained Melvin Belli, the well-known San Francisco lawyer, and counter-sued, charging mental cruelty and incompatibility. He needn't have bothered. The case was thrown out of court on the grounds that neither party lived in Mexico. In spite of which, Barbara fell in love with Cuernavaca and bought an estate there.

Estate? It is a fairy-tale palace with twenty acres of green hills and fantastic views of the snow-covered volcanic mountains. She called it "Sumiya." For many years, Barbara said, she had wanted to build a Japanese palace and call it Sumiya—translated, "the House on the Corner." During one of her many visits to the Orient she had seen the real Sumiya in Kyoto, built for one of the great courtesans of Japan whose clients were the top echelon of Japanese society. Barbara returned to Japan with a host of architects, builders, and designers, and personally selected the imperial lacquered furniture and priceless screens. The graphite tiles for the roof were made, numbered, and shipped off to Cuernavaca, also the rocks, chosen by the high priest of the Riyonji Temple in Kyoto. When these arrived in Mexico, a puzzled Customs man exclaimed, "But we have rocks in Mexico, why import them from Japan?" He would have been more confused if he had seen them planted deep in the earth with only an eighth of each matching rock showing above ground.

Peacocks and cranes roam around the acreage and sometimes dip a tentative foot in the huge swimming pool. The peacocks are not only decorative but serve as watchdogs. Did you know that peacocks scream at night, which is very scaring for strangers?

It would take a book to describe adequately the interior of Sumiya, with its white Thai-silk upholstery with silk cushions in bright colors, the superb screens, the Japanese-style theater—for the showing of films and stage presentations; at one time Barbara imported a famous group of Kabuki players from Tokyo to entertain her guests. The dining room, separated by exquisite antique Japanese screens, has a long row of low, lacquered teak dining tables. Guests sit on cushions at floor level with a well in which to put their feet. The fantastic Garden of Contemplation—if only Barbara would go there *before* a marriage instead of after—has dark lacquered teak floors and ceilings, while outside are all those one-eighth tops of the rocks from the Riyonji temple priest.

Finally, with the divorce going back and forth in Mexico—one report states the divorce *was* in Mexico but it was not valid anywhere else—Barbara shed the prince she now found uncharming in a Paris court, on October 31, 1951. The poor boy didn't get anything, and, to add to his mortification, he had to pay the $300 court costs! The divorce was granted on the usual French charge of "abandonment." "And this divorce," gloated Babs, "is good *anywhere*."

Although Barbara called Igor a mean man, Cholly Knickerbocker, in a 1954 *Journal-American* column, stated that the prince was actually kind and considerate, especially as Barbara had been sick during most of the marriage. Well now, wouldn't you think that the love-prone heiress would have had enough of European titled husbands? Not at all. She fell in love with Prince Henri de la Tour d'Auvergne, who was many years her junior. Fortunately for Barbara, she tired of him before he could get her to the altar.

At this time, according to a newspaper report, Barbara stated dolefully, "I have never really had a home. My mother committed suicide when I was five, and my father's only thought was of money. He hated me because the inheritance was mine, and I believe he would have been happy if I had died before I was twenty-one." To a friend, Barbara asked, "Don't you think I'm beautiful enough to get a man even though I hadn't a cent? Or wouldn't men look at me if I were poor?"

With Barbara's looks, kindness, and dependence on a man, perhaps she would have done better had she been poor. She might even have married a rich man and have had a happy marriage with him. It was a pity that she was attracted to impoverished noblemen who were brought up with the idea of marrying an American heiress. A title and position in exchange for money. It was considered a good bargain for both. The bartering is still going on, as you will see in some of the following chapters. It is rarely successful. The heiresses wake up too late to discover they've been "taken." This is not always true of the rich men who marry poor girls. The marriage very often goes on to the end, especially if the lady has married for money —why settle for a few million when you can have it all? In time.

After the Igor disaster, what with the diets and pills, Barbara was down to eighty-six pounds when her friend, heiress Doris Duke, persuaded her to recuperate at her $3 million "Shangri-La" in Hawaii. With Diamond Head for a background, the disillusioned lady announced that she would never marry again. "You can't go on being a fool forever. It makes me sad to think of all the silly things I've done. I hate to look at myself in the mirror. Money alone can't bring you happiness, but money alone has not brought me unhappiness. I won't say my husbands thought only of my money, but it had a certain fascination for them." *Quelle* understatement!

And then Miss Hutton met Porfirio Rubirosa. No title, but important in the diplomatic service of his native Santo Domingo and simply dripping with charm. He was wooing Zsa Zsa Gabor at the time, but Barbara fell headlong in love with the great lover, and nothing would satisfy her but marriage. It was obvious from the start that Rubi was not in love with her. As Zsa Zsa said in a cruel moment of perception to the press, "Rubi loves me, I love George Sanders, but who loves Barbara?"

But before going into the sad Hutton-Rubirosa saga and Rubi's brief marriage to Doris Duke, who had the title of the Richest Girl in the World, which she may still have, we will dispose of Barbara's last two marriages, almost as quickly as she did.

Barbara had announced that she would marry Baron Gottfried von Cramm as soon as he was allowed to enter the United States. In those days if you tried to visit America with a man who was not your husband, and vice versa, our virtuous officials said, "No, you can't come in, you would corrupt our morals."

Barbara had known the famed Davis Cup tennis player since 1937 and he was someone to fall back on between marriages. Without waiting for his U.S. visa, which never came through, they were married in a secret ceremony in the town hall near

Versailles. Their wedding regalia was on the mournful side. She wore a black tailored suit. He wore a dark-blue business suit. Von Cramm's brother Siegfried was a witness, also J. van den Kemp, the curator of the Palace of Versailles.

For Barbara's first marriage she was given away by a Woolworth cousin, but the witnesses for the six following marriages were almost all strangers. At the Hotel Ritz in Paris, there was a reception for twenty friends. For this occasion the bride wore a black satin gown, highlighted with an orchid, a double strand of pearls, diamond earrings, a diamond bracelet, and her gold wedding ring. (I wonder what Miss Hutton does with all the rings? Does she wear the same one for each marriage?) She must have changed twice at the party, because the *Daily Express* of London described her get-up as a blue velvet Balenciaga suit.

It was now time for the rumors. But Barbara denied them, saying she was happy with von Cramm and that she was dancing for the first time in years. But when she arrived from Europe with her son, Lance, and the thirty-year-old Philip Van Rensselaer, the New York socialite, the rumors naturally started up again. "We are just good friends," stated Barbara to the New York reporters who swarmed all over them on the good ship *United States*.

More queries when Babs and Philip flew to her home in Cuernavaca. The marriage to von Cramm was still okay, Barbara insisted, and introduced the press to her other good travel friend, James Douglas. It was James who took her back to London in November, 1958. Mr. Douglas was twenty-eight, Barbara forty-six.

You usually know when a woman is in love or contemplating another marriage. She cuts down on the food and alcohol—not that Barbara was ever a heavy drinker—and she buys new clothes. Barbara carried off more than half of the Lanvin-Castillo fall-winter collection in Paris. She was not in love but obviously hoping to be. She was still married to von Cramm, but in name only. No details of the divorce in 1960 are available. Neither of them has ever discussed it, for publication or to anyone.

How long could Miss Hutton remain single? She was dating various distinguished gentlemen, but in 1964 she took the plunge again. It was inevitable that Barbara would again marry a foreigner. All of her seven husbands were born outside the United States.

If only Miss Hutton had spent more time in her native land, she might have had a happy and lasting marriage. The American of the species is much less likely to be an heiress hunter. But she was always traveling abroad. When she fell for Vietnamese Prince Doan Vinh de Champacak, she whisked him to the home in Cuernavaca and married him there in 1964.

Four years seems to be the maximum for a Barbara Hutton marriage, and after a year's separation she filed a divorce suit in Mexico against the prince, but dropped it for a good reason. She was not strong enough for another battle in the courts, as she was still recuperating from a fall in which she had fractured her right hip, and would have had to be carried into court. The hip was set badly, and in the summer of 1971 the unfortunate lady underwent further surgery at the Cedars-Sinai Medical Center in Los Angeles.

A few months ago, a newspaper reader spotted a photograph of Barbara, in Spain, being carried into her car. Was there something wrong? he wrote to the paper. The published reply was that Barbara had been carried to cars for years. However in the late fall of 1972 she attended many parties, dressed to the teeth, at cousin Woolie Donahue's Palm Beach block-long oceanfront mansion. But she had to be supported by Woolie on one side and his wife, Mary, on the other. When Woolie died soon after, it was another heartbreak for Barbara.

She suffers from insomnia and rarely falls asleep before five or six in the morning. When she spent her summers in Paris—she recently sold her home there—she would ring for her chauffeur, Jean Flysens, to come to her bedroom and talk and read to her. No romance and no hanky-panky. He has his own home, plus a pretty wife aged twenty. Barbara paid him 24,000 francs a year, whether she was in France or not, and an extra 1,000 francs a month when she was. Jean is also a private agent for the French government and carries a gun. After his marriage he bought himself a fine home in Versailles.

Barbara is happiest when she is living in Cuernavaca. Or helping people in unfortunate circumstances. During the war, she brought over British friends, dozens of them, to live at her expense in California. Some of them never went back.

Recently she was hospitalized in San Francisco. Two women who had gone to school with her, and had kept in touch over the years, visited her in hospital. When Barbara was discharged, she gave one an expensive sapphire and diamond clip, the other a costly pair of sapphire earrings. The women were overwhelmed, and one protested, "You shouldn't have done that, it's too much." Added the other, "Who do you think you are, Doris Duke?"

7. *Rubi*

Zsa Zsa Gabor was in London. So was I. She telephoned to ask, would I have lunch with her and her "friend," Porfirio Rubirosa. "I have my eleven-year-old daughter with me," I told her. "Never mind, dollink," she said in her assured Hungarian accent. "Bring her along. I'm sure that Rubi would luff to meet her."

I wasn't quite sure whether I wanted Wendy to meet Rubi. Then I thought it might be interesting for her to see how the fast, fashionable other half lives. I took her with me to Les Ambassadeurs at 5 Hamilton Place, Mayfair.

Rubi kissed our hands and I saw Wendy furtively rub it off on her dress. I hoped he hadn't seen the gesture. We settled down to a long chatter from Zsa Zsa, who was nice to Wendy but not as nice as Rubirosa was.

At close intervals he interrupted Zsa Zsa's flow to lean toward my daughter and say softly, *"Ah, comme elle est mignonne!"* or *"Elle est charmante!"* My daughter, a good French scholar, glared at me furiously after each compliment. But by the time the meal was over, she was chatting amiably with the world's Great Loverboy who had already been married and divorced three times, from Flor de Ora Trujillo, the daughter of the Dominican dictator, French actress Danielle Darrieux, to the rich

Doris Duke. His marriages with Barbara Hutton and Odile Rodin were still to come.

Wendy asked me many questions later about Rubi, which I answered discreetly. I could see that he had charmed her, as he had me, Zsa Zsa, and the numberless women he encounters. All done effortlessly. He was probably a charming baby. I am sure that women rushed to coo over him in the cradle.

Details of the early life of the late Porfirio Rubirosa are scarce. It is believed that he was born in 1903 or 1905—as he grew older, he became younger—somewhere in the Dominican Republic. According to early reports, his father was first a coffee planter, then an army officer, and ultimately a diplomat stationed in Paris, where Rubi lived as a youngster. At seventeen, he spent a year at a university in his native land, then went into the army. At twenty he was a captain, and Generalissimo Rafael Trujillo selected him to be his private aide.

Behind the veiled sexy eyes, Rubi was always on the lookout for promotion and power. If you want to succeed in business, you sometimes marry the boss's daughter. Rubirosa married the dictator's sixteen-year-old daughter, Flor. They were promptly sent to the Dominican embassy in Berlin, where the groom was installed as the *numero uno* secretary. Then later to Paris in the same position.

It was impossible for Rubi to be faithful to one woman, and he was soon looking up the young ladies he had known during his father's regime. Flor decided that this way of life was too much to bear and returned to Papa for what was politely termed "an extended vacation."

When the marriage ended officially in 1938, her husband explained to the press, "Invitations began pouring in, but my wife was too young to cope." They remained friends. He was always too charming to dislike.

There is no report of a dowry with the marriage to Flor, but I believe he received a large settlement. It is the custom in Spanish-speaking countries to pack the daughter off with a big bundle of banknotes, and for Pop to pay off when she returns. Or perhaps you don't need a dowry when the bride's father is her country's dictator. Before his marriages to the Misses Duke and Hutton, Rubi signed documents disclaiming any interest in their fortunes, except for the dowry and what he received during the marriages: two lovely French homes—a town house in Paris from Barbara, a small estate in the country from Doris—several strings of polo ponies, a plane, jewelry, etc., etc.

Some time in the mid-fifties, I visited Rubi at the chic house in the Rue Bellefasse. Manservants, maidservants, and, as hostess, Miss Gabor. We had an exquisite lunch, and afterward went to the polo club in the Bois de Boulogne, where Rubi distinguished himself by shooting two goals.

Zsa Zsa, to my surprise, informed me that she "luffed" horses and horseback riding and was exercising Rubi's ponies every morning in the Bois. She then went into a long story of how she had ridden horses all her life, starting when she was little more than a baby. I always thought the middle Gabor sister was a complete lady of the boudoir, without outside sporting interests. But her mother had done well in Budapest, knew many influential people, and could certainly afford to give her daughters riding lessons.

Nonetheless, when Zsa Zsa, the last of the Gabors to come to the United States, arrived, she said her journey was paid for by a string of pearls, one pearl a day to the men who helped her escape from the Nazis. Nasty people said it was one *affair* a day, but as Zsa Zsa is noted for always telling the truth, I'll accept her story.

Rubirosa and his marriage to film star Mlle. Darrieux. They met in Paris while he was chargé d'affaires for the Dominican Republic. It was a hectic courtship and marriage and lasted through the German occupation. Rubi was known for his courage and chivalry where the ladies were concerned. He had need of both for Danielle.

After an alleged insult from a Nazi officer to the petite French actress, Rubi punched him. This episode landed him in an internment camp, but he soon put his diplomatic immunity in motion and was freed. The diplomatic dodge was a godsend for the man whose bravado landed him in some difficult situations.

Rubi and Danielle were married in September, 1942, at the Vichy town hall. (Flor Trujillo, still a friend, helped him get the divorce from her—difficult to obtain in a Catholic country.) Danielle had just been divorced from Henry Decoin, the French film director. The bride and groom gave their ages as twenty-five, although Rubi was thirty-seven or thirty-nine. The witnesses were Mrs. Douglas MacArthur, II, wife of the general, and the Brazilian Ambassador, Señor L. M. de Souza Dantas.

Danielle divorced Rubi in the spring of '47. Always maintaining his image, he allowed his wife to inform the press that he had acted like a gentleman, agreeing to her request to divorce him because she wanted to remarry.

This gesture was not as altruistic as it seems. Rubi had already met Doris Duke and his mind had been made up for some time. The announcement came from the Dominican consulate in Paris —that Miss Duke, former wife of James R. Cromwell (his mother was the multimillionairess Mrs. Edward Stotesbury of Philadelphia and Palm Beach), whom she had married in 1934, and chargé d'affaires Rubirosa would marry at the earliest opportunity.

Doris was twenty-two when she had married poor little rich boy James Cromwell, who had recently been divorced from another rich girl, Delphine Dodge of the automobile family. Doris and Jimmy met at Bar Harbor when she was a gawky sixteen. When the engagement was announced, Jimmy stated, "It was love at first sight."

The spectacular million dollar house, Shangri-La, at Diamond Head in Hawaii, was built in 1937. It was to be the dream house for Doris and Mr. Cromwell. The Moroccan-Persian-style mansion features two stone camels at the doorway, with water flowing from the Pacific up to the flight of mosaic Moorish-style steps.

They had to leave when Cormwell became U.S. envoy to Canada. Doris was pregnant at the beginning of 1940, but the baby girl was born three months prematurely and died one day later. The tragedy helped to sour the marriage, and they separated soon after. The battle for the divorce lasted three years.

Doris, three inches taller than Rubirosa, her groom-to-be, had a difficult time ridding herself of Mr. Cromwell, who loved to play the drums, and when he died, his mother put a toy drum in his coffin. Cromwell first won a "limited" decree in New Jersey, claiming desertion. Doris then divorced him in Reno, charging mental cruelty. He then filed in New Jersey for an absolute decree, which at the time apparently satisfied all parties, especially Rubirosa, who was anxious to hitch his marital wagon to the hundred-million-dollar heiress.

She had met Rubi in Rome, introduced by the marriage push-button man Freddie McEvoy, and then in Paris where for a while Doris was fashion editor for *Harper's Bazaar*—Rubi had followed her there. On the marriage register, her age was given as thirty-four, Rubi's as thirty-nine, an omission of three years, which wasn't too much considering the vanity of the groom.

The ceremony at the Dominican consulate by the consul-general featured ten wedding guests and about a hundred reporters and photographers. Rubi gave Doris a gold ring studded with rubies. She gave him a gold wedding band, perhaps to remind him that he was a married man and she would always love him. "Always" proved to be thirteen months.

Technically, as the marriage took place on Dominican territory, Doris not only had to promise to obey her husband, but her fortune would belong to him—except for that pre-marriage notarized contract. Rubi was nervous—it was not every day that he hit the Great Jackpot. To calm his jitters, he smoked a cigarette during the first part of the ceremony, extinguishing it just in time to place the ring on her finger!

A story about the wedding in *The New York Times* estimated the third Mrs. Rubirosa's fortune as between $50 and $200 million. We should all be sandwiched between those two figures.

Trouble in their paradise started almost immediately. Two days after the marriage to Rubi, Mr. Cromwell claimed that Doris's New Jersey divorce was not legal and therefore he would be entitled to her New Jersey properties if she should die before him. Fortunately she didn't. But this rich woman might not have missed it, although the Duke estate in New Jersey totals 2,500 acres, with forty-two miles of roads and woods, and a thirty-room stone house containing a movie theater, an indoor swimming pool, and an indoor tennis court. The house is about a mile from the front gate, which is always securely locked. There is an entryphone at the gate, and when a special guest phoned to say he had arrived, Doris went in her car to meet him, and, the newspaper story goes, after pressing the button to open the gate, the car went out of control and the nearsighted heiress ran over him.

Strange how the fathers of these rich girls die young. Is it because they work too hard making the fortune to leave to their daughters? A well-fixed man of my acquaintance explained why he was amassing his fortune: "to leave to my daughter so she can tell any man to go to hell." When Doris was thirteen, her father, James Buchanan Duke, passed away, leaving the child the Doris Duke Trust, valued at more than $30 million. Also a trusteeship of the Duke Endowment—a gift of $40 million, with all the accumulated interest. Plus a railroad car named Doris, a New York Tudor castle on Fifth Avenue, "Rough Point" in Newport, Rhode Island, and the Rudy Vallee home, "Falcon's Lair," in the Hollywood hills.

Doris, born in 1912, was privately tutored as a child. She studied French and Italian, the piano and the accordion. As she grew older she loved music, mostly jazz. One year Doris traveled with a Negro band and appeared with them in blackface. Some years ago she was reputedly interested in a jazz pianist. Between fourteen and eighteen she attended the fashionable Brearley and Fermata schools, although her father insisted that simplicity should be the keynote of her childhood, and perhaps this is why she has had a more fulfilled life than Barbara Hutton.

"Nothing makes people unhappier than luxury," Mr. Duke told his shy, solemn daughter, and, "How can you be happy if you are not busy?" Also, "Satisfied ambition is an awful thing."

Doris made her debut into society the same year as Miss Hutton. The rich blondes have known each other from childhood and have always been good friends. Her debut was in Newport (like Barbara she was then "presented" at Buckingham Palace). Three orchestras were brought to the home in Rhode Island to play for the four hundred guests.

In her father's will, Doris was to receive one third of his fortune at the age of twenty-one, another third when she was twenty-five, another at thirty, to protect her from the fortune-grabbers. He did not know Rubirosa! But Doris was never as easy a target for the spongers of both sexes as Miss Hutton was and probably still is.

At twenty-one, Doris was described as tall, slim, shy, solemn-faced, with honey-blond hair and an oversize chin. Did she later have surgery to bring it into line with her more classical features? She was popular with those who realized she was near-sighted. Some acquaintances considered her snobbish, simply because she would pass them by. "Snob," they would mutter, and tell nasty stories about her. Men and women with impaired vision sometimes half-close their eyes to see clearly. These people are noted for their "bedroom eyes." Warren Beatty is a good example.

Doris has always been businesslike, calm in crisis, and usually careful with her money. When you are rich and careful you sometimes get a reputation for stinginess. "I'm not stingy," she declared, "I'm just afraid of being an easy mark. People wouldn't have money long if they didn't ask how much things cost and then refuse to buy half of them."

Unlike Miss Hutton, Doris believes that it is not enough to give money to charitable causes, you must give yourself. During World War II she worked for the United Seaman's Service. Pay: one dollar a year. She was a correspondent for International News Service in the Balkans. "I couldn't live with myself if I didn't do something real to help in this war. This may sound funny to you, but I honestly believe that I'm happier now than I've ever been in my life. I feel that I'm doing something worthwhile, earning the right to be friends with a lot of swell, interesting people. I guess I've discovered that it's fun to work."

On September 1, 1947, while the leaves were turning brown on the Paris boulevards, Miss Duke ecstatically signed her name Mrs. Porfirio Rubirosa, in a Dominican embassy ceremony. Legally Rubi could have taken her for all her millions. But these rich women have shrewd lawyers. In any case, you can usually get the wealthy wife to give a golden handshake when she wants the divorce. The marriage lasted just over one year.

Eighteen days after the wedding, Rubi was accused of smuggling millions of dollars' worth of jewels out of Spain during the Civil War of the late thirties. The accuser was one Manuel Fernandez Aldao of Madrid, owner of a large firm of jewelers. I imagine he believed that Rubirosa's rich wife would pay up rather than face the scandal of a lawsuit. Manuel appealed to General Trujillo to use his influence to have the gems returned, but the dictator refused to cooperate, and perhaps Rubi's claim to being rich in his own right was true.

The story of the jewels: Emilio A. Morel, former Dominican ambassador to Spain, stated that Rubirosa, traveling as a private citizen, had gone to Madrid and taken them out of the country in his diplomatic pouch and therefore was not searched when he arrived in Paris. Morel had fled to France, saying that he was in fear of his life. Rubi was chosen by the Dominican envoy in Madrid to deliver the jewels to Manuel in Paris, who later stated that he did not receive all of the gems. Rubirosa denied the charge.

He had traveled to Paris from Madrid by car, with a Polish friend on a false passport as Rubi's chauffeur. Rubi arrived in the French capital alone and explained that his friend had been killed by a guard. "And I barely escaped with my life." The disappointed Manuel stated, "Rubirosa went into Spain a poor man, but when he came out he was rich enough to buy his wife Flor some expensive pieces of jewelry."

Back to September, 1946. 'Twas said that the United States State Department was not ecstatic over Miss Duke's marriage to the boyo from Santo Domingo. Perhaps they were worried that the huge taxation on her estate would be siphoned into Trujillo's pocket.

It was reported that Miss Duke's passport would be taken from her, but this did not happen. It was soon evident that the marriage was in trouble. Doris divorced Rubi on October 27, 1948, in Reno, where she had maintained a residence since 1945.

If there was an out-of-court settlement it was not mentioned by the judge issuing the decree. It is what these men get *during* the marriage that can make a rich girl less rich. In fact, Doris emphasized this, saying, "He now has ample financial means and is well able to take care of himself."

In the divorce suit she charged Charm Boy with treating her "with extreme cruelty, entirely mental in character [he would never strike a woman] which injured her general health." In America when you get a divorce you can ask for any one of your previous names back, and Doris was granted the right to be a Duke again.

It seemed like a reconciliation when Rubi stayed at the estate in New Jersey in 1951. But they both stated truthfully, "It's not a renewed romance, just friendship." When the sexual flame has been extinguished it can rarely be relit, even for a Rubi. Doris has not remarried, and she is no longer enamored of the jazz musician. I met the latter recently, and from my view of him I can't believe that Doris was ever seriously interested. For the shy girl it was friendship and a mutual love of music. Doris is a collector of jazz records and the sweet music of the twenties.

She is the custodian of the late Vincent Youman's music—"Tea for Two" and "Flying Down to Rio" are among the well-remembered tunes.

Before Rubirosa could marry again, he was named corespondent in two divorce suits. According to newspaper reports, in 1952 rich Richard J. Reynolds, Jr., sued his wife, Marianne—another poor girl—on the grounds that she and Rubi had been together in a hotel room in Paris, presumably in bed. In November of 1953, the well-known society golfer Robert Sweeny named Rubi as the man who had destroyed his marriage to the former Joanne Connelley, New York's most beautiful debutante of 1948. And yet he could sometimes be lonely. A male friend of Rubi's told me, "We were in New York together and I was taking Sharman Douglas to the opening of *My Fair Lady*. Rubi asked me to get him two tickets and said, 'Can you get me a girl? I don't know any girls in New York.'" He must have lost his little black book.

In August of 1953, Zsa Zsa Gabor was vacationing with Rubirosa in the South of France. A reporter confused her name with Garbo and called Miss Gabor to ask for an interview. Zsa Zsa gave him a much better story than the "I vant to be alone" Greta. Zsa Zsa was then married but separated from George Sanders. Rubi still had his job at the Dominican embassy in Paris.

From her own accounts, all of Zsa Zsa's marriages and romances were stormy and difficult—a press director of the Turkish government; Conrad Hilton, who at one time committed her to a mental home featuring, said Zsa Zsa, straitjackets; George Sanders, who insulted her in front of guests or anywhere; Herbert Hutner, who gave her an engagement ring costing $150,000 that she still wears; and her short marriage with Joshua Cosden II or III, I forget which, of Texas.

When General Trujillo was assassinated, some of the jewels he had given Zsa Zsa came to light. She was called a nasty name by a member of Congress. But none of Zsa Zsa's romances and marriages were as tempestuous as the affair with Rubi. He really was deeply in love with her and she was amazed when he told her of his intention to marry Miss Hutton. Rubi had met Barbara in Europe—introduced by the ubiquitous McEvoy—during his long romance with Miss Gabor, but for months he was able to keep both ladies in ignorance of each other.

Zsa Zsa is a blabbermouth, to put it mildly. "Rubi had style, hadn't he?" she said recently to British columnist Roddy Mann. "I was there," she added, "when Doris Duke wrote out a check for $3 million to try to bring him back to her." Rubi, according to Zsa Zsa, tore up the check in front of Doris, and, Miss Gabor told Roddy, King Farouk of Egypt—in exile—had said, "Even though I was a king I would never have done that."

Although Zsa Zsa was consorting openly with Rubirosa, George Sanders did not name him when he divorced the amusing, garrulous woman of whom the late Oscar Levant said, "She enjoys a permanent middle age."

The night before Rubi flew to New York to ask Barbara to be his wife, he was with Zsa Zsa in Las Vegas. "He told me that if I would not marry him right away, he would go to New York and marry Barbara. I told him I luff my career and I vant to stay in America, that I'm a vorking woman and I can't be around people who don't vork!" At this time, because of the Sweeny divorce scandal, Rubi was no longer with the Dominican embassy in Paris.

Zsa Zsa's version of the shiner she received from Rubi: "He got so mad at me for turning him down that he hit me and gave me a black eye outside my hotel suite [at the Frontier Hotel in Las Vegas]. To make him madder, I told him I still luffed George." (She was saddened and shocked by his suicide.)

"I told Rubi that Barbara would be brave to marry him, 'although for a rich woman you're the best pastime she could have.'" Rubi had a different story for the reporters. "I had already proposed to Barbara two weeks before, and I was not doing it out of pique because Zsa Zsa refused to marry me. In fact I never asked her to marry me." Last word from Miss Gabor after Rubi's death: "He was always a gentleman. He was born a century too early, that's all."

The marriage to Miss Hutton took place at the Dominican consul general's home on Park Avenue in New York. The brief ceremony made her a Dominican subject—she had been a Danish citizen with Reventlow. "But," said Rubi at the time, "we have both signed a premarital arrangement where she keeps her property and I keep mine. I have property, you know." Instead of saying "I do" during the ceremony, they both said "*Sí.*" With the marriage to Babs, Rubi's previous escapades were forgiven by his native government. He was given back his job in the diplomatic service in Paris. But first, at the airport, Rubirosa wheeled his bride—she had fractured her ankle—to the privately chartered plane for the honeymoon trip to Palm Beach, where they stayed at the villa owned by the Maharaja of Baroda, who was then in France.

Rubi's wedding ring for Barbara was a gold band set with the usual rubies. Hers to him was a plain gold ring. Her wedding present was a string of polo ponies to add to his stables at Neuilly near Paris. The ponies had a workout in Florida at the Gulf-stream Polo Club. Everyone was impressed with his playing—he was the high scorer. Babs watched from the sidelines in her wheelchair and remained in the villa at night while Rubi sampled the nightclubs.

The fights began forty-eight hours after the marriage. Within a few weeks, Barbara moved into the exclusive Everglades Club, and soon after wired the Hotel Pierre in New York to expect her back shortly. But Rubi, who had returned from a jaunt to swinging Miami with his ex-brother-in-law, Trujillo's son, remained in the maharaja's villa. He was still playing polo and taking trips around Florida in the $200,000 plane that Barbara had given him.

On March 13, 1954, exactly seventy-two days after saying "*Sí*," Barbara announced from the Pierre in New York, where she asked to be known as plain Miss Hutton, "We regret that we have mutually decided it is wisest for us to separate. Our separation is entirely friendly." Again Rubi stated that his poor (rich) wife had wanted a life that was too quiet for him. Surely he had know that Miss Hutton was not a gadabout, that she had been ill for many years. So there could be one reason for his marriage to her. Money.

Naturally he insisted that he had paid for the plane and the ponies, but I strongly doubt that. Even a cache of jewels will ultimately run out, and Rubi always believed in having the best of everything. This is important when wooing a rich woman, even if you have to go into hock to do it. But it is no use getting into debt unless you have the calculated charm to bewitch the heiresses who want something unique in the men they marry.

Rubirosa, reading the innuendos and attacks in the newspapers, remarked tartly, "Never again will I marry a woman of wealth. Perhaps it is better that I marry a poor girl." He did. But first a resumption with Zsa Zsa. She was in Paris with the forgiveness sign on the door of her hotel suite. He was coming back to her, she told the world. On May 6, 1954, they both announced that they would marry as soon as their two divorces were final.

They decided—for publicity—to fly back to New York in *that* plane, Rubi's twin-engine B-25, but unfortunately one engine conked out—I doubt whether the small plane could have made it, it was a converted World War II bomber—and they had to settle for a commercial plane. It would have been more romantic to arrive in their own plane, but thank God the press was at the airport.

A few weeks later, Barbara flew to her home in Tangier. The publicity had distressed her. Later that year, Rubi and Zsa Zsa were together in Ciudad Trujillo. And early in the new year his divorce proceedings started. Rubi obtained the uncontested final decree in the midsummer of 1955.

Fourteen and a half months later, Rubi kept his promise to marry a poor girl. He was rich from two of his marriages and could afford the experiment. This happens all the time. A man receives millions from the rich woman he married. They divorce or she dies, and then he marries a girl—poor usually—whom he genuinely loves.

It reminds me of Grace Moore, who died in a plane crash during the war. Everything went to the impoverished Spaniard she had recently wed. Soon after her death he married a young Spanish girl and at last report was still living happily with her in Spain.

Odile Rodin, a pretty French actress—her real last name was Berard—was nineteen years old when Rubi, now giving his age as forty-seven, which was more or less correct, married her in a civil ceremony at Longchamps near Paris. The mayor officiated this time, not the Dominican consul, which meant that Odile could keep her French nationality and her money, only she didn't have much.

A few friends were present, among them Prince Aly Khan (without Bettina), the Duke de Cadoval, dressmaker Geneviève Fath, Count Guy d'Archangues, and some others who had worked with Rubi and were not important enough to be mentioned.

Rubi met Odile in Paris in the summer of '56, when she was about to play the second feminine lead in *Fabien* by Marcel Pagnol. Rubi was recuperating from an injury incurred while playing polo and was wearing a neck brace, an elegant one, of course. It made him look even more adorable. Complete with brace, he attended Odile's opening night and led the applause at her entrance on stage.

For the first time, Señor Rubirosa was truly happy. This time *he* was on the giving end, and he liked it better than squeezing millions of dollars from rich women. Two years later he was appointed Dominican ambassador to Cuba. He had now risen to the top of his profession. Rubi's session as ambassador was not entirely smooth going. A bomb was thrown into the Dominican embassy in Havana during his tenure as Cuban ambassador in the spring of 1959 and some windows in the embassy were broken. Earlier, their suite at the Plaza Hotel in New York was robbed. The thieves took Odile's $23,000 diamond and ruby necklace and earrings, plus her $7,000 mink coat.

It was an unlucky day for Rubi when Trujillo, Sr., died in May, 1961. Junior inherited the job, but Rubi's diplomatic career was never the same. He was fired by a council consisting of Trujillo foes—Daddy would have stood firm, Junior couldn't. Rubi was caught with his diplomatic pants down. Down? They were off, and now sans immunity. The New York district attorney announced that Mr. Rubirosa would be subject to an investigation if he put one foot in New York.

It was an old crime, the 1935 murder of Sergio Bencosme, an anti-Trujillo exile. Rubi, always a brave man—one of his charms for women—nevertheless flew to New York to clear his name. But before leaving Santo Domingo, he somehow managed to get a temporary diplomat's visa, just in case. He was subpoenaed to appear before a grand jury, which also questioned him about the mysterious disappearance in March, 1956, of Dr. Jesus de Galindez, another anti-Trujillo man. Dr. de Galindez was a lecturer at Columbia University. Rubi promptly revealed his diplomatic immunity and was excused from appearing before the grand jury! Why do women love rogues?

Odile has married again. Her new husband is Paulo Marinho, a Brazilian financier.

Before saying "*Requiescat in Pace*" to Porfirio, we should take a brief look at his marriage broker, Freddie McEvoy. Through Freddie, Rubi had met two enormously rich American ladies, and Freddie did so well that later he was able to indulge himself by marrying a working girl, Claude Stefani. You can be sure that this self-seeking man was in love with Claude, because he drowned while trying unsuccessfully to save her when his $250,000 yacht *Kangaroo* was blown up off the coast of Tangier. Also among the dead: his wife's maid and three crew members. The tall, handsome McEvoy was a close friend of Errol Flynn, and, like Flynn, was born in Australia.

No one has ever discovered whether Freddie received money for introducing poor boys to rich girls. Both Freddie and Errol were sharp operators in money-making schemes pre, during, and after World War II. Freddie especially, who touched on or was concerned with the beautiful people of the thirties and forties until he died a hero's death on November 7, 1951. He was forty-seven.

The yacht, formerly called *Black Joke*, was suspected of gun-, drug-, and whiskey-running. The police investigating the tragedy discovered that the masts of the yacht had been cut through. Miss Hutton, still a close friend of Freddie's, was in Tangier at the time and was very upset. Mr. Flynn, who was in the United States, cabled that he would pay all the funeral expenses for his pal—the fortune had gone on riotous living—and adopt his stepson. The Moroccan police authorities filed murder charges against "persons unknown."

McEvoy first came to Europe in his early twenties. He was accompanied by his mother and his ailing brother Theo. They lived modestly in Nice on the French Riviera. Freddie was noticed at once by the rich widows who were looking for a gigolo to escort them and their dogs. In Australia he had worked as a lifeguard on the beaches. He had a movie-star smile and a fine physique. Millionairesses everywhere, from Cuba, Brazil, England, Italy, America, sought the young men who wanted gold—the women in search of the sun and the sons of bitches in search of rich old ladies, who were so lonely and so rich they *wanted* to be exploited. Freddie, with his physical attributes and easy line of talk, was the gleam in every lonely wealthy woman's eyes. When the Riviera season packed up, the old women and their young men moved on to other playgrounds—Venice, Rome, London, Paris, Palm Beach, and California.

The men liked Freddie for his excellent tennis, golfing, and swimming. He was the British bob-sledding champion at St. Moritz. Like Dr. Stephen Ward, who also came to a sticky end, Freddie's great joy was to mingle with the rich. He would do anything for them, and for his elegant but poor men friends. He was always dressed appropriately for each occasion. He was accepted by the millionaires as one of them—he had attended the exclusive Stonyhurst School—and he would soon be a millionaire himself.

A bizarre story is told of a dinner party in the South of France when Freddie was seated next to the American heiress Mrs. Beatrice Cartwright. She was a Benjamin of Standard Oil, a staggeringly rich family. He held her hand under the table and at one point guided it to his undone fly and whispered, "If you ever want to see this again, give me $5,000." They were married in June, 1940, and divorced October, 1942. But she sent money to Freddie until the day he died. Beatrice passed away in August of 1956.

McEvoy obviously loved the smell of oil. He found it again in his marriage to eighteen-year-old Irene Wrightsman. Her father is oil billionaire Charles Wrightsman, whose wife had worked as a bit player in films. Freddie was then thirty-nine. Not long after the marriage, Irene committed suicide.

Freddie's secret with women? Adventure-loving, full of energy, he was always on the go, always organizing something. He knew everybody and everything about them. He had a hot line into the pockets and conditions of the rich girls. Like, "Okay, boys, Barbara Hutton needs a husband." Ditto for Miss Duke. He considered himself a friend to the rich and poor.

Freddie is dead, all his wives are dead. He brought misery to many people and he died penniless. There's a moral here somewhere.

8. Throwaway Chic — Mrs. Loel Guinness

SHE WAS BORN Gloria Rubio, sixty years ago, in Vera Cruz, Mexico. Her mother was a seamstress, or a milliner—the story varies—in a back street in the city. One of the few women in whom she confides describes her childhood as "excessively poor."

The young Gloria was not beautiful. The neck that one day would support millions of dollars' worth of jewels, was considered too long. She was small for her age, a wispy, thin-boned girl, with a Nefertiti profile and dark flashing eyes that seemed too big for her face.

Today, and since her marriage to multimillionaire Loel Guinness twenty-three years ago, Gloria has been considered by the fashion experts to be the most elegant woman in the world. "Throwaway chic," Jacques Fath called it.

The red hair has lost some of the burnished look, there are some lines on the taut fact, but she is still attractive, and this very special woman is courted, admired, and respected wherever she goes, and she goes everywhere—but only to the best everywhere, as social climbers in five countries have learned to their chagrin.

Among the luxuries Gloria Guinness shares with her husband, Loel, are a yacht that they keep in the South of France, a plane, a helicopter, and homes in various parts of the world—a pied-à-terre at the Waldorf Towers, where Gloria once lived in a servant's room (all she could afford for the cachet of the address—who would know the difference when they met her in the lobby?), a house in the Swiss town of Epalingues in the hills above Lausanne, an apartment in Paris, a farm in Normandy, France, and until very recently a large estate in Florida, and two homes in Acapulco, Mexico.

When I reel off the addresses, it reminds me of all the French kings named Louis, who were always getting into their coaches and galloping off to one of the royal estates sprinkled throughout France. It isn't quite the same for the rich people of this book, but, like the kings of France, they are always traveling to the homes they own, presumably to endow them with some atmosphere of warmth and livability.

Gloria's favorite domicile is the house in Switzerland, where, she says, "I can live simply—wear old clothes and Chanel suits." My choice would have been the fantastic estate known as "Gemini" in Manalapan, the luxurious suburb of Palm Beach, Florida, about ten miles south of Worth Avenue. It is far enough away to avoid the perennial balls for charity—if you are one mile from Worth Avenue, diehard Palm Beachers exclaim, "How can you live so far from town?"

Let me tell you about Gemini—in astrology it signifies "the twins," in this case the ocean and the lake. It takes fifteen servants to run when the owners are absent, twenty-one when they are in residence. Because Florida is becoming too popular, Gemini was very recently put on the market. The asking price was $1,600,000. It has been bought by a Dupont—naturally—for $750,000. Cheap.

The estate is considered among the finest in the world. On one side of Gemini there is 1,500 feet of ocean. On the other side is Lake Worth. Gemini has its own private island close by, with two helicopter launching pads. One part of the residence is geared to ocean living, the other to the gardens and the lake. The huge heated and filtered copper-lined pool, fifty by twenty-five feet, is filled with seawater.

The two parts are connected with an underground living room. The thirty-nine-room house includes six bedrooms and six baths, servants' rooms and baths, marble floors, and fireplaces everywhere—it sometimes gets cold in Florida. On the grounds, which are beautifully landscaped, there is a pitch and putting green. There are two large parking lots.

Personally, I would settle for the apartment over the garage, which has a glassed-in sun porch, a kitchen, two bedrooms and bath, and its own garage with space for two cars.

The furniture was sold with the house, for which it was custom-made. The style throughout is contemporary Palm Beach, lots of glass with stuffed settees and armchairs. You could build another cottage on the East Terrace loggia overlooking the ocean. The servants have a bathroom for each bedroom, a dining room, and a laundry. At one time, Gloria's mother might have been satisfied for her to be one of the servants in such a magnificent house. I have not seen the two mansions in Acapulco —why would they want two?—but I am sure they are equally grand.

Gloria's climb to the top could only have been accomplished by severe discipline and ruthless determination. You must have both to succeed as the little peasant girl has done. An ambitious mother is also helpful. Some great actresses had mothers who pushed them into stardom, thereby working out their own acting frustrations. Gloria's mother believed that her daughter, with her fine features, could one day be a great lady. The child had long tapering fingers, but the poor in Mexico have never heard of soft water. Every night, putting her daughter to bed, Mama Rubio rubbed cream into the small hands to make them smooth and aristocratic to the touch. This is one of the few facts that Gloria has revealed about her childhood. She does not discuss her early years, except to state that her father was a writer in Mexico.

A decade before World War II, Gloria surfaced in Mexico City and mingled with the international set. It was then the golden era of mixed international society, with a sprinkling of Americans who had left the United States because of various illegal business deals, such as the late A. C. Blumenthal, the financial promoter who was wanted in Washington on a federal charge. Sharp-witted and tremendously chic, Gloria was popular with the expatriates, and, encouraged by Blumenthal, she went to Hollywood and appeared in a movie that flopped. Realizing there was no future for her in films, Gloria, with two Mexican girl friends, took off for New York, hoping to find fame and especially fortune. They all did. One girl married an oil millionaire, the other a steel magnate. Gloria, who wanted elegance as well as riches, took off for Paris, where she obtained work as a model, which has always opened the door to the wealthy. Gloria, at 5 feet 7½ inches, still weighs 107 pounds, the right height and weight for a clothes horse.

On a weekend in the South of France, she met the wife of a director for Garbo films. This woman was to introduce her in Berlin to Count Franz Egon von Furstenberg, a German whom she married and with whom she had a daughter, Dolores.

With World War II threatening to explode, the countess, now separated from the count, went to live in Madrid, and it was there that she met Prince Ahmed Fakrey, who became her second husband. Fakrey was rich and related to the Egyptian royal family. He draped her in jewels, and all the time Gloria was learning from the society in which she found herself, although she still has a singsong trace of a Mexican accent. As a young woman she had a great admiration for Mrs. Reginald Fellows—Daisy—a lady who moved in Prince of Wales circles. Gloria was always talking about her, and she copied her style of dress and behavior. Especially the simplicity of her clothes. Daisy should perhaps have received some of the fashion prizes later awarded to her disciple.

Princess Ahmed lived in Egypt with her prince, but when they tried to leave the country, the government—this was about the time of the expulsion of King Farouk—stepped in. They were allowed to go, but the jewels must stay behind.

Gloria was separated from the prince, but still married to him, when she met and fell in love with Loel Guinness, the merchant banker, who is not related to the beer Guinnesses. Loel's father Benjamin died in 1947. The international financier left his son an estimated $200 million. In his will he requested his heir to establish Swiss residence, or "try Panama, Australia, or even Timbuctu. In any case, safeguard your freedom of movement."

Loel was an obedient son. The Loel Guinnesses have sets of clothes and toiletries in each of their six homes and only carry a passport when they travel.

Gloria was named as the other woman in the divorce brought by Loel's second wife, the former Lady Isobel Manners, daughter of the ninth Duke of Rutland. His first wife was the Honorable Joan Yarde-Buller, daughter of Lord Churston, who later married Prince Aly Khan. Loel had two sons and a daughter from his previous marriages, and when his son Patrick, whose mother's husband was Prince Aly, married Gloria's daughter, Dolores, Loel's stepdaughter, it required a mathematician to sort out the various relationships.

"It all sounds very confusing," said the former Joan Aly Khan, "until you work it out. Mr. Guinness is the bridegroom's father. He is also stepfather to the bride. I am the bridegroom's mother, but I am not the stepmother of the bride because Mr. Guinness married her mother after our divorce." Patrick Guinness, surveying his relatives, stated smilingly, "We are all the best of friends." In 1965 Patrick was killed in Switzerland in a car crash, leaving Loel's son Billy as his only surviving male heir.

Dolores's wedding present from stepfather Loel was a diamond and sapphire *parure* consisting of necklace, bracelet, earrings, and clip. Rather weighty for an eighteen-year-old bride. The bride was given away by her father, Count von Furstenberg. The guests included the Duke and Duchess of Windsor, the Greek shipping millionaire Stavros Niarchos, the Aga Khan, and Sir Gladwyn Jebb, the British ambassador in Paris, and Lady Jebb.

Loel's only daughter Lindy married the Marquess of Dufferin and Ava (family name Guinness), thus uniting banking and beer. Dolores has since married the young Prince Sadruddin Khan, brother of Karim, the present Aga Khan. I refuse to figure out this new relationship!

But we are ahead of the story. When Mama Gloria married Loel Guinness in April, 1951, he gave his age as forty-four. Hers, thirty-eight. The press described her as a Paris model who had lived in Berlin before the war with her then husband, Count von Furstenberg, who during the war was aide de camp to Otto Abetz when Abetz ruled occupied France. The marriage to Fakrey had been by proxy. It was recognized in Mexico but not in Egypt. After the war was over, Gloria settled in Paris, where she was a frequent visitor to the British embassy and where she met Mr. Guinness. Sir Alfred Duff Cooper was then British ambassador to France. It was he who introduced Gloria, his good friend, to Mr. Guinness. The British government had been worried about the Duff Cooper friendship because of von Furstenberg's work in Nazi-occupied France. Was it possible they considered Gloria a spy, and was she relaying secrets to Germany? She was not, and Duff Cooper, married to the famed beauty Lady Diana, was too much of a patriot to give away his country's secrets, even to Gloria, whom he liked very much.

Loel and Gloria each had to get divorces before they were free to marry. The ceremony took place in the South of France. The honeymoon was spent on the Guinness yacht, *Sea Fury*. Gloria arrived on deck the perfect yachtswoman, in gray flannel pants, loose cotton coolie jacket, dark sweater, and pearls for the extra touch of throwaway chic. Loel's current yacht, the *Calisto*, with its crew of eight, was rented by Rex Harrison off Morocco when he was courting Elizabeth Harris (Mrs. Richard), now his wife.

In 1963 Gloria became a contributing editor to the American *Harper's Bazaar*. Her first article was titled "Elegance in All Countries." In November, 1967, Gloria won a $1,000 prize in New York for her article in *Harper's*, "The Short, Short, Short Life of the Short, Short, Short Skirt." She stated that her own skirts were "just a teeny weeny bit below my knees." But when she collected her prize money, her skirt length was an inch above her knee. Sometimes what a woman says and what she does are not the same.

Recently twenty-nine of her *Harper's* pieces were published in a small book, titled *Glorious Guinness*, in which she wrote: "Elegance is in the brain as in the body, as in Jesus Christ, our only example of possessing all three." Adding that "Jesus was elegant."

Gloria loved the midi length, which rested somewhere on or below the calf. She prophesied, "It will catch on. A woman in Paris wearing any other length would be considered unfashionable." This is one of the few times in Gloria's fashion-conscious life that she has been wrong. The midi looked awful, cutting a woman's leg to show the least attractive part. I don't remember any legs that looked good in it. Even the maxi was better. At least those awful long hemlines cover *all* the leg.

Gloria, as quoted in the London *Evening News:* "I order my clothes from sketches, except for Balenciaga suits and coats, which I must see for myself." She describes her "working" clothes as "Castillo navy wool pants, navy pullovers, and a pink- and white-check shirt." (She financed the Castillo couturier house in the mid-sixties.) In London she wears black and grays, or black with white. In Palm Beach recently she was seen in a large-brimmed black hat and a sweeping black cape. Black is not usually worn in Palm Beach except for evening functions.

"The idea of clothes," Gloria has said, "is not to spend all of your husband's money. You can look elegant in a blouse and skirt." Also: "The idea of clothes is not to bring the message, it is the woman who must bring the message."

Gloria was reportedly annoyed when Jackie Onassis was listed at one time as the best-dressed woman in the world, with herself in second place. She had some words on the subject at a dinner party at Mrs. Kitty (Bache) Gilbert's home. Not too many, because Gloria rarely says anything unfavorable about another woman. While she prefers the company of powerful men, she believes in having women friends, especially in the United States, where they run the social show. Her current choices for the most elegantly dressed women in America are Mrs. Babe Paley and Mrs. Charles Wrightsman.

In dress, as in many other areas, Gloria believes that "a woman's job is to please the man," which should cause more than a few words from the Women's Libbers. Also, and I agree with Gloria, "the best age for a woman is when she is in her thirties."

Gloria, now in her early sixties, is still elegant and chic. She has no use at all for the sloppy hippies of both sexes. "I'd be horrified if I had a child or grandchild who was a hippie. Just looking at them makes me sick. I believe the press is to blame for so much drug action today."

Sounds a bit stuffy, but Gloria is not prunes and prisms or

starched and hoity-toity. She plays the latest jazz and rock and roll records, and dances wildly. She speeds in her cars—"but the policemen know me! I love music. I love food. I love everything." All except outdoor sports. The only time she was in a pool was when her children were young and they swam at Aly Khan's estate in the South of France. She has tried tennis and golf, but admits, "I'm bad at them all." Besides, she does not want to develop her muscles. She prefers to remain feminine-looking.

She was asked, "Do you have a hobby?" "Yes, one," she replied. "Myself. I'm very self-centered." She once wrote a play to be produced in London. "But"—with disarming candor—"my husband wouldn't let me. He said he didn't want to be left alone for weeks while the play was on the road, and he didn't want to spend his weekends in Manchester and Birmingham. I decided I would rather have the husband than the play."

Gloria reads a lot and has written a nonfiction book, *The China Birds*. She would like to write a novel. How about one based on her own incredible life?

9. *"Till Death Do Us Part" — Nina and Joanne*

NINA DYER and Joanne Connelley were poor beautiful girls who each married twice for money—Nina, English, born in Ceylon, Joanne, the American Debutante of the Year. They both died young of an overdose of sleeping pills.

Miss Connelley came to New York via the Brentwood Academy on Long Island. Her mother was a saleslady in a dress shop. Nonetheless, Joanne, with the aid of a press agent, was able to make her society debut with 115 bona fide debutantes at the Cotillion dance in New York. It was the era where beauty allied to publicity was as important as background.

Joanne was one of the lovely debs who haunted the Stork Club in the great hey-hey days of proprietor Sherman Billingsley. The ubiquitous Ted Howard, always on the prowl for possible clients, spotted the blue-eyed blonde there and introduced himself.

"I beaued her around," he told me casually. "I decided to make her the most talked-about debutante of the year. Mind you, we had some competition—Pamela Curran, another beauty and rival, and Jacqueline Bouvier were also making their debuts at the Cotillion.

"I was worried about Joanne's mother being a saleslady, but I was sure we could overcome that. The listing that year was Joanne, Pamela, Jackie. The runners-up," said Ted, grinning, "didn't have Ted Howard to publicize them." During the week of Joanne's debut, her P.R. friend landed her on the cover of *Life* magazine. It was a triumph and a disaster for Mr. Howard.

The gorgeous girl on the cover attracted the popular rich men about town, among them the designer Oleg Cassini (who had married Gene Tierney), Frank Shields, the handsome tennis player, and rich international playboy and golfing champion Robert Sweeny. His rivals did not take Robert too seriously because of his reputation for pursuing only important women. He had had a round with Barbara Hutton and with the famed beauty Lady Sylvia Ashley. Ted made sure that Joanne knew all this. She promised him she would keep her cool.

"I spent money on her for dancing and singing lessons. I knew that once I had landed her on the *Life* cover I could get her some screen tests. I had three lined up for her. This made her more important to Sweeny. They eloped the following week."

Robert's brother, Charles, had married Margaret Whigham, who was debutante of *her* year in London. Inevitably, the two Sweeny brothers were later divorced from their debutantes of the year. Joanne named one of her best friends as the corespondent. Robert, counter-suing, named that happy boulevardier Mr. Rubirosa. Miss Whigham went on to marry the Duke of Argyll —what a messy divorce that was!—and Joanne married Jaime Ortez-Patino, the Bolivian diamond and tin multimillionaire. And what a firecracker of a divorce *that* was. At the age of twenty-seven, Joanne was found dead in her bed in Switzerland. But we are ahead of the story.

Eighteen-year-old Joanne married Mr. Sweeny at the imposing Saint Edward's Church in Palm Beach. Her mother had announced that it would be a small wedding. But there were 300 guests present, including Marjorie Post, who was Mrs. Joseph E. Davies then (she died in 1973), and Mrs. Joseph Kennedy, wives respectively of former ambassadors to Russia and England.

Joanne's father was not present, but her stepfather was, relegated to an unreserved pew, and he was not invited to the reception. She was given away by the rich, social Winston Guest.

The following year, Joanne gave birth to a daughter. The marriage was reported on the rocks in 1953, by which time she had two children. In the divorce settlement Joanne received custody of the girls, plus a handsome financial settlement.

The next spring, in Paris, she married Jaime Ortez-Patino. She was twenty-three, Jaime two years older. On the wedding night, she swallowed twenty sleeping pills. On June 14, 1954, the police were searching for her. She had disappeared from a nursing home in Rome. "I put her in the clinic to recover from another overdose of sleeping pills," Patino told the police through an avalanche of tears. They had been married for only two months, and he still loved her.

Joanne had been taking at least twelve pills a night since the breakup of her marriage to Sweeny, and, because they had become less and less effective, twice that amount, the doctor assured Jaime, would not kill her. When she fled from the clinic, she took with her, stated Patino, "all our jewels, including mine," adding, "she told me on our honeymoon that she would never give up the drugs. She called them pills. She took so many that she was never really normal. She was a little better in the clinic, so I went off to play bridge and arranged for her to leave the home, but when I returned, she had gone."

The following day, she was reported in London with her mother and trying for a reconciliation with her first husband, Mr. Sweeny. A newspaper account revealed that she had spent the weekend in Sweeny's empty flat in London, then gone to Paris. Her close friends George de Randich and his wife, Doria, informed a newsman that Joanne had escaped with Doria to London to get away from Patino, who Joanne said "beat her all the time, that she was an American and didn't enjoy being slapped." The beating proved to be a figment of Joanne's befuddled brain.

The de Randiches had accompanied the Patinos on their honeymoon—Jaime and Joanne in their Cadillac, George and Doria in their Alfa Romeo. There had been trouble from the start, Joanne sometimes refusing to ride in the same car with her husband. In any case, he preferred to speak in French or Spanish, which Joanne did not understand, although he could understand English.

She was too young and he was too rich, although his money was controlled by an uncle, Antenor Patino, who had been against the marriage. Soon after Joanne's escape from the nursing home in Rome, Jaime filed suit for divorce in Paris on grounds of desertion. She immediately counter-sued in Switzerland, claiming cruelty. Can you wonder why I sometimes weep when I see a couple, so radiant as they exchange their vows, so sure their love will last for ever?

According to Swiss law, there must be an attempt at reconciliation before the case can be heard. Joanne was there, but Patino boycotted the hearing. His fortune, the court learned, was estimated at $60 million, but Joanne stated tearfully that she had not married him for his money, and it might have been true, because at the beginning she agreed to a monthly allowance of $500, whittled down from $4,000.

At the subsequent divorce hearing, Joanne claimed that she had not received a cent of the allowance, and furthermore he had put the money from her first marriage into his own name, and that he had only given her four pieces of jewelry, the other thirty-two were from Mr. Sweeny.

The reason Patino got away with the $500 a month for Joanne was that he had pleaded he was the poor son of a billionaire. To prove his claim of "poverty," he took a job as a furniture salesman for a factory based in Lausanne.

When love flies out the window, lawsuits sometimes fly into court. On August 31—we are still in 1954—Jaime filed criminal charges of defamation of character against Joanne. She had given an interview to an Italian magazine, claiming that Patino had beaten her and caused her to have a miscarriage.

When the case came to court in Milan, Joanne was absent. She was in the Cedars of Lebanon Hospital in Hollywood—she had finally made it to the film city, but not as Ted Howard had envisaged. Even though Patino had brought the suit, he also stayed away. The judge was naturally annoyed. "They started all this fuss," he complained, "and they don't even bother to show up." Nonetheless, he decided against Joanne, gave her an eight months' suspended sentence, with payment of $800 damages to Jaime, plus $232 court costs and a fine of $112.

Meanwhile, Patino was suing Joanne in the London courts for the return of his jewelry. Men can be so gallant! The court ruled that she must put her $90,000 diamond engagement ring on deposit with the London branch of the Chase Manhattan Bank until the ownership of the gem could be decided. I had always thought that once you married the man, the engagement ring was yours for keeps. Apparently not. This proved to be a legal ploy to have all the jewelry held on deposit. Hell hath no fury like the splitting up of the property of a once-in-love couple.

It was now Joanne's turn to bring a lawsuit in London, demanding damages for being unable to wear her jewelry. Patino's lawyer then stated that his client would claim *all* of the jewelry on the grounds of "breach of matrimonial obligations." Joanne counter-claimed. He counter-sued against her counter-claim. Then another libel suit in London by Patino against Joanne because of a story that had appeared in a British newspaper, not only claiming that he beat her but "violently raped her."

"Not true," said Patino, and referring back to their strange honeymoon night, he insisted that after she had swallowed the sleeping pills, she had pushed him away from her, screaming, "Leave me alone." He said it was all so different from their pre-marriage relationship, which had been "rather intimate." For good measure, he added that Joanne was a "worthless woman," who did everything for money.

The once happy debutante, wrapped against the cold in a mink coat, her hat featuring a thick veil, listened silently with a faint glimmer of a smile as he said he was aware of his wrong-doing in the prenuptial living together. He also trotted out the old bromide of blaming the mother for their troubles. In his choice phrase: "It was the mother, the same old mother, always the mother."

Another newspaper asserted that he was really referring to his own mother, who had opposed the marriage. Take your choice. As for the beating when she was pregnant: "She was making a scene in the hotel lobby, and I had to restrain her. She was behaving like a spoiled brat."

When Joanne did not appear at the final hearing, Patino was awarded $56,000 damages, even though Joanne completely withdrew the libelous adjectives. Mr. Howard, in New York, reading all the dreadful details of the suits and counter-suits, must have wished he had not triggered Joanne into the world of riches that proved so disastrous for his client.

The sad battles ended on June 16, 1957, when all the lawsuits in France, Italy, Belgium, and Switzerland were called off with an announced "amicable divorce" agreement—Joanne to receive $67,000, but no alimony, and allowed to retain the engagement ring and a matching bracelet. Two and a half weeks later, she was dead.

A clerk in the district court in Cernier, Switzerland, revealed that she had died of an overdose of pills—whether intentionally or accidentally was not known. Results of autopsies are not published in Switzerland. The divorce decree would have been final in three days. Her maid had gone to her bedroom that morning in the home she had rented in Montmollin, and found Joanne ill. A doctor was called, but before he arrived she died with the peace that comes from the last rites of the Catholic Church. I'm glad that her mother was with her.

At the Requiem Mass on July 9, 1957, in Our Lady Chapel in Saint Patrick's Cathedral in New York, her first husband, Robert Sweeny, was among the mourners. She was buried in the Gate of Heaven Cemetery, Valhalla, Westchester County.

As Marilyn Monroe could not cope with fame—she died similarly from sleeping pills—so Joanne Connelley, who was just as beautiful, could not handle what had at first seemed an exciting, glamorous life. Both girls might still be alive today if the fates had left them where they were.

"Operation Casket"

Nina Dyer was a woman without a past. She lost it during her climb to the Rich People. She never discussed her mother, who was thought to have died when she was a baby. Her father, she said when questioned, managed a tea plantation in Colombo, Ceylon. Sometimes she said he was a lawyer. She was quoted as saying that he had died when she was ten, when she was sent off to a boarding school in South Africa. It sounds as phony as some of the witnesses in the Watergate Senate hearing. After her death, Nina's father, William Aldrich, who proved to be an electronics engineer, claimed her $8 million estate, which she had left to a home for cats.

Nina, born in Ceylon, was described as a "cat person," with her dark hair, feline movements, and hard green eyes. She received a panther from her first husband, German industrial tycoon Baron von Thyssen, who said, "Take away the fur and you wouldn't know which was which."

She was a beautiful object to be admired from a distance. She was coveted by rich men who wanted to add her to their collection of priceless treasures. Nina seemed incapable of love, which made the conquest more exciting for the men who hoped to melt her into matrimony. It was easier than they knew. While Nina claimed that she had no interest in money, her untouchable, unobtainable attitude was the magnet that drew the spoiled, wealthy men.

During her lifetime, the cat lady was as cold as her body after she died at her home in Paris, in July of 1965. She had not cared enough about any human being to leave anything to remember her by. An acquaintance explained, "When the good fairies gathered around her cradle, they gave her beauty, fame, wealth, but they forgot humanity."

Of course she became a model at the age of nineteen when she arrived in London from South Africa, and of course when she became rich she angrily denied this, although she had worked in Paris as a photographic model for Dior and Balmain, among other couturiers. What Nina did for a living matters less than her two unusual marriages. She was twenty-three when she was introduced to the famous industrialist-playboy Baron von Thyssen at a party in Paris. They married in June, 1954, and separated ten months later. The given cause—incompatibility.

During the brief months of bliss, he had showered her with jewels, and given her a menagerie of birds and beasts. For less than a year of reluctant sex on her part she received $2.5 million in the divorce settlement. She was also allowed to keep her wedding presents from the baron, which included the black panther

"Tiamo"—it means "I love you" in Italian; an island in the Caribbean that was also called "Tiamo"; a three-row necklace of 151 black pearls, and two expensive cars.

When her next husband, Prince Sadruddin, the half brother of Prince Aly Khan, was asked how he liked living in a zoo, he replied half-seriously, "I'd like to feed the hummingbirds to the parrots, the parrots to the rare blue pekinese, the peke to the baby leopard, and the leopard to the panther, which I would then give to a zoo." The leopard was ultimately given to Princess Grace and Prince Rainier for the zoo in Monaco.

Nina and Sadruddin were married on August 27, 1957. The marriage lasted five years, during which time they were fairly happy, or seemed to be. Summer tourists on the French Riviera saw the tall, slim brunette at ten o'clock every morning skimming over the Mediterranean on water skis. Not many people were close to her. She was nicknamed "la Mystérieuse" or "the Cold One." Even her jewels, which included a million dollars' worth of emeralds, seemed cold when she wore them at the parties they attended. She rarely talked to the press, and that was only at the prodding of the prince, who said, "Darling, I know you are shy"—her excuse—"but your life has been a Cinderella story, and everyone is interested in that."

The Sadruddins were irritated by the nonstop press reports of the jewels given her by von Thyssen. "Rich men love to give presents," protested Nina. "If you admire something, it usually arrives on your doorstep the next day, tied up in blue ribbons." She had admired Pelleu, the Caribbean Island. "We were sailing near it on a cruise, a tiny island with nothing on it except coconut trees." It lay in a quiet lagoon, on a ribbon of white beach, shaded by tall palm trees. "Without thinking, I said, 'What a lovely spot! I feel I could live there for the rest of my life.'" A few days later, von Thyssen presented Nina with the title to the island.

At another rare interview, she was asked, "How do you marry a millionaire?" She replied, "You must be simple and dignified.[She was the latter, but never simple.] Rich people and important people are really very simple, with simple tastes," she continued. "Some people think I'm a schemer." She immediately denied it. "I'm just lucky. Luck comes my way without my doing anything about it. The big things in life come my way. This has been true all my grown-up life."

At the same time she changed the story of her mother dying when she was two years old. "She died in a car crash when I was twenty-four." This would have been after the first marriage, which, she claimed, broke up because von Thyssen had too many business interests and was always away from home. But they managed when he was home to attend all the jet-set parties. While being a successful businessman, von Thyssen was, and still is, a super playboy. The pace, even for Nina, was too much.

"La Mystérieuse" had met Sadruddin at Prince Aly's annual party in Paris, following the Grand Prix, the horse racing event of the year. She said they fell in love immediately, as she had with the baron. Her friends say it was not true in either case. And rather guiltily: "If you asked me how much Sadri has, I'd say, your guess is as good as mine." All she wanted, Nina said, was to be a good wife and mother to their children. They did not have any, and the only child in whom she ever showed an interest was the three-year-old daughter of her housekeeper and chauffeur.

The wedding to the prince was a simple affair, only twenty guests. Aly did not attend. "He has too many appointments in Paris. He will come along later," said his secretary. Actually, he was not in Paris; he just did not like his future sister-in-law. The wedding was memorable in that for the first time at an important occasion Nina did not wear any of von Thyssen's magnificent jewels. The sparkle was in the prince's eyes, and from her new diamond engagement ring.

While money meant nothing to her, she said, it was nice that the prince had given her a $15,000 Italian sports car, and that he had a magnificent château at Gstaad near Geneva, and a villa in the South of France. No, she would not ever want to be the Begum, wife of the Aga Khan.

If you remember, the old Aga was in a quandary as to who should inherit his title. It would not be Aly, who was too much of a playboy to assume the obligations to his religious followers. It would be either Karim or Sadruddin. As you know, the inheritor was Karim, who also married a model, the former Jeanne

Stuart, who had married Lord Crighton-Stuart, and is now known as Princess Selima.

Nina loved horse racing and had bought a horse at the Dublin Yearling Sales for $20,000. She and Sadruddin spent their winters in his château in Gstaad. But when they parted early in 1960—in the settlement she received half a million dollars—she lived in Paris, he in Geneva and Gstaad. Her thirst for skiing had been quenched when she broke her leg on the snow slopes, her reason for not attending the funeral of Prince Aly in May, 1960. Her social round continued until the end, and her acquaintances had no idea she was contemplating suicide. The man who discovered the body was delivering wigs from her hairdresser.

The tickets for the auction of Nina's property cost three dollars, champagne included. It was called "Operation Casket," which incidentally was covered with two thousand dollars' worth of red roses from her ex-husbands. Among the items, the black pearls fetched $500,000. Among the buyers were Archdukes Michael and Joseph of Hapsburg, Professor de Watteville—Sophia Loren's gynecologist—and Bolivian tin and diamond millionaire Jaime Ortez-Patino, who had quite obviously recovered from the suicide of his first wife, Joanne Connelley.

10. Three Little Girls from School — Linda, Bettina, and Alicia

I WAS LEAVING by the car exit of the MGM studios in Culver City as Linda Christian was walking in. She carried a cardboard box. She greeted me cordially. There was a mischievous glint in her green eyes. "Would you like to know what's inside?" she demanded. She had just returned from Mexico after a discreetly publicized visit to a Very Important Politician, who had been instrumental in getting her a contract at the studio. I made a guess. "Jewels?" She opened the box. The diamond necklace with matching earrings flashed in the Hollywood sun. "From — — —?" I asked. "Yes," happily.

At the height of Linda's romance with the prominent Mexican, Franklin D. Roosevelt reportedly cabled him, "If you don't stop giving jewels to Miss Christian we'll stop sending aid to Mexico!" It's a good story—if true.

Linda has been in love with many men. She married two of them and has been completely candid about all her relationships, whether inside or outside the wedding ring. She believes in living life to the full. She answers questions truthfully, and perhaps this is why I have always found her interesting as well as beautiful. She is also extremely intelligent and well educated. She lives in Rome now and I have not seen her for a few years, but a young Italian actor told me recently that Linda, now fifty years old and a grandmother, is still very attractive, with men of all ages and usually rich swirling happily around the bright glow of her personality.

Linda speaks English, French, Italian, German, and Spanish, as well as Dutch—she was born in Holland of Dutch-Mexican parents. She needs them to converse with the men of different nationalities she has known and loved. They have usually been rich and sophisticated, but once in a while Linda has fallen in love with a small income—such as that possessed by British actor Edmund Purdom, whom she married after his divorce from Alicia Purdom, thereby doing Alicia a great favor, which we will come to later.

Linda's romance in Mexico was over—perhaps the politician needed U.S. aid more than he needed Linda—and, never a girl to sit around and mope when all those lovely men were out there waiting to know her (her first job in Hollywood had been at RKO, where the aging Noah Dietrich, partner of Howard Hughes, had befriended her), she took off for Rome for some work and fun.

Linda's first mate was the late handsome movie star Tyrone Power. He was in Rome making a movie, and she was anxious to meet him. He was fairly wealthy, earning a top salary at 20th Century-Fox—not a millionaire then, but he was the best-looking man in a city of handsome males.

Ty was trying to catch up with a well-known Italian beauty who would not, however, give him the time of day. Newspapers and magazines were full of photographs of Linda with this and that important film executive. All right, the next best and perhaps the best. He started sending Linda flowers, plus expensive crocodile handbags.

The number one Italian beauty declined Ty's invitation to dine with him at the Forum restaurant, where the fiddlers wander among the tables playing romantic tunes. She went there with another man. At the very next table were Mr. Power and Miss Christian. This was their first date, although they had met previously at a cocktail party with Linda's sister Ariadne, who had told the world she had fallen in love with the gorgeous Hollywood star. The more discreet—and smarter—Linda kept her impressions to herself.

Linda and Tyrone were married in January, 1949, at the Santa Francesca Catholic Church in Rome. They were divorced six years later, when Tyrone was forty-two, Linda twenty-eight, and their children, Romina and Taryn, two and four respectively.

During their marriage they gave several parties at their elegant home in Bel Aire with the nude statue of Linda proudly displayed in the garden illuminated with hidden lights. It was rather startling to enter the gates and be immediately confronted with the naked white marble Mrs. Power.

It seemed like a happy marriage. Linda was always on the set of Ty's current film, where they chatted lovingly between takes. I was surprised when they divorced, on May 4, 1955—the grounds: "he became distant and cool." Linda received a $1 million settlement (Ty was then at the height of his superstardom) with Linda getting custody of the children for ten months of the year, two months for Ty. I wonder what he would have thought if he had seen that birthday suit photograph of Romina in a bathtub a few years ago when she was starting her film career?

After his death in 1958 during the filming of *Solomon and Sheba* in Spain, Linda was in deep mourning. During her later marriage to Edmund Purdom the only photographs in her bedroom were of Tyrone. Edmund must have been excessively virile to be able to perform his marital duties under the challenging eyes of his predecessor.

Linda's romances were mostly with millionaires. They included Prince Aly Khan, Baby—I have never known his real first name—Pignatari, John Schlesinger, Jr., Jorge Guinle, Marquis Alfonso de Portago, Errol Flynn, and Glenn Ford.

She was with Glenn one starry Hollywood night not too long ago when she called film columnist Harrison Carroll to tell him that she and Glenn were planning to marry. She had just asked the sleepy actor, "Do you love me enough to marry me?"—you know how men are when they are enamored of a lady, they always say I love you. "Of course I do," mumbled Mr. Ford. It was 3 A.M. Linda reached for the phone to tell the columnist "Glenn and I are going to be married." He had heard this statement from Linda before about other men, and he asked, "Is Glenn there? Okay, put him on."

All Glenn wanted to do at that hour was to kiss Linda goodnight and go to sleep. When Harrison asked him, "Is it true that you and Linda are going to marry?" he replied, "Yes, yes," and rushed off to bed. He awakened at six in the morning with a splitting headache. "My God!"—suddenly remembering.

The columnist would be sleeping, so Glenn waited until later in the day—Mr. Ford is always considerate—then dialed the number and asked, "What did I say?" Harrison told him. "No, no," cried Glenn, "it was not me talking, it was Jack Daniels" (that lovely whiskey). But the story was already in the *Herald Express*.

When Linda was in love with Pignatari, who is regarded as the Howard Hughes of Brazil, she called a press conference to announce, "I am engaged to a tough guy in South America" and, as an afterthought, to prove how much in love she was, "a woman in Brazil cannot get alimony."

The story was printed all over and especially in South America. This was too much for Baby, and he imported a thousand laborers from Hong Kong to picket Linda at her hotel. The placards they carried exhorted, "Go home, Linda." Which she did—tearfully. She is not as tough as people believe.

But during the romance it was all fun and games for the handsome couple. The free-wheeling Baby spent $10,000 one night in Paris for a party of five that included Linda. It started at the famous nightclub "L'Eléphant Blanc," where Baby played the drums and then hired the whole band to his suite at the Prince de Galles Hotel. At five in the morning they all ran down the hotel corridors pounding on the doors, then into the street with the band playing and back to the suite, where a Dior model passed out on Baby's bed.

Linda sometimes took from the rich to give to the poor. Pignatari had given her a beautiful watch, which she gave to a young man to sell for his fare to leave the country. She had loved the watch. Later, the watch was returned to her. Miss Christian once described herself as a female playboy. She was also a great traveler and, usually with the man she loved in the party, visited many parts of the world—Hong Kong, Cairo, Mexico, South America, France, Italy, and so on. You name it, Linda was there.

Linda was deeply in love with the Marquis Alfonso (Fon) de Portago, whose American mother was CCC—Commercial Credit Company of the United States. Ma was worth between $4 and $5 hundred million. Fon, a Rubirosa-type charmer, assured Linda that his wife, from whom he was separated, was taking steps to divorce him. Linda brought a girl friend to chaperone them at their first lunch date. A chaperone for lunch? But it made Portago more eager to get her alone. They went to St. Moritz, where Fon displayed his various athletic skills—skiing, bobsledding, and nose-diving down the dangerous Cresta slope. Linda is all female and loves a strong man. Fon had his Achilles heel, or rather tooth. He shrank from sessions with the dentist. He had a large cavity in a back tooth that showed when he laughed. Linda insisted he visit his dentist and held his hand during the drilling. It is little things like this that endear and make you indispensable to a rich man—or a man, period. One night after a car-racing triumph, Fon asked Linda to marry him. She says she hesitated, and you know what happens to a hesitator. Before his divorce was final, like so many rich playboys before and after him, he was killed in an auto race, the Mille Miglia. "Be fore my eyes," sobbed Linda. "I was plunged into a state of hysterical emptiness. It was Aly Khan who saved me."

Aly, one of the great loves of Linda's life, was to suffer the same fate as Fon. It was the way he would have liked to die, in a fast car with a beautiful woman by his side. His girl, Bettina, the famous model, who was in the car with him, was injured, but not seriously. At that time, the romance between Aly and Linda had dissolved into friendship and she could talk about his death calmly. She was not shocked, she said.

And reminiscing about Aly: "I was enriched by our relationship. I found the real man under the playboy surface. I was his confidante, his ally in the everyday struggle against conformity." He was a fatalist, she informed the press. "He told me to live every day as if it were my last. That way I would fulfill my pact with life."

Linda was not jealous of the other women in Aly's life, which included Gene Tierney ("Gene never bored me," he told me once); Rita Hayworth, whom he married and found dull without her film-star glamor label; Kim Novak, whom I visited in New York at Aly's lovely house in the East Sixties; and, of course, Zsa Zsa.

Linda had met Aly at a supper dance he gave in Cannes during the summer of 1948. She was taken there by Tyrone Power, with whom she had been in love for six months. Aly asked Linda to dance—and he must have been a great dancer because she did not marry Tyrone until the prince had flitted to another lady.

Kim Novak also met Aly at a dance in Cannes and, according to Linda, was immediately swept off her feet. This is interesting in view of what Bettina, Aly's girl, said when a man asked her to dance with him at a party in Paris. "I only dance with the prince." All his girls danced only with the prince.

Bettina was the right kind of woman for Aly. Before meeting him she had married and divorced the Italian photographer Graziani. She was too pretty to bloom alone. There were romances with the publisher Guy Schoeller and the late Bob Capa of *Life* magazine. Then came Aly, and for Bettina there could be no other man. "We had five intensely happy years," she said sadly after his death. She had been helped in handling Aly by the Begum Aga Khan, who like herself also came from modest circumstances and was a model. Like most strong women, neither the Begum nor Bettina faded into neurosis after the death of their man, and each continued living a good life.

Bettina, chic, slender, intelligent, and quiet, sold the house he left her, the Green Lodge home in Chantilly near his racing stables, and built herself a dream of a whitewashed villa on the beach in Sardinia. The shutters are light blue, the walls inside are white. The rooms surround a shaded courtyard, and above are the blue skies of Sardinia. Much of the furniture was brought from Green Lodge, including Aly's favorite portrait of herself.

Bettina does not have to work, but dislikes idleness. Her prince left her $250,000, in addition to the country house. But she is now fulfilling one of her earlier ambitions, to be a designer. If Aly had lived longer, they would have married. His father, the

Aga, was promoting the marriage. In talking of Bettina to Aly, he always said, "Your wife." "He promised to marry me," Bettina confided to a friend, "and never in all the time I knew him did he break his word." One reason why Aly liked her so much was the way she handled the ladies who admired him and with whom he sometimes had affairs. He was half Moslem, remember. "If I bitched about them, Aly would have lost interest in me." The other women in Aly's life were immaterial to Bettina. She had the best years with her Prince Charming. And as Linda said, "No one could ever imagine Aly as an old man."

Perhaps Bettina was the woman she was because of her happy childhood in Brittany. She was born Simone Bodlin. Her family were poor but were content living the simple life in the country. Her father was a railway clerk, her mother the village schoolteacher. When Bettina grew into slim womanhood, she went to Paris with the blessing of her family, and soon became a top model for Jacques Fath, Givenchy, and other famed couturiers. She is an honest, warm woman, placid—"a freckled freshness" is how she has been described.

Bettina is very feminine and, as you know, French women are expert in handling men. They use their femininity to the nth degree, and the men don't realize that the women are controlling them. After Rita Hayworth's temperamental tantrums and jealousy, Bettina was very soothing to Aly, who was not as young and dashing as he had been. Eight months after his death, Bettina appeared in a special TV show in Paris, "The Elegant Ladies of Paris."

"I am completely content," she said recently. She confessed she missed Aly's horses. It had been fun going to the courses with the racehorse owner. Lately she was seen at Longchamps with another owner, Omar Sharif. She is now fifty-two, travels a great deal, and hopes to marry again. "A woman can only give of her best," she says, "when she forms part of a couple. She is only really happy when she feels she is indispensable to the man she loves."

Two years ago there was a rumored romance with a twenty-nine-year-old Italian playboy, Paolo Vassallo, seventeen years her junior. They were like a couple of teen-agers having fun in the sun. Before Paolo, it was reported that she would marry

Count Lorenzo Attolico, but he was married and divorce in Italy was not possible then. She is still looking.

Not so incidentally, the last words spoken by Aly Khan as he lay dying were, "Is she safe?" She is, and I hope she always will be.

The serenity of Bettina is in sharp contrast to Linda. Bettina is content with what she has, Linda was always reaching for more. She claims to have turned down marriage proposals from Aristotle Onassis, Henry Ford, and Howard Hughes. She said they were bores.

Linda was always desirable—'twas said that her mother started teaching her when she was fourteen how to interest men, as Madame Jolie Gabor taught her trio of daughters. Linda always played it cool when she did not fancy the man and that is usually when the rich want you, they want something special, something to be exclusively theirs.

Sex is usually its own reward. Passionate women—and men—don't stop to think, is this good for my future? They want the sex and to hell with money. Up until and past middle age they take the mate they want. But when old age creeps in by a hidden door they sometimes wish they had been smarter in the game of sex. (The case of a close friend of mine who gave away a million dollars' worth of sex before she realized she could have used it for marriage to a rich man. It was too late and she is still working for her cake and jam although approaching seventy.)

Linda has been proud of her beautiful daughters, Romina and Taryn, but she did not approve of Romina's marriage in 1970 to a pop singer whom Linda was reported in print as calling an ape with big ears, and she tried to stop the wedding on the grounds that Romina was too young. Her daughter was furious and when the baby arrived refused to allow her mother to meet her child until two years later.

In 1968 Linda became ill when her beloved poodle was killed in unexplained circumstances. A neighbor implied that Linda in a tantrum had thrown the dog to its death from the balcony of her apartment, an allegation strongly denied by Linda. This sort of thing sometimes happens to a beautiful girl who is always in the news. Homely women who dream secretly of being a femme fatale become jealous and spread ugly stories. The awful things I have heard about Linda, Elizabeth Taylor, Marilyn Monroe, even pure Doris Day and Debbie Reynolds. The latter became colorful only when her son Todd shot himself with a gun she had bought. Demure Debbie with a gun? The publicity didn't hurt the musical remake of *Irene* in which she was starring on Broadway.

Because Linda has taken so many chances in her life, there has been a lot of bad luck, more bad than good. For instance, Robert Schlesinger, the son of Mrs. Harrison Williams, who inherited $10 million in 1935 from her second husband, was in love with Linda and gave her jewels in excess of $100,000, but his check for the gems bounced. The shop demanded the return of the jewels, but Linda, according to press reports at the time, struggled to keep them. "A gift is a gift," she was reported as saying. She was ultimately persuaded to return them for a payment of $30,000.

Unlike Mrs. Burton, Linda has always been more interested in the value of the gems she collects. Elizabeth will never sell hers —when she goes to her final bejeweled resting place, her children will sell them and collect millions. Linda's kids will be lucky if they get her wedding rings. Not long ago, her mink coat was stolen and sold for $300. In 1963, Linda filed a $150,000 suit for damages against the Plaza Hotel in New York in connection with a loss of jewelry. A friend in London loaned her a beautiful home. Linda went away for the weekend and she returned to an empty house; everything had been taken out, from the grand piano to a bedside radio.

She tried to sell an Epstein sculpture of her head at Christie's recently, but the bidding did not reach the reserve price. In 1959 United Artists arranged for her two daughters from the marriage with Tyrone to receive 2 percent of the gross from *Solomon and Sheba,* the film in which he had been starring in Spain when he collapsed and died. If you remember, Yul Brynner took over the part and demanded and got $1 million—he had the company in a bind. So what with having to scrap all the scenes with Tyrone and remake the film with Yul, and the fact that it was a big flop, the 2 percent didn't mean anything.

Linda was never in a hit movie. As she became better known,

her roles increased, and in 1956 she starred in a TV play with Edmund Purdom. It was called *A Piece of Cake*, and Linda had her cake and ate it (she was to marry Purdom in 1957). She made a movie with Robert Taylor, *The House of the Seven Hawks*. There were few customers at the box office. Another film, *The Moment of Truth*—it was about bullfighting—was shown at the London Film Festival of 1965. The general opinion of the critics was that "it is too cruel, too savage, too sadistic, and too awful. Ban it."

Linda is usually hard up for cash. She spends money as though it were going out of style. A few years ago, court officials in Rome seized her furniture because of an alleged failure to pay for two fur coats. Girls like Linda get credit because the shopkeepers believe they will find someone to pay. I understand that Miss Christian has lately taken up a new hobby. There was Power, Pignatari, Purdom, and now there is Painting.

Alicia Purdom Clark and Linda are alike in many ways. They are both cool and calculating, both beautiful—Alicia blonde, of Polish ancestry, Linda brunette, with the best of her Mexican and Dutch lineage. They also have the same ability to attract rich powerful men. And they both married Mr. Purdom, who was poor by comparison with their other conquests.

Alicia's actual name is Alicja Kopsznska. At first she called herself Barbara, then Alicia Darr for her professional name as an actress and painter. Alicia fell in love with Purdom after seeing him in *The Egyptian*. She was determined to meet him and asked a press agent at MGM to allow her to sit in at an interview scheduled for Edmund with a journalist. "I'll have to check it first with Mr. Purdom and the journalist," he told her. By the time he came back to Alicia with an affirmative she replied, "Oh, don't bother, I met him last night."

Purdom was handsome and gentle—this can be pleasing to certain women. And even women who want to marry or be supported by rich men sometimes go off the track and fall genuinely in love. Alicia married Edmund in Hollywood where he was under contract to MGM. After *The Egyptian* he starred in *The Student Prince*. Edmund did the acting and Mario Lanza, who was too fat for the part, did the singing. Alicia was then an actress playing small roles in films. It was a stormy time.

"Marriage to Edmund just didn't work from the start. It was impossible to have two careers in the same family," said Alicia, which is rather funny. Personally, I can't remember one film in which Mrs. Purdom appeared. After the divorce she was reported in love with Jacques Charrier, who had been married to Brigitte Bardot, the sex kitten. Alicia boasted, "I think he is forgetting Brigitte."

Purdom's first wife, Tita, at one time claimed that Edmund was spending $1,000 a week on Miss Christian—if you are getting confused over this triangle, so am I. Tita also claimed in court that her two children from the marriage with Purdom were starving, while their father was showering Linda with money.

Poor Mr. Purdom, he was always being sued by the women who loved him in courts all over the world—London, Rome, Mexico, Switzerland, Naples, New York. At one time when Alicia was bringing a suit for separation in London, she named a redheaded actress as the other woman. Whether she was or wasn't was never proved, because there was another reconciliation with Edmund.

But when he was in love with Linda, and vice versa, he was anxious for a divorce from Alicia, which finally took place in Mexico, whereupon he married Miss Christian. Within months, Alicia made her great capture of Mr. Alfred Corning Clark, the Singer Sewing heir. Until she married him she was always hard up and trying to find ways of making money. After her final separation and divorce from Purdom, she claimed she was broke, "with only five dollars to my name. I hope," she added sadly, "to sell some of my paintings in New York."

How she met Mr. Clark is a good object lesson in How to Marry Rich. She was at loose ends and living in New York, and still trying to sell her paintings, when a friend said to her, "You should marry again." And, thoughtfully, "Why don't you go to the Guggenheim Museum? You meet a fine [rich] class of men there." Shortly before this, Alicia, who rarely waited for what she wanted, had said to another friend, "I'd like to meet Mr. Clark, will you find someone who knows him to introduce me?" The wish is father to the deed. Without waiting, she stationed herself outside the Guggenheim Museum and waited for the man she wanted. She was lucky. Clark was inside. It was raining when he came out, and seeing the lovely drenched blonde, he offered her shelter under his umbrella. They married soon after. He died thirteen days after the marriage, leaving his bride with $10 million, plus his paintings, among them Rembrandts and Picassos. Also all the jewelry, his and hers, which included the egg-sized diamond engagement ring. Clark had made the will the day *before* he took Alicia to bed and board.

Soon after his death, an impoverished titled Frenchman announced that he wanted to marry the widowed Mrs. Clark. "And," he said virtuously, "I won't let her money stand in our way." They had known each other some years before. Alicia sent word to him in Paris to forget her, "as I have forgotten him."

Now she was rich and could settle into expensive obscurity, but Alicia seemed still somewhat in love with Mr. Purdom, who had now been divorced by Miss Christian and was wooing Norma, previous wife of the five-times-wed Mr. Clark!

When Edmund was at the Palace Hotel in St. Moritz, Alicia appeared and marched into his bedroom. The idea was to find him with Norma. But Edmund was alone and asked her to leave. She refused, and he called the management. The owner, Andrea Badrutt, was polite but firm and insisted she go to another hotel. As Alicia dramatically told the reporters, she went "in the snow" to the police station to lodge a complaint.

A cop accompanied her back to the hotel. Purdom showed the law his small single room, "too small, as you can see, for two people." Alicia then went across to the Carlton Hotel, while Purdom told Badrutt, "On no account is she to be allowed to return here." The last I heard of Edmund was that he was living in Capri, where he owns a record shop.

In 1965 the battling lady sued a male friend for $100,000. He had told her, Alicia stated, that he was about to marry into the Aston Martin auto family and offered to get her one of their cars at a $3,000 discount. No matter how rich they are, they still want a bargain. Alicia gave him a check for $12,500. But she complained that he registered the car in his own name and refused to give it up. She won the case.

There were rumors that Alicia would marry the Duke of Marlborough (father of the present duke), whose wife had recently died. "No," denied the duke, "the tradition in my country is you don't marry for a year after your wife dies." Soon after the end of the year he married Mrs. Laura Canfield, whose third husband had died a year before.

Laura was a poor relation of an aristocratic family when she married her first husband, David, Viscount Long of Wraxall. I had met him in St. Moritz during what I call my society period, and on one of my visits to London from New York he invited me to dinner with Laura and her sister Anne and her husband, Lord Shane O'Neill. Anne also did well in the matrimonial stakes with marriages to two peers of the realm, O'Neill and Viscount Rothermere, and a third marriage to Ian Fleming.

While the others were talking, David told me of his rather sudden decision to marry Laura. "We were out riding, and when we returned to the stables, Laura realized that her horse had gone lame. She put her arms around his neck and cried. I found that irresistible." I suppose the moral of this is that to get the peer, you cry on the neck of the horse.

Back to Alicia. The Italian magazine *Ore*, which is not always correct, published an interview purportedly with her in which she stated that before President John Kennedy married Jackie he had wanted to marry her. When the piece was published, Alicia claimed that she had been misquoted, but it was possible. John and his brother, Robert, were great admirers of beautiful women. JFK certainly knew Alicia, Linda, and Marilyn Monroe—very well—and other entrancing ladies. If he had married one of them, could he have become President of the United States? I leave the answer to you.

11. Where There Was Hope, There Was Sikkim

THE LADY who came to dinner handed her coat to the king and curtsied to the butler! An embarrassing moment? Not at all. The King of Sikkim laughed. At another time, he walked into the White Elephant Club in London's Curzon Street and was told there was no table for him. "I'm with these friends," he said, apologetically. His hosts were well known in the London jet set, but at that time were absolutely broke. "Oh, that's all right then," said the maître d' and stood aside for them to pass.

These anecdotes give an idea of the royal personage who, on March 20, 1963, married wealthy socialite Hope Cook of New York and Seal Harbor, Maine, in Gangtok, the capital of Sikkim. The prince was a widower. The Tibetan noblewoman he had married in 1950 died after giving birth to a daughter in 1957. There were two sons from that marriage. He had announced his engagement to Hope in November, 1961. She had expected to be the bride of the prince—he had not yet inherited the throne—early in 1962. But the people of Sikkim, a tiny kingdom about the size of Delaware, were strongly opposed to the marriage. Every queen had been Tibetan for the past four hundred years. The diplomatic Buddhist astrologers decided that 1962 was a "black year," and postponed the nuptials for eighteen months, no doubt hoping that it would all go away.

The government of India, the protector of the mountainous country after the British moved out, was also perturbed. Uprisings could cause problems with China, which had recently moved into Tibet. However, Peking was quite pleased with the match, hoping that this would be a signal to annex Sikkim, together with the neighboring two small kingdoms of Nepal and Bhutan.

The more obstacles presented to Maharaj-Prince Kumar Sikkim Palden Thondup Namgyal, the more determined he was to marry the girl he had met in the tea lounge of the Windamere Hotel in Darjeeling, India. She was not only taller than he, but she was richer. Another worry for the Sikkimese was that Miss Cooke was a Protestant, an Episcopalian. The stubborn heir to the throne ignored the clamor, and in a palace ceremony, placed a diamond engagement ring on Hope's fourth finger, left hand. Both the ring and the palace are small by Hutton, Duke, or Elizabeth Taylor standards—fifteen rooms in all for the palace, with a garage containing two jeeps and a blue Mercedes-Benz limousine. The ring cost $2,000.

Miss Cooke, aged twenty-one, a senior at Sarah Lawrence College, had taken her junior year in Sikkim to study Oriental languages. She had been raised by her uncle and aunt, the Selden Chapins, after the death of her grandparents, the Winchester Noyes. Her mother had died when Hope was aged two. Her family ancestry goes back almost as far as her husband's—to Francis Cooke, who sailed to America on the *Mayflower*, and the Noyes family, who founded Newbury, Massachusetts, in 1634. Mr. Chapin, in the U.S. diplomatic corps, had served as ambassador to the Netherlands, Panama, Iran, and Peru.

Hope graduated from the Community High School in Teheran and was presented to society in 1958 at the Debutante's Ball in Washington, D.C. After the teaparty in the Windamere, Hope returned to Sarah Lawrence for her last year. But she and the prince corresponded—there is nothing like letter-writing to keep the flame burning.

On a visit to the United States, which always makes a big to-do when an American girl marries a European king or prince, Hope stated solemnly, in her slightly-above-a-whisper voice, that her fiancé was a "very wise and good man." While not changing her religion, she would raise their children as Buddhists.

Her grateful fiancé stated that although his country allowed polygamy, he would have one wife (at a time) only. In turn, Hope sent a check for $2,000 to the Indian National Defense Fund when Sikkim was under a state of emergency because of border clashes between India and China.

Before the marriage, a statement was given to the press that Hope, whose royal title would be Princess Hopla, Consort of the Deities, would rank equally with Princess Grace, the wife of the ruler of Monaco, a kingdom that is even smaller than Sikkim, but would outrank the Duchess of Windsor.

It was a spectacular wedding, following the custom of the country. A dozen chefs were brought from Calcutta, the orchestra from Bombay. The four-day wingding cost the government about $5,000. This small sum (for royalty) was another irritation for the impoverished people of Sikkim. The prince remarked, "I wish we could have a Christian ceremony where, once the ceremony is over, the couple are left in peace. This will be a long and tiring thing."

As part of the ceremony they exchanged twelve-foot-long white silk scarves, which were placed around their necks. The allotted money did not go far in entertaining the 15,000 guests, which included John K. Galbraith (then American Ambassador to India) among the two hundred foreign guests. Four hundred chickens, one hundred goats, and two hundred pigs were slaughtered for the royal feast. The National Congress Party protested the killing of the birds and beasts—especially as the groom had not consulted them.

Hope was immediately made aware of the position occupied by women in Sikkim. While the high lama chanted the service, the king sat cross-legged on one platform, the bride one step down in an attempted cross-legged position. Neither had to say "I do," or promise to love, honor, and obey. This was implicit, for Hope anyway. The setting was a monastery, hung with gold cloth and red tapestries, before a huge statue of Buddha.

The prince wore a Tibetan dress of bright yellow silk and gold brocade. I am sure you are longing to know what the bride wore—an all-white brocade traditional wraparound garment, heavily ornamented gold bracelets, and a heavy gold belt that held a small dagger. The ceremony was seen by the Sikkim people and those in surrounding kingdoms via closed-circuit television.

One of the guests said, "She is embarking on a personal adventure that makes Princess Grace Kelly seem almost tamely Ruritanian." Hope said, "I have taken a one-way ticket to Sikkim, where my heart now belongs." Belongs! Looking at her now, you get the impression she invented the country. She is more Sikkimese than the native-born. Her clothes, her speech, the way she repeats a word, her pride in her husband and his kingdom all spell "Sikkim." She has no problem now sitting cross-legged, and crouches in the native way when she walks. Her speech is barely audible. It's almost a hiss. She is a chain-smoker, a habit she did not contract in Sikkim, but after-hours from her nursing social work. When the father of the prince died of cancer in December, 1963, the husband of Princess Hopla became the Absolute Ruler. He prefers to be called Chogyal, which also mean "Ruler." She is Gyalmo—"Consort."

Priests in the mountains proclaimed the royal marriage on six-foot-long horns, echoing across the valleys, which must have scared the birds and the sheep who graze on the sparse slopes. Sheep are most important to the economy of Sikkim. "They don't have enough land for grazing for twelve months of the year, so we encourage the sheep to go into Tibet," says the king. "They prefer green pastures, but we always make sure they will return. When the Chinese invaded Tibet, they put up barriers to keep out the animals. Our big industry is the wool from the sheep, so you can imagine the unstable condition of our economy."

There has been trouble in that part of the world for a thousand years. Last year, the people rebelled again, and it was almost Seal Harbor here we come. But the King called on Mother India, and, as of going to print, matters have settled down, although for several months the king and his family were confined to the palace for their protection.

But Hope, Hopla, or Hopey, as her friends call her, made a vow that she would grow old in the Himalayas—she brought along two rocking chairs for this purpose. (Sikkim is ten thousand feet high up in the mountains. It is hard to reach. First you must get a visa from India, then fly to Calcutta and transfer to a jeep to drive a whole day around the sharp, ever-rising, curving, unpaved, practically impassable roads. The air is fresh, the streams are unpolluted, and the people are healthy and live to a good old age.)

At one time, the king, who is aware of conditions in his country, was interested in Communism. He went to Moscow to find out what it could mean for his people. He decided against it. He prefers the paternalistic method of ruling, to be the father of his country, the feudal lord who takes care of his serfs.

While living carefully on a small budget—$5,000 is allotted annually for food and drink—they have a good life. From the king: "We are not rich. We travel on government money, but it's never enough. We have to rely on our friends to feed us and"—laughing—"we beg, borrow, and steal to make do." The king, an Eastern man with an Eastern philosophy, has tried to cope with his duties in Western Oxford-educated manner. "Unlike Tibet," he has said, "there is no landed aristocracy in my country. This is not possible in a poor country." Queen Hopla contributes to the family finances with the fortune she inherited from her family.

It has been a good deal for the king, but it would be wrong to say that she has given more in money than she has received in happiness. "Hopey was always a little out of place in the West," said a school chum. "She's always been crazy about the Orient, and feels right at home on a cloud." The palace, with its beautiful grounds, has been a Shangri-La for the former Miss Cooke, who seems to have become darker of complexion as the years go by. She was once described as a "fair-skinned brunette with a Myrna Loy nose and large gray eyes."

There have been two children from the marriage, a boy, Paldun, and a girl, Princess Hope Leezum, but Queen Hope is equally interested in the two grown-up boys and girl from her husband's first marriage. The stepsons are Kunzang Jigme Tenzing, twenty-three, and Tobgyawal Wangchuk, twenty-two; the daughter, Yangchen Dolma, is aged eighteen. They were all educated in England.

Paldun was born in February, 1964. Hope took the baby to America, to show him off to her relatives. Wearing a national dress of green silk to meet the reporters, she said, "No, I am not bored. I truly, truly, truly like my role of consort to the king. I have many domestic duties which I enjoy. I am also writing a history of Sikkim."

One reporter described her as "still the same shy, reserved, freckle-faced girl." She was asked, "How do I address you?" Hope replied, in the smallest whisper, "Your Highness, I believe." When asked what she had thought of the king at their first meeting, she replied, "I was immediately impressed by his charming manners, so typical of the East. Call it love at first sight." And added, "He proposed to me on the dance floor. I said, 'Yes, yes, yes.' There was no grand design on my part to catch a king. I just fell in love with sad, sad, sad eyes and sad smile, and disjointed and beautifully courteous manners." She referred to the Sikkimese affectionately as "my people."

While astrologers gave the dates for the engagement and the wedding, Hope believes that the signs of the zodiac have nothing to do with their happiness. (She is Cancer and he was born on the cusp of Taurus and Gemini.) "The important factor that makes us get on so well is that we were both the second children in our families" and "life gets better every year." The king's older brother died before he ascended the throne. She was asked, would she leave Sikkim if the king—he is fifteen years older—were to die. It was not a happy question, but she whispered gently, "I'll think about that if the time comes."

As of going to press, she and her children were in the United States for medical and political reasons, but I am sure she and the king will soon be together.

12. The British Royals

Anne and Mark

ANNE IS a rich princess, Mark a poor lieutenant in the army. His pay as an officer in the Queen's Dragoon Guards is about $6,250 a year. Mark's father, Major Phillips, is better off. He is a director of three companies, including the well-known sausage makers, T. Wall & Son. He is an expert on pigs and in charge of buying the pig meat for the company. Dad lives in a pretty sixteenth-century farmhouse in the little village of Great Somerford in Wiltshire—Wiltshire bacon is famous all over Europe. He earns between $50,000 and $60,000 a year—not a fortune by royal or today's inflationary standards. Anne's pre-marriage annuity of $37,500 was raised on her marriage to $87,500. She also received a large supplement from the queen, her mother, who is one of the richest women in the world, and who also married a poor man.

The engagement of Princess Anne, only daughter of Queen Elizabeth II and Prince Philip, to Lieutenant Mark Phillips was announced officially on Tuesday, May 29 of last year. The marriage took place last November 14, which was also the twenty-fifth birthday of her older brother, Charles, Prince of Wales.

In bygone days, a royal princess married for reasons of state, to form an alliance with another powerful country. The princesses were usually married off in their cradles—as Mary of Scotland was to the Dauphin of France. Mary was shipped to France as a child and brought up with her future husband, who was little older than she. They married at the ripe age of sixteen, but soon after, he committed the fatal sin of dying.

Happily today, princesses are allowed to grow up first, and to choose their own husbands. Princess Anne was a young maiden of twenty-two when her engagement was announced. She had known Mark for several years through their mutual love of horses, having met him casually in 1968, then more frequently from 1971.

Several rich royal ladies and gentlemen have tied the knot with a poor spouse, especially in the present House of Windsor. There was Edward VIII, who married Wally Simpson. Prince Richard of Gloucester married a Danish secretary. The late Duke of Kent took the impoverished Princess Marina of Greece for his bride after a frowned-upon courtship of American piano player Edythe Baker. Lord Snowdon, a well-educated, pleasant photographer, ran into a fortune when he married Princess Margaret, the queen's sister. Princess Alexandra had rich relatives; her husband, Angus Ogilvy, is the brother of the not-so-rich Earl of Airlie. There will be more marriages, no doubt, of a royal Windsor and a poorer consort. It could certainly happen for the present Prince of Wales who, because of his sense of duty to the Britsh crown, might prefer a poor princess to a rich nonroyal. But you never can tell, love is where you find it, and you never know when Cupid will go into action.

There is no doubt about Mark's love for Anne, or hers for him. At the beginning he was rendered practically speechless by the romance. I can still see him on television, grinning like a charming idiot, and trying to answer the questions posed by the sharp reporters. The words were strangled in his throat, although I did manage to catch "Iwaspetrified" in reply to the question of how he felt when asking Prince Philip for the hand of his daughter. When asked about his future prospects, he giggled and ventriloquized, "What prospects?"

Mostly Anne answered for him. She is used to this sort of

thing. Mark will have to get used to it. Can you imagine how this embarrassed man will sound when there is an announcement of a baby! I won't watch, I won't listen. I pray he will be left alone at that shy-making moment, unless Princess Anne has managed to teach him some of her own savoir faire.

Do you remember their first public kiss when Mark was stationed in Germany? No, they were not going to meet, said Buckingham Palace. But of course they did, all the time. When lovers are in the same country, try to stop them. The handsome lieutenant barely brushed her lips, but Anne went limp and swooning at such close proximity. The second kiss in Germany was more casual. Anne hadn't cared for the photo showing her eagerness to surrender to her man. She is as royal as her mother, and such revelation of inner tumult is not permitted in public.

When you marry a British princess, you are not only accepted into the inner circle of royalty, but you also gain a title. Mark will probably be created an earl, in which case their oldest son will be a viscount, and all the daughters will have the prefix Lady. (It would be inconceivable for the queen's grandchildren to be addressed as plain Mr., Mrs., Miss, or Ms.)

Even before the engagement was announced, Mark knew that he would be transferred to an executive job at the Military College of Sandhurst, from which he graduated a couple of years ago. His wife, therefore, does not have to lead the usual lonely life of a spouse of a British officer at home or abroad. He is able to see Anne every night for dinner, bed, and breakfast at their home at Sandhurst. This pleases the couple, who are still more or less on their honeymoon.

It is not a bad life for a man if he has an absorbing work interest of his own. The husbands of princesses do not attend all of the royal functions with their wives. Their public appearances are limited mostly to escorting the royal ladies to a film premiere for charity or a play. It will be fun seeing them compete together at the various horse shows. Anne has beaten her husband on several occasions. As his wife, will she be smart enough to let him win? No man, even a commoner, likes to come in second to his bride.

Margaret Jones

Everyone was wondering why Queen Elizabeth was frowning. Had she disapproved of the marriage? I forgot the bride and groom and concentrated on the queen. She was clearly put out. She had thumbed down her sister's wedding plans before, but then Margaret had been in love with Captain Peter Townsend, a divorced man, and not all the queen's horses or all the queen's men could put that marriage together in the Church of England, of which Elizabeth is titular head. Why was Margaret always choosing the wrong man? It was very tiresome of her.

Elizabeth herself had married the penniless Prince Philip, but at least he was a prince and related to her dear Uncle Dicky Mountbatten. In fact, Philip was her own cousin, many, many times removed to be sure, but he was an aristocrat, and it showed even in the way he walked with his hands clasped behind him. Philip never floundered. But Margaret's groom, Antony Armstrong-Jones, was short, ordinary-looking, and popular in such a Bohemian crowd, my dear. He actually lived in Pimlico!

True, Tony was a good photographer. It was really Elizabeth's own fault that she was now sitting in the front row of the section in Westminster Abbey reserved for royalty, while the bridal couple knelt in front of her own dear Archbishop of Canterbury, taking their marriage vows. They looked for all the world like a toy bride and groom on a wedding cake. It was *she* who had consented to Mr. Jones taking portraits of her young son Charles and younger daughter Anne, and then Margaret. If only the globe at which her children had been looking intently in the photograph had been a crystal ball to foretell this day, she would have sent Mr. Photographer Jones packing. But they had all come to like him. He was respectful and easy to have around. Too easy. And what was that story about his attentions to a certain Miss Jacqui Chan?

If Her Majesty had asked me at that moment while the trumpets blared ecstatically, I could have told her about Miss Chan. Only a week before, I had taken Jacqui to lunch to learn about Tony's past intentions pre the sudden engagement to Princess

Margaret. The pretty Chinese-born actress had been seen everywhere with Tony, and I, for one, had assumed that they were lovers.

I was in London to cover the wedding of the queen's sister, and I was trying to interview some, or even one, of the people concerned. The queen and Prince Philip were out of the question. I had lived long enough in England to know that. Tony, aware of his new status, had clammed up, although I had met him casually in New York at a cocktail party when, as Mr. Armstrong-Jones, he was taking photographs for the slick magazines. But he had been briefed on what *not* to say, which was NOTHING.

Where was the soft underbelly—as Churchill used to say—of the situation? Miss Chan, obviously. But Dorothy Kilgallen had been trying to get to her without success. I was writing for the *New York Mirror*, Dorothy, a veteran reporter and columnist, for the *New York Journal*.

We had often been in competition for the same story. She was a good reporter in the traditional sense. But I was more adventurous and persistent, from the first time that we were on the same story—the trial of the German Bruno Hauptmann, charged with the kidnapping of the infant son of Charles and Anne Lindbergh.

When the Scottish nurse was due in the witness box, all the hundreds of reporters were trying for an interview with her. The lawyers were in a quandary, but finally, during a brief interval in court, decided that one reporter from Scotland would get the interview and give it to the rest. I decided to be that reporter. "Quick," I said to the man sitting next to me, "what is a good Scottish name?" "What is the matter with Graham?" he flashed. I became an instant reporter for the *Glasgow Herald*. But Dorothy and the others made such a fuss when I was chosen for the job that no one got it.

But this time around, I got Jacqui. She had been appearing in the West End production of *The World of Suzie Wong*. Because reporters around the world were trying to reach her, she left the show following the announcement of Tony's engagement to royalty. A kindly man at the stage door gave me her home number.

I called, and I called, and I called. Each time, a voice with a Chinese accent would say, "Miss Chan not here." Strategy was required. I telephoned my friend Ross Hunter in Hollywood—he is the successful producer of film musicals. "Will you give Miss Chan a role in *The Flower Drum Song*—which he was about to start for Universal Films. "Gladly," he replied. It would be a sharp piece of publicity.

I picked up the phone, dialed the Chan number, and without bothering with preliminaries, said, shrieked almost, "We want you in Hollywood for a film." Silence. "Ross Hunter," I added, then: "This is Sheilah Graham, I have come all the way from Hollywood to interview you." I had, in a way. I asked her to lunch with me, and she said, "Yes."

Jacqui had a lot to tell me. Right up to the week before the queen announced the engagement of her sister Margaret, she had been receiving visits from Tony. She spoke very highly of him, but had been as surprised as nearly everyone else that he had captured Princess Margaret for his bride-to-be. "They are so different," Miss Chan mused, adding positively, "it won't last."

It has, for fourteen years—the marriage took place May 6, 1960. There have been some strained times, when it seemed certain that Tony, created the Earl of Snowdon, and his princess-countess would separate. They seem to have an arrangement. They live together in the exclusive Kensington Palace area and appear together at the important functions—Tony was at Balmoral for the weekend family party before the announcement of Princess Anne's engagement to Mark, but he is not a frequent visitor to Windsor Castle or Buckingham Palace. They have some similar interests—music and ballet—but more or less lead their own lives. She will pop off to the Bahamas, he to New York on photographic assignments, then join her perhaps for a week and the flight home.

Tony is not at all interested in horses, except from an aesthetic point of view—his in-laws, as you know, are daffy about horses. Tony and Margaret have friends in common and both adore Peter Sellers. They like small, intimate parties. They sometimes call unexpectedly on friends and stay for a bite—they did this more in the early years. Margaret obviously does not consult Tony about her clothes. His taste in these matters is instinctive. Hers is haphazard.

You don't often see Prince Philip with Tony, and if anything he was less enthusiastic about the match than his wife. But outwardly, all is serene, and the children of the Snowdon marriage come to the birthday parties and such for their young cousins, Prince Andrew and Prince Edward, the Duke of Kent's brood, and Princess Alexandra's offspring. It all looks like one, big, happy family, and as far as the children are concerned, it is.

While Princess Margaret becomes somewhat more imperious with each passing year—she is not as plump as she was and perhaps that is why she and Tony today are seen more together—he has remained the Bohemian charmer. He had this little white minicar, and I was a passenger after our photographic session at the London *Sunday Times* for the serialization of my book *College of One*. While taking the pictures in the expensive studio built for him by the prestigious newspaper, he was so down-to-earth and pleasant that soon I was telling him my whole life story. Afterward, he presented me with a copy of his book *Private View*, and offered to give me a lift toward my destination.

He was going to Saint James's Street to meet someone in a club for lunch. Talk about a ride of terror! I was nervous as he weaved in and out of the traffic at a fast pace, torn between the headline I egotistically envisaged, "Sheilah Graham Dies with the Queen's Brother-in-Law," and my desire to stay alive.

Tony is easy to like and I would advise Margaret to hang on to him. There are lost of beautiful people ready to race away with him. Rich beautiful people.

Pragger-Wagger and the Woman I Love

One of love's mysteries is why a man falls for this woman and not for that woman. And vice versa. Lady Thelma Furness was so confident that the then Prince of Wales—"Pragger-Wagger," his friend called him—was all hers, that she actually precipitated Wallis Warfield of Baltimore, Maryland, U.S.A., into the prince's arms, asking her to take care of him while she was in America, because "he'll be so lonely without me."

Wallis was not pretty, and to judge by the descriptions of writers who knew her when, she was the mousy type, the face you would never pick out in a crowd. Dark thin hair, parted in the middle, skinny (but not as thin as she became later in the mistaken idea that she would look younger), totally unambitious, or so it seemed. Sometimes you need a spark to fan your potential. You suddenly give the right answer to the wrong question. Beware of these women whom you regard as safe when you introduce them to your best beau. They have to try twice as hard and make up in concealed effort what they lack in looks.

Wally had come to London in the early thirties with her second husband, Ernest Simpson. She had divorced her first, as she would do Ernie in due course. London was full of rich American ladies in those days. Any respected American lady had an entree to this U.S. circle.

Mr. Simpson, a comfortable, but not rich businessman, enjoyed escorting his wife to dinner and dance parties to homes such as those of the American-born Lady Emerald Cunard, and Lady Thelma Furness, who was one of the beautiful Morgan twins. Wally was popular in a negative way. Quite obviously, she would not be a threat for the women hoping to attract the attentions of the glamorous prince. In any case, you would need the courage of a lioness to attempt to woo him from the tough-minded Thelma, who had been having a good time with the prince for several years.

You can imagine Thelma's dismay, on returning from America, to hear the rumors of a close friendship between her plain protégée and Thelma's lover. Not only that, but when she telephoned the prince wanting to say, "Darling, I'm back!" she could not get through to him. Edward could be petulant, autocratic, and unfeeling when he was through with a lady.

The blond, good-looking prince was a dream of every ambitious mama for her daughter. I remember one article in a New York magazine, titled, "I Danced with the Prince of Wales." He was loved by women and liked by men, there was nothing sissyish about him. He had been trained for his future kingship, and while he drank a certain amount, and fell off his horse frequently enough to be the subject of jokes, he had the stamp of authority that ladies have always liked in a man.

It was soon clear to fashionable London that Mrs. Simpson

had the dear boy completely under her thin thumb. She even made him dance to her tune in public, telling him to take a cigar out of his breast pocket, because "it bulges." She could tell him when he'd had enough to drink, which no one except his mother, Queen Mary, had the courage to do. He ignored his royal Mama, but obeyed his American commoner.

When Wally was to be late for lunch at Maxim's in Paris, she commanded Edward, "No drinks until I arrive." Entering and finding him sozzled, she hauled off and slapped him. The prince fell under the table and it took two waiters to put him back into his seat.

How did she get him interested in the first place? When you are hoping to attract a man, the number one move can be the most important. Rich men especially—the Prince of Wales was loaded with money and property—do not like to be kowtowed to. They are attracted to people who can stand up to them, male as well as female, and who will take no nonsense from them, the people who will *not* accept crumbs from the rich man's table.

According to a guest who was there when Wally was introduced to the prince at a winter party in the home of Lady Furness, the talk went as follows. Looking for a conversation opener, the prince said, "I suppose you miss American central heating in England." To which the lady replied, coolly, "I would have expected something more original from the Prince of Wales."

Every sophisticated woman knows that this is a ploy for attention. Disagree with a man, or put him down, it makes him believe you are more clever than he is. To put down the future King of England was gambling for high stakes. Was the mousy Mrs. Simpson, with large hands, no chic at that time, and who moved ungracefully, out to get him?

Accounts at the time of the marriage reveal that after that first meeting they did not see each other for another six months. I am sure this is wrong. The injection had taken. He became the weaker half of the new alliance. At the beginning, Mr. Simpson always accompanied his wife and the prince.

The late Lord Furness had been aware of his wife's affair. Thelma was so candid and uncalculating that she had immediately informed her husband of the liaison. It wouldn't do to have a divorce and name the Prince of Wales as the corespondent—these scandals belonged to the era of Edward VII. Besides, Furness liked the prince, so, to avoid what could be embarrassing to all parties, he would telephone Thelma from the club, to ask if it was okay to come home. Now, there's a thoughtful husband for you.

But American husbands are, shall we say, less "civilized," less decadent might be the better word. When Ernie realized that Wally was seeing the prince, he separated from her and returned to the United States. Now Wally and the prince, with his circle of friends, were together most of the time. She was a visitor to the yacht and Fort Belvedere—his home in Sunningdale, Berkshire, where she soon began compiling the menus, giving orders to the servants, and rearranging the furniture: it was amazing how fast she learned about the ways of the British upper class, of which the prince was the most upper.

The "scandal" erupted in the American newspapers when Wally went on a long cruise with the future king. They were now in effect telling the world, and in particular England, to mind its own business.

If Mrs. Simpson had been born an Englishwoman instead of the more independent American, she would have known it was impossible for the King of England—he had succeeded his father, but was not yet crowned—to marry a woman who had been divorced. Once would have been enough, but this was twice. Her friends in America were divorcing all the time, and if they wished they could marry the President himself. She was a virtuous lady from Baltimore, and once Mr. Simpson had allowed her to divorce him, she believed there was nothing to stop her marriage to the king. He needed her so much. I doubt whether his hair was cut without first consulting Wally. As he said in his "Woman I love" speech on his abdication, he literally could not have done his duty as king without the help of the now indispensable Mrs. Simpson. At a dinner party given by Lady Granard, the daughter of the rich Ogden Mills of the United States, Lord Granard turned to his table neighbor, Mrs. Winston Churchill, and attacked Mrs. Simpson. She replied angrily, "If you feel that way, why did you invite her to your house and put her on your right?"

An Englishwoman would have been proud to be the recognized mistress of the king. It had happened so often before—Nell Gwynn, Mrs. Fitzherbert, Daisy, Countess of Warwick, and Mrs. Alice Keppel. They wore the title of mistress as a badge of honor. But Wally was an American. It would have to be marriage or nothing.

Did she realize that the king would not let her go, no matter how much pressure Stanley Baldwin's government put on him? Is that why the wise lady went to France, knowing he would follow?—every woman knows this, although she has stated in her memoirs that she left the king to free him for his royal heritage. Nonsense! She would be his wife or nothing.

Neither were young, he forty-one, she a year younger. After the marriage he tried to have her acknowledged as a Royal Highness, but when the offer was finally made it was too late. Her first visit to London years later after the marriage was to be with him during his three operations for detached retina sections. It is ironical that the Duchess of Windsor, so beloved by the man who was trained to be King of England, was invited to Buckingham Palace only after his death. She attended the funeral at Windsor, and everyone, from Queen Elizabeth to the man in the street, was kind and at long last accepted her.

The Duchess did not stay long. She returned to Paris, to the rented house near the Bois, and to Le Moulin ("The Mill), their estate nearby in the country. She was shattered with grief, and soon had the FOR SALE sign on the country house where she had lived like a queen, servants in livery, the finest of everything, and loved by the duke. It was originally for sale at $1 million. The price was halved when a year elapsed without a buyer. It was sold recently for something under $300,000.

In a way the duke had also served as one of her servants. When they traveled to New York and Palm Beach, his butler Fletcher brought the royal tea caddy, and the duke made the morning tea himself, which he took to the duchess in bed. In the TV documentary (filmed a year before the duke died) in the garden and house of Le Moulin, the duchess answered many of the questions addressed to the duke. She was being very bossy, I thought. Actually, she was helping him. In his later years, the duke's speech was very slow and she did not want the world to know this.

Wally is a well-off widow, not super rich, but with several million dollars in cash and property. Also the magnificent jewels the duke gave her during their courtship and after. At seventy-six, she seems lonely—although there was a printed rumor that she might marry John Utter, the duke's secretary for fourteen years, which I thought was ridiculous. She had her own man for thirty-six years and, by some of our standards today, that equaled a lifetime. They were years of togetherness, which was lucky, because having given up a throne for "the woman I love," they were knotted together for life.

Birgitte and Richard

There was no such do-or-die decision for Prince Richard of Gloucester when he married a pretty, blond, Danish secretary, Birgitte van Deurs. Richard, a first cousin of the queen—his father and hers were brothers—met Miss van Deurs at a Cambridge tea party when he was an undergraduate, and saw each other frequently in the same circle of friends.

Birgitte had been studying at the Cambridge Language School, but she suddenly returned to Copenhagen. No, it was not a ploy to have him come running after. She was sure he would be unable to marry her, but they corresponded, and on her return in 1970, the friendship, it was reported, had "ripened into romance."

The engagement was announced on February 16, 1972, after six months of will-they-won't-they speculation. Because Richard is ninth in line to the succession, the queen had to give her consent. The engagement also had to be formally approved by the Privy Council. Unlike Wally, Birgitte on her marriage became Her Royal Highness, Princess Richard of Gloucester. They are a quiet couple. Their private life is kept well out of the public eye. Birgitte is not at all trendy, prefers home life to a career, makes many of her own clothes, and had previously studied domestic science, cooking, housekeeping, and sewing for one year in Copenhagen.

The prince, like the Marquess of Londonderry, is very left-wing. He is not popular with the friends of his mother, the Duchess of Gloucester. His clothes are comfortable, but definitely not Carnaby Street, Kings Road or Savile Row. While they married in a leap year, the prince did the proposing, but there is no need for her to join Women's Lib, although Richard likes to cook. His chief hobby is photography. Before his marriage he published a book, *On Public View*, with a hundred photographs of British statues.

Richard's main work is as an architect, and he is employed by a firm with headquarters in Rotherhithe, East London, which is where they have built a house. At the office he is called plain Richard Gloucester. Before this they had lived in his small flat in Camden Town, an unfashionable neighborhood in the northwest of London, certainly not as grand as Kensington Palace, where the Snowdons are quartered. By coincidence, Rotherhithe is where Princess Margaret and Tony rendezvoused in their premarital hideaway. Richard is a sports car enthusiast—he is president of the Advanced Motorists Club. They are both good skiers.

Birgitte's parents were divorced when she was five years old. She took her mother's name of van Deurs. Her father is a Henrichsen. Both parents came to the wedding, which took place in pouring rain at the small church in Barnwell, Suffolk. The village is so tiny—360 residents—that the local railroad was recently closed.

The wedding was small by royal standards, only seventy-five guests. He is the second son of the Duke of Gloucester. His older brother, Prince William, was best man (he died in a plane racing accident soon after). The guests had to slosh their way through the rain and the mud to the big house where his mother, the duchess, held the reception.

Neither Queen Elizabeth nor Prince Philip attended the wedding, or the reception. They were in Scotland with Princess Anne. But Britain is a small country, and there was nothing to stop the trio from flying to Barnwell in one of the Queen's Own Flight. The Duke and Duchess of Kent—Richard's first cousins—did not appear either. They remained at their home in Wimbledon. Perhaps it was considered infra dig by some of the royal family to attend the wedding of a secretary.

But Margaret, God bless her, came, all in flouncy yellow, with a yellow-trimmed plastic umbrella. Elizabeth, the Queen

Mother, in white with a white transparent brolly, was there to see her nephew taken in marriage. While the queen was absent, her dress designer, Norman Hartnell, was present to put the finishing touches to the bridal gown his assistants had made for the new princess—white Swiss organdie with a white veil, and white flowers to carry. The bridegroom's father, the Duke of Gloucester, had a legitimate reason for being absent—he has been a cripple for several years.

Richard is not rich. As a royal son, the duke receives an annuity of £45,000, but his children get nothing from Parliament except what they earn for doing the royal chores—small wonder they are always doing them. As a secretary, Birgitte made $75 a week. Now the pretty blond princess is earning much more because of the many functions at which they, or she, do their duty for the crown.

It seems that every day I see the name of Birgitte and/or Richard at occasions such as the Swan Feast of the Vintners' Company, in the City of London, or the Order of Saint John in Clerkenwell; Princess Richard presenting certificates to the Junior Red Cross Cadets; a reception by the British Public Schools Exploring Society in Golders Green; the Eighth International Reinforced Plastics Conference at the Metropole Hotel in Brighton; a dinner at the Fiji–United Kingdom Association in Bloomsbury; or a housing development in the East End of London.

The former secretary has her own lady-in-waiting at these affairs. Certainly not at home—there wouldn't be room for her, or the money to pay her wages. But on parade, Her Royal Highness behaves as though born to the blue blood of her husband. She is a charming representative for the royals, and who knows by what chain of circumstances she could become Queen of England. She would then be a very rich girl indeed, but this is a case where love is more important than money.

Elizabeth and Philip

While Prince Philip is apparently in love with Queen Elizabeth, he also enjoys the appurtenances of enormous wealth.

This cousin of the ex-King of Greece didn't have many beans to his name when he entered the Royal Naval College at Dartmouth in 1939. He met the then Princess Elizabeth when she visited the college in that year. He was eighteen years old. She was thirteen. As the nephew of Earl Mountbatten, once known as Prince Louis Battenberg, he is distantly related to the royal family of Britain. Elizabeth and her prince are fourth cousins once removed through descendants of King George III, third cousins through the line from Queen Victoria, and second cousins once removed through King Christian IX of Denmark.

Philip and Elizabeth corresponded during World War II when he served with the navy, but it did not mean too much. They were too young, and the king and queen chose to ignore the matter. After the war, when King George of Greece spoke to them on behalf of his young relative, there was no encouragement from George VI of England.

Prince Philip accepted the decision and started courting the beautiful Cobina Wright, Jr., named for her mother, who had been a great beauty and, before the Wall Street crash, enormously wealthy. At this time, mother and daughter were still moving in social circles, but the home larder was pretty empty.

The fact that Philip wanted to marry the junior Wright proves he had no money motives in later repursuing the very rich Princess Elizabeth. Philip was so poor that the senior Cobina did not consider him a good match for her blond, blue-eyed daughter! In Venice, Italy, she advised him to forget Junior. "You have a more fruitful destiny," she told him with ESP prophecy. Mother, then writing a society gossip column, and daughter were invited to the wedding with Elizabeth.

At a house party at the country home of the late Sir Harold Wernher, Uncle Dicky Mountbatten made sure that his nephew would be alone with the future queen. The adolescent spark was fanned to a flame, and from that time he belonged to Elizabeth, who had been closely guarded and had not met too many young men of her own age. They still had to wait. Elizabeth accompanied her parents on a tour of South Africa, and by the time they returned, they knew that this was the real thing for their daughter and Philip. The engagement was announced on July 10, 1947, with the wedding solemnized in Westminster

Abbey on November 20, 1947—twenty-six years almost to the day of the marriage of Anne and Mark.

It has been a good marriage, and there were great celebrations recently when the queen and her husband celebrated their Silver Jubilee. Prince Philip has proved a fine consort for his queen. He has supported her in every way, at home, in public, and is an excellent father for their four children. He is one of the diminishing number of masculine men. He has managed to find time for his favorite sports, which are sailing and polo. He has a good sense of humor and uses it to great advantage in his public speeches. Some of it has rubbed off on the queen, for whom he will always be Prince Charming. As a former British subject, I say, "Long May They Reign."

13. Saint or Sinner? — Jackie Onassis

SHE IS greedy. Stingy. Extravagant. Autocratic. Arrogant. She loves publicity. She hates publicity. She is vain. Heartless. Selfish. Cruel. Lazy. Impossible. You name it. Jackie has been called it. But only since her surprise marriage in October, 1968, to Greek multimillionaire shipowner Aristotle Socrates Onassis. The event triggered a succession of uncomplimentary literature. Before that date, she was praised as charming, a great hostess, a beautiful woman of good taste, always on the best-dressed lists, kind, a good mother, a good wife, brave, admirable, respected, and a great help to her husband, John F. Kennedy, in the United States and all over the world.

Which is the truth? In my opinion, she is a combination of both, part saint, part sinner, as we all are. Did she marry for money? Many believe she did. But so have thousands of other beautiful—and homely—women. Let her who is without guilt cast the first uncomplimentary adjective.

I admit to being amazed and shocked as most of the public was when Jackie's mother, Mrs. Hugh Auchincloss, announced that her daughter and Ari planned to be married. She had been regarded as a special woman, ever since November 22, 1963, when the assassin's bullet in Dallas, Texas, had stained her garments with the blood of her husband, the President of the United States.

At a moment when most women would fall apart, Jackie, after two seconds of panic, behaved splendidly, crouching over his body, cradling his poor head in her lap, and in the subsequent agonizing hours and days behaving not only like the First Lady of the land, but as the Greatest Lady. I will never forget her courage at the funeral, or tiny John, Jr.'s salute, as the cortege passedby. Let none of us ever forget her magnificence.

Of course Jackie has failings. Who hasn't? And it is a sad trait of human fallibility that we find it more interesting to learn the worst than the best of people in high places—especially those who are born in good circumstances and in addition have the temerity to marry very rich.

Jackie has always loved high living. She has always wanted the wealth of the world. Now she has it. She wanted to spend money without any thought of adding it up, without running a total. Now she can. She has been called the "calculating, man-killer type," meaning that sex means less to her than the goodies of rich living. Also that she is cold and aloof, which, as I have already mentioned, causes a chase by a rich man—if you are beautiful, that is. She always has been. Her photographs as a child show the dark good looks she inherited from her father, John Verou Bouvier, "Handsome Black Jack," who, before his death shortly after she married JFK, was a well-to-do New York stockbroker with a seat on the exchange. Her mother, the former Janet Lee, was the attractive New York socialite daughter of rich real estate bankers.

Jacqueline Lee Bouvier was born on July 28, 1929, at the height of the season in the fashionable Southampton, Long Island, New York, resort. Her parents were Catholic and Republican. At her debut in 1947, she was described by a society reporter as "a regal brunette with classic features and the daintiness of Dresden porcelain. She has poise . . . is soft-spoken and intelligent. . . . Her background is strictly old guard."

She had attended the best private schools, with a couple of

years at Vassar before the craving for excitement inherited from her spirited father caused her to take off for Paris with her younger sister, Lee. "They were out for a good time," a friend who knew them then informed me.

Jackie was also good at photography and took a job with the Washington *Times-Herald* at the princely sum of $42 a week—she needed the extra cash, as she always needed extra cash. Her camera covered the coronation of Queen Elizabeth II.

There are two printed versions of how she met Senator John Kennedy. One, that she interviewed him in Boston for her newspaper. The other, that they met at a dinner party, and that John leaned across the asparagus and asked the dark-eyed beauty for a date. Both occurred.

They were married on September 12, 1953. It was a spectacular wedding at her mother's home, Hammersmith Farm in Newport, Rhode Island, with their close friend, Archbishop Cushing, officiating. Jackie was twenty-four at this first wedding. Her gown was in eggshell silk taffeta with little cap sleeves and an off-the-shoulder neckline. The wide skirt fell from a tightly fitted waist, with row upon row of ruffles on the bouffant skirt.

The Kennedys honeymooned in Acapulco, where John caught an enormous sailfish, which Jackie had mounted and delivered to his office in Washington. She was happy to be pregnant in 1955 because this absolved her from the chores of a politician's wife. There was a miscarriage, and another in 1956. When Caroline was born the following year they were delighted and John gave his wife the present of a house in the fashionable Washington suburb of Georgetown. She at once went to work on her favorite hobby of decorating and redecorating.

According to her secretary, Mary Gallagher, in her book *My Life with Jacqueline Kennedy*, JFK grumbled at the constant changing of the furniture and decor and exploded, "Dammit, Jackie, why is it that the rooms in this house are never completely livable all at the same time?"

When Jackie moved into the White House she was in a constant state of bliss because now she had a truly large canvas on which to express her ideas.

Do you remember the television special in which the First

Lady took us from room to room to show off the changes she had made so painstakingly? "As the Kennedys moved in," wrote Pierre Salinger, "so did the carpenters." I remember the special chiefly because I was surprised by her little-girl voice, slow and lisping—it reminded me of Marilyn Monroe at her most helpless.

Some men love a babyish voice in a woman—it makes them seem in need of protection—but I was somewhat irritated. I had heard of the steel behind the wide-eyed wistfulness. It is true that she is selfish. She has rarely undertaken any project in which she was not interested personally.

From Mary Gallagher's book: "People told me of 99 things I had to do as First Lady, and I haven't done one of them." It was nothing to boast about. When she was pregnant with John, she was under doctor's orders to be absent from her husband's activities while he was campaigning for the presidency.

Mrs. Kennedy's extravagance with clothes brought a continual protest from her husband. In 1961, she spent $105,446.14 on clothing herself and more—$121,446—in 1962. The outfits were designed by Oleg Cassini, whom Gene Tierney married early in her Hollywood career. Jackie sometimes bought herself a Dior or a Balenciaga, but her favorite was Cassini. In the same year, she spent about $40,000 on her hair. There was criticism. Expostulated Jackie, "What do my hairdos have to do with my husband's ability to be President?"

She was always angry when criticized by people in and outside her own small circle. JFK could take opposition somewhat better. He was also more gregarious. While he upbraided Jackie in private for her extravagance, he always defended her in public. There was only one time I know of when he put his foot down with her, when Jackie had his private elevator decorated with fancy wallpaper. He made her change it to the off-white color of the state dining room.

Jackie has always competed with her younger sister, Lee, especially in the dress department. They are like schoolgirls when indulging in their favorite sport of shopping, then as now. Jackie was seen recently in Palm Beach with Onassis, darting in and out of the shops on Worth Avenue like a hummingbird, he complacently carrying the parcels.

But, as Arthur M. Schlesinger, Jr., wrote in his book *A Thou-*

sand Days, describing a dinner with the Kennedys at Hyannis-
port in 1959: "In the course of the evening I realized that
underneath a veil of lovely inconsequence she [Mrs. John Ken-
nedy] concealed tremendous awareness, an all-seeing eye, and a
ruthless judgment. Her response to life was aesthetic, rather than
intellectual or moralistic."

In addition to their clothes, there are other areas in which
the sisters compete. When Jackie married a senator, Lee married
a prince—Radziwill, the Polish nobleman, with his family crest
embroidered on his underpants. When last heard from, they
were divorcing. When Jack Kennedy became President, Lee
created her own furor by deciding to become an actress. She
was dreadful. The reviews for her stage appearance in *Laura* in
Chicago were scathing.

Lee and the prince were separated when she became a regular
visitor on the Onassis yacht, the *Christina*. It was believed in
jet-set circles that when she divorced Radziwill, she would become Mrs. Aristotle Onassis. Could this have triggered Jackie's
interest in the shipping and plane magnate? She had visited the
yacht with her husband, John, and sister, Lee, so it was not
considered unusual that she was a frequent passenger on the
yacht after the President's death. Besides, she was well chaperoned by Lee.

This is when, in my opinion, it occurred to Ari that it would
be a more exciting match for him to marry the woman whose
charm, beauty, and clothes had been publicized all over the
world. She could be as good a business asset for him as she had
been a plus for President Kennedy on his missions abroad.

The wedding itself was a fantastic affair. Journalists from all
over the world tried to converge on the tiny island of Skorpios,
which according to reports was given to Jackie, with the house—
the only house on the island—as a present from Ari. There was an
army of guards to maintain the privacy of the event. Fat chance,
although some reporters who tried to land were dumped into
the sea. Jackie was thirty-nine, Ari claimed to be sixty-two, although his passport stated his age as sixty-eight, an age difference
of almost thirty years. But he is amusing and women have always liked him.

After Mrs. Auchincloss announced the engagement of her

daughter to Onassis, about ninety passengers were thrown off an Olympic Airline jet to accommodate the wedding party flying to Athens. The couple were married in a Greek Orthodox ceremony, which caused some problems for Jackie, a Roman Catholic. The reception took place aboard the *Christina*, in the midst of which Jackie appeared wearing one of her famed short-line dresses, a ruby ring that was described as "almost too big to lift," plus earrings of rubies the size of the ring, and diamond bracelets from which hung cabuchon rubies.

Jackie brought her two small children to the ceremony and reception. Caroline was enchanted with the jewels and, hugging her mother, exclaimed, "You're both so pretty." Whereupon the new Mrs. Onassis took off her ruby ring and gave it to Caroline to try on and play with. The mother was already careless with money, having so much. If the little girl lost the ring, *tant pis*, as they say in French, which Jackie, who attended the Sorbonne and lived in Paris, knew intimately.

It is significant that, after the marriage to Jackie, Ari immediately made a $400 million package deal, based on his Panamian company Omega, which had a nominal value of $166,000, with the Greek government, all of whose members were delighted to meet his new, gracious wife.

Some nasty-minded people believe that Onassis married Jackie to soften the U.S. tax authorities, with whom he has had problems. His two children were American citizens and their trust funds had to be settled in America. Thus a great deal of Onassis's reported $500 million remains in the United States. His son Alexander was working for his father when he died in a plane crash. His daughter, having divorced her Hollywood husband, Meyer Bolker, went to work in her father's New York office. In the trust fund she was to inherit $75 million on reaching the age of twenty-one. But after his marriage to Jackie, the wily Ari managed to prolong the date at which the money will be hers. "A man," he said quite indignantly, "must also provide for his wife." Apparently he has.

A certain Christian Kafarakis, formerly for ten years chief steward on the Onassis yacht, had access to the marriage contract, which was, he reported, "so complicated that it required 170 clauses." To shelter his wife "from want," if Onassis ever leaves Jackie, he must give her almost $10 million for every year of their marriage. If she leaves him, she would get a total of $18 million, that is, if the parting comes before five years of marriage. They have had five years and are still together, although there have been some reports of trouble. If they stay together longer and Jackie leaves him, she is to get an additional $75,000 a year for ten years. If he dies while they are still married, she will inherit $100 million. But what intrigued me most about the steward's revelations is that the marriage contract stipulated that they were to have separate bedrooms and spend only a certain amount of time together. Ari denied it but took no action. How much of this is true, the Onassises are not telling, but it is a fact that they are often apart in their various homes and together for important and sometimes sad occasions, such as the funeral of Alexander.

Do women love Onassis for himself or for his money? He is short, and looks like a wizened gray monkey. I am sure Jackie likes him, but I find it hard to believe that she *loves* him, certainly not as much as she had loved John Kennedy, who reportedly had affairs with other women, Marilyn Monroe among them. I believe that Jackie is not a passionate woman—her passions are in her head, for the arts, for historical knowledge, antiques, music, paintings, which she can now buy by the dozen. Ari is a rags-to-riches man, but self-taught and self-cultivated, with some of the same interests as Jackie.

Before the marriage to Jackie he was known as one of those Greek shipping magnates, and as the husband of the former Tina Livanos, who divorced him in 1960 to become the Marquess of Blandford—"Sonny," heir to the Duke of Marlborough. Perhaps Ari was better known as the great and good friend of opera star Maria Callas, who was the hostess on the yacht when he entertained Winston Churchill.

Elderly husbands are prone to shower their pretty young wives with every kind of gift, especially gems. For her first Christmas in Greece, with the kids along for the festivities on Skorpios, Ari gifted Jackie with earrings to match the diamond and ruby bracelets. When Jackie celebrated her fortieth birthday, Ari gave her jeweled earrings depicting Apollo 11's visit to the moon, featuring a forty-karat diamond. The earrings had a sapphire-studded earth, to clip on her ears, with a moon, decorated with rubies, hanging from a chain, and a miniature Apollo ship attached to a thin gold thread to circle the earth and drop to the moon. To get all this on a delicate lady's lobes, her ears would have to be as big as a donkey's. But Jackie managed it. Where there's a will there's a way, as I don't have to tell you.

In the same year, for no reason at all, Ari bought his wife a villa at Lagonisi, overlooking the Aegean Sea on the road to the Temple of Poseidon. A few months ago, Jackie acquired yet another roof over her head—a château in Touraine in the southern region of France.

For a Christmas present he gave her not one diamond but a whole diamond mine! Small wonder that Jackie wrote to the U.S. Treasury that she would no longer be needing her President's widow's pension of $10,000 a year. There had been some talk in government circles that perhaps she was no longer entitled to the pension, being married to Ari.

Jackie was now more in the news than ever, but without the protection she had received as First Lady, and as the widow of the assassinated President. The reporters and photographers followed every step she took outside her New York home on Fifth Avenue. I remember the fuss when she visited the West Fifty-seventh Street movie house, showing the pornographic Swedish film *I Am Curious Yellow*. She had gone there in the afternoon, wearing a yellow suede jacket and mini, hoping to be unobserved. She had been curious but not yellow, as the photographer waiting for her to come out realized when she bashed him and his camera to the sidewalk with, he claimed, a judo throw.

More recently she was dragged into court to rebut the claim for damages from a photographer—I will not give him further publicity by naming him—who, she claimed, made her life hell and frightened her children, dogging their steps wherever they went in New York. Her guards, paid for by Onassis, finally pushed him away. She counter-sued and won her case against the man, who was ordered to stay fifty feet away from her at all times, and a hundred feet from her children. The footage was recently reduced.

While Jackie enjoys spending money at a fast pace, and is glad to be without some of her Kennedy in-laws—she loathed touch football and the feeling of belonging to a clan—there is always some problem that is highly publicized. Her letters to Roswell Gilpatric (President Kennedy's deputy defense chief) were put up for auction by Charles Hamilton, who deals in autographs and letters of the famous. He had bought them from someone who claimed to have found them in a wastepaper basket. The letters, which started "Dear Ros," spanned the five years between 1963 and 1968 and the correspondence, which seemed to be from one friend to another, were interpreted as love letters, because she ended them "with my love." This is done for people you like, not necessarily love.

Before her marriage to Onassis there was gossip when Lord Harlech was seen frequently in her company, and it looked like a romance, but Jackie turned him down. Harlech, who had been British ambassador to Washington, was comfortably off, but not a hundredth part as rich as Ari. From an age point of view, and physically, it could have been a good match. But Jackie preferred at that time to remain the widow of President John Kennedy.

It took a certain amount of courage for her to marry the elderly Onassis. Apart from the public, what would the Kennedy family say? Mrs. Rose Kennedy, in her eighties, immediately stated that she approved of the marriage, and that Jackie had discussed it with her before the announcement was made. Matriarch Rose spent New Year's Eve of 1969 with Jackie and Ari in Greece.

Ted Kennedy, Jackie's last remaining Kennedy brother-in-law, has always accepted everything Jackie does. To him she is the super-goddess who can do no wrong, and while he might have wished her to be more active in brother John's political life at the beginning of their marriage, she more than did her duty in his last years. Later she campaigned for Bobby Kennedy, although her fear of crowds is well known.

Once in Europe she actually fainted when the crowding and jostling became too much. When leaving Claridge's Hotel in London, she would crouch on the floor of the limousine to avoid being recognized.

Jackie has few women friends. Her closest men friends are

the amusing, squeaky-voiced author Truman Capote and musician and maestro Leonard Bernstein, who composed a special Mass for the opening in Washington of the John F. Kennedy Center for the Performing Arts. Jackie had not planned to be present, but changed her mind at Bernstein's urging, then changed her mind again and did not appear.

She is her own woman, as the President, and his father, soon learned. She disliked Joe's way of ruling his family, and always stood up to the old man. When he put Le Pavillon out of bounds for the family because the then proprietor, Henri Soulé, refused to have photographs taken there of her husband's birthday party, Jackie ignored his request, which she thought was petty, and continued to patronize the restaurant. But even though she would not take any nonsense from Joe, she admired him. And he liked her for her spunk, which none of the other members of his family dared to display.

There have been several reports of an impending divorce between Jackie and Ari. The most serious was when they had a verbal battle in '72 at the London Airport. Ari claimed there was not a rift. "I would say we are a happily married couple, and happily married couples often fight. I'm afraid this story comes from some of my lesser friends, who seem to be trying either to bury me or divorce me." The chatter still goes on, and I wouldn't bet against it, except for the lovely money Jackie inherits if she is still married to him when he dies.

At Easter in 1973, it was reported that Onassis had been assassinated, "like Jackie's previous husband and brother-in-law." The news made all the European newspapers. I was in Palm Beach at the time and can vouch for Ari being with Jackie on the *Christina*, which was tied up in the harbor. Did you know that Jackie's bedroom on the yacht features wall-to-wall mirrored closets, so she can see herself from every angle, and that her stateroom, decorated in grays and greens, is the only one on the boat with a tub in the adjoining bathroom? And what a tub! It is composed of mosaic tiles from Spain. The *Christina* also features Ari's $4 million painting collection, including the Rubens in his study. The small swimming pool is in mosaic with a painted bull at the bottom. The yacht can accommodate the Onassis jet plane.

When they were last in Palm Beach, Jackie perfected her

water skiing and hired a skiing instructor to take back with her to Greece to continue the lessons for herself and the children. Water skiing is now her—and Lee's—favorite sport.

There has been a complete reconciliation with all the Kennedys. Mother Rose and her daughter Jean came to the Onassis fourth wedding anniversary party at El Morocco in October, 1972. Everyone in New York was scrambling for an invitation to the event, which was the highlight of the season.

In November of the same year, an enterprising and cheeky European photographer managed to snap the nude Jackie preparing to swim from her island. Of course the pictures were published in an Italian magazine. Ari admitted that the photographs in the magazine, which was sold out immediately, were probably authentic. He added, "I have to take my pants off to put on my bathing suit sometimes; she does too." Jackie was furious.

"Will I never have any privacy?" she demanded. Well, she has everything else. You weigh the one against the other and decide which you want most. Jackie made this decision when she married politician John F. Kennedy, and again when she married Croesus himself, Aristotle S. Onassis.

14. *I'm Just a Girl in a Gilded Cage — Gregg Dodge Moran*

EVERYONE WAS LOOKING for the bridegroom. He had stormed out of the wedding reception, drunk and defiant. They found him at two in the morning, waving an empty liquor bottle on the roof of The Colony, one of Palm Beach's oldest and most proper hotels. Major Horace Dodge, the fifty-three-year-old problem child of the seventy-five-year-old Mrs. Horace Dodge, Sr., was celebrating his marriage to and almost instant departure from former showgirl Gregg Sherwood.

It had been an unusual wedding reception. Major Horace was inebriated when he arrived for the ceremony at his mother's $3 million oceanside mansion. He was barely able to mumble, "I do," in an "I don't" sort of voice.

Afterward, his blond bride helped to support him into the exclusive Everglades Club, already closed for the season, with the Terrace opened for the heir to the motorcar company in faraway Detroit.

One of the twenty-four embarrassed guests describes the scene. "Horace was quarreling with Gregg when they came in, and he kept it up. When her friends came to her defense, he threw things at them."

The waiters wanted to call the police. Fortunately for everyone involved, Horace decided to leave, shouting foul language all the way to Worth Avenue. The blushing bride was left behind, sobbing into her caviar and champagne. Some of the guests thought she was laughing. Gregg always had a sense of humor.

Drunk or not, the major had married her. She was now a member of one of the richest families in the world. The Dodge fortune at one time was put at $600 million. Her financial problems would now be over, so she thought. She had not reckoned on the old lady, who held the purse strings in a tight clutch.

Mrs. Anna Dodge was like another matriarch, Mrs. Jessie Donahue—"they with the gold to give doled him out silver." The Donahue sons, as with Horace, had to go to Mama for every cent. Woolie Donahue's last wife, Mary Hartline, had twirled a baton in a circus band, but she had married a rich man before Woolie and still owns nine construction companies and actually had more money to spend than her mother-in-law allowed her husband. These mothers make weaklings of their sons, who hate their mothers but are always dependent on them, an intolerable situation for a grown man.

It was not surprising that Horace, Jr., found early consolation in alcohol. It was a dreadful marriage for a girl who was looking for the comfort and security of love backed by wealth. Should I put the money first? How could she love a man who was usually drunk pre and post their marriage? But she had. His father had indulged in the same form of escape.

I had been in love with Scott Fitzgerald, who drank. But he was sober when I met him and he remained sober for three months afterward, by which time I was hooked. If he had been drinking when I first saw him, I would not have fallen in love with him. And later during the frightening alcoholic benders I was glad that we were not married. So Gregg was to learn on her wedding day that happiness was not part of the package, and when the major died there was nothing for Gregg but a file of debts. Horace had always hated paying bills. He let them run for a year, then took them all to Mama who paid them, grudgingly.

In the spring of 1965, she married a handsome former police-man, Danny Moran, from the Bronx in New York. He is fifteen years her junior. What he lacks in years and money, he makes up in looks—he's a Dick Tracy type—black hair that grows low on his forehead, the bluest eyes, and a strong vibrant body.

But we are ahead of the trials and tribulations of our blond, blue-eyed beauty, who finally was rich in her own right when she sued her mother-in-law for $11 million after the major's death, claiming that his mama had alienated her husband from her. Gregg settled happily for $9 million.

Some of the people in Palm Beach who don't like Gregg have insisted to me that she is not as rich as she claims, but when I visited her last May on her estate, which covers four big lots totaling 525 feet of oceanfront, she showed me statements that seemed to my dazzled eyes to add up to *more* than $9 million.

Danny was there, and seemed somewhat uptight, though more relaxed than he had been earlier with his wife's rich friends. He used to fidget a lot and tug at his collar, but now his hands were still, except when he made me a Tom Collins behind the huge gleaming bar in the playroom, which also serves as living room, dining room, and center of entertainment.

The bar pavilion is at one end of the frontage. At the other end, another pavilion contains two bedrooms, a large one for Danny and Gregg, the other for a guest—mostly Gregg's mother—and two bathrooms. The space in between is taken up with an enormous parking space—it can take one hundred cars—and a hundred-by-fifty-foot seawater swimming pool, which is emptied every four days and replenished from the ocean. The pool was built in the twenties by Mrs. Jesse Donahue, who used four lots to build a beach house. Jesse's estate on the other side of the road, on South Ocean Boulevard, is now occupied alone by Mary Donahue. Woolie died in the fall of 1972 while watch-ing the news on television—and I'm not surprised. Gregg bought the "beach house" for $175,000 and put in improvements costing $100,000. Today she could sell it for more than a million dollars.

"All these homes on the oceanside seem to be valued at more than a million dollars. How can people afford them?" I asked Gregg.

"For every person who goes broke," she answered, "there's

another coming over the bridge with a fistful of dollars." She recently purchased Magda Gabor's estate in Southampton, Long Island.

Gregg told me some of the highlights of her life. Her real name is Fjelstad. I would guess her age to be around fifty or so, but she looks younger. She came from Beloit, Wisconsin, and lived with her Polish-born parents in a small house at the foot of a hill, at the top of which the rich folk had their homes.

"One day," she told her mother, "I'll buy you one of those houses up there." True to the fairy-tale tradiiton, she did. The homes on the hill were a constant reminder of her own poverty, and of her determination to be rich.

Where do you start? Pretty girls can surface from their bleak backgrounds via a beauty contest. Gregg, as Miss Wisconsin, placed fifth according to news reports of the Miss America contest in Atlantic City. "I was third," Gregg assured me. John Powers, of the famed modeling agency, was one of the judges and offered her a job.

"I was on 176 magazine covers," Gregg boasted. "I was the Chesterfield girl for three years, although I never smoked." To make more money, after modeling by day, she became a show-girl at the Vanity Fair Night Club, doing two shows a night. "Tired? Never! I was thrilled to be chosen and loved my salary of $350 a week.

"I was signed by RKO for *The Jean Harlow Story*. [At that time the studio was owned by Howard Hughes.] I sat out there [Hollywood] and sat and sat." (I remember meeting her then at a cocktail party—she was, and still is, on the round, soft side.) "My best friends in Hollywood were Mary and Charlie Morrison—as you know, he owned the Mocambo" (a fancy, dimly lit night haunt on the Strip, patronized in those early days by the famous personalities in the film city).

"One day, I'm sitting in the beauty parlor, my feet in a basin for a pedicure, a girl doing my nails, my hair in curlers and still wet under the dryer, when they tell me, 'Mr. Hughes is on the phone.' 'Which Mr. Hughes?' I asked. 'Howard Hughes.' I had almost forgotten I was under contract to him and that I had been brought to Hollywood for his *Jean Harlow Story*. The message: I must see him right away—not at RKO (he never set foot inside it, as you know) but at Paul Hesse's photography studio on the Strip.

"I put a towel around my head and rushed there. The sun was in my eyes, but I recognized Mr. Hughes, who said, 'Just stay in the sunlight.' I was annoyed. 'Mr. Hughes,' I said, 'this is unfair. I've been sitting out here waiting to see you for months and months, and now, for you to see me like this!'

" 'You look just like her,' he replied. I was no longer angry. My moment had come. 'Jean Harlow?' I asked. 'No, Lana Turner.' He was going with her at the time. I walked out on my contract."

Gregg had reached Hollywood after her unsuccessful second marriage. The first, to a boy when she was in high school, had been annulled by her mother. The second was with Walter Sherwin, who managed the New York Yankees' downtown ticket office. He was earning a good salary and making more on the side after his marriage to Gregg in July, 1948. She gave her age as twenty-three. He was thirty-nine. A year later, Gregg announced she would sue for divorce on the grounds of incompatibility.

Walter had been proud of his beautiful wife. At one of the rare times she visited him in his office, he begged her to stay as he was expecting some important people and he wanted to show her off. According to what Walter told a friend, she became irritated by his insistence and replied, "What have I got to do with those creeps," and left.

Early in 1950, Sherwin, who had been missing from the office, was arrested on charges of embezzling $43,687 in baseball receipts. "I had to do it," he explained, "to keep Gregg in furs and jewels, and I bought her parents a house in Beloit."

Gregg had kept her promise. The house was on top of the hill, but it was not paid for. Neither were the furs and jewels. In the summer a judgment was filed against Walter in favor of an interior decorator who had made over a penthouse for Walter and Gregg at 40 Central Park South. The couple were ordered to pay $2,228.

On his next job, Sherwin was earning $90 a week and in Gregg's view they were no longer married, as she had obtained a Mexican divorce. She was still modeling and showgirling in nightclubs. The Powers Agency sent some of the girls to Palm Beach to model clothes for a charity event. This is when Gregg met Mr. Dodge, who was still married, although separated from the former Clara-Mae Tinsley. Mrs. Dodge, Jr., obliged by stating that she was suing Horace for a divorce.

There was unpleasant publicity for Gregg in February, 1951, when Mr. Sherwin pleaded guilty to first-degree larceny and was given a suspended sentence on condition that he cooperate with an insurance company trying to locate the money embezzled. The hapless Yankees ticket man explained that he had negotiated large loans from ticket brokers on promises to give them preferential treatment if the Yankees got into the World Series—which they did not. He must have failed to cooperate, because he served time in prison and died soon after his release. Of a broken heart, 'twas said. Apparently he had loved Gregg to the end.

At the time of the meeting between Horace and Gregg, he had been married four times. Number one was Lois Knowlson, a Detroit socialite. Muriel Sisman, another socialite, held the number two spot. Next came Martha (Mickey) Devine, a showgirl and model. Clara-Mae Tinsley was an army nurse who met Horace in London during World War II. Like her predecessors and successor, Clara-Mae received a million-dollar trust fund from the capacious pocket of Mrs. Dodge, Sr. They could spend the interest but not the capital, but no matter what happened, none of the five wives of the major would ever starve.

In September of 1952, Clara-Mae brought her suit for divorce on the grounds of "cruelty and abandonment." In the settlement, Clara was to receive $30,000 a year for life. It would be the equivalent today of $100,000. At the time, the impatient Gregg and Horace were staying together—chaperoned, they said—at the Colony Hotel in Palm Beach, on top of which Horace would soon be seen waving his bottle.

While the senior Mrs. Dodge, Anna, had been violently against the marriage of her son to Mickey—it took him eight years to get her legally to bed and board—the old lady had no objections to the marriage with Gregg, reportedly because Gregg had persuaded Horace to switch from the hard stuff to beer.

You can imagine how the yearning-to-be-rich Gregg went to

1. *"Sylvia looked somewhat like Clark's previous wife, Carole Lombard." Lady Sylvia Ashley and Clark Gable on honeymoon. (United Press International)*

2.

2. *"She wanted to be an actress." Mary Lou Schroeder Hosford with her husband-to-be, Cornelius Vanderbilt Whitney. (United Press International)*

3. *"Hunt had found a pearl through the smoke of the cigarettes she sold." Huntington Hartford with Marjorie Steele, 19, when they disclosed their marriage. (United Press International)*

4. *Mama must have said, "Marry a multimillionaire." Babe (Barbara) Cushing Paley and husband William. (Wide World Photos)*

4.

5. *"The poor servant girl and the rich nice son of her employer."*
Steven Rockefeller marries Anne Marie Rasmussen. (United Press
International)

6. *"She won a Lithuanian beauty contest at the Chicago 1933 World's Fair." Bobo and Winthrop Rockefeller after their surprise marriage. (Wide World Photos)*

7. *"How to marry Howard Hughes." First, Jean Peters married Stuart Cramer III. (United Press International)*
8. *"In a milieu populated by wealthy men, Mildred Brown was pursued by them, including the candy and restaurant heir, George Schrafft." (United Press International)*
9. *"A Nefertiti profile and dark flashing eyes." Gloria Rubio becomes Mrs. Loel Guinness. (Wide World Photos)*

10. "If I had only known how pretty I was." Barbara Hutton's first wedding—to Prince Alexis Mdivani. (United Press International)

11. "He was the handsomest man I'd ever seen." Barbara and second husband, Count Kurt von Haugwitz-Reventlow. (United Press International)

12. "Cash and Cary." Barbara with third husband, Cary Grant. (United Press International)

13. "Would men look at me if I were poor?" Barbara and Prince Igor Troubetzkoy, her fourth. (United Press International)

14. "*I feel as if someone has hit me over the head.*" *Rubirosa, Barbara's fifth, on their wedding day. (United Press International)*

15. "*He was someone to fall back on between marriages.*" *Barbara with sixth husband, Baron Gottfried von Cramm. (United Press International)*

16. "*You are never sure . . .*" *Barbara with her seventh and latest, Prince Doan Vinh. (United Press International)*

17. "Doris Duke ecstatically signed her name Mrs. Porfirio Rubirosa." (United Press International)
18. "He got so mad at me for turning him down, he gave me a black eye." Zsa Zsa with Rubirosa. (United Press International)
19. "Once in a while, Linda has fallen in love with a small income." Linda Christian and actor-husband Edmund Purdom on a Hollywood set. (United Press International)

20. "On the wedding night she swallowed twenty sleeping pills."
    Joanne Connelley and Jaime Ortez-Patino announcing their mar-
    riage. (United Press International)
21. "She settled happily for nine million." Gregg Sherwood Dodge, her
    son, and her new husband, Daniel D. Moran. (United Press
    International)

22. "It began with a bizarre murder." Nancy Oakes de Marigny with Count Alfred after verdict of "not guilty." (Wide World Photos)
23. "Where there was Hope, there was Sikkim." The marriage of Hope Cooke and the Crown Prince. (United Press International)

24. *"I only dance with the prince." Bettina with Prince Aly Khan. (United Press International)*
25. *"For the first time, she did not wear any of von Thyssen's jewels." The former Nina Dyer and Prince Sadruddin at their wedding reception. (United Press International)*
26. *"On her toes." Doreen Wells, the future Marchioness of Londonderry. (United Press International)*

25.

27. "He didn't have many beans to his name." Prince Philip and bride, Princess Elizabeth, wed at Westminster Abbey. (United Press International)
28. "At first he was rendered practically speechless by the romance." Captain Mark Phillips and Princess Anne before marriage, in Buckingham Palace. (United Press International)
29. "Only a week before, I had taken Jacqui to lunch to learn about Tony's past intentions . . ." Antony Armstrong-Jones, photographer, and Jacqui Chan, actress. (United Press International)
30. "While she becomes somewhat more imperious, he has remained the Bohemian charmer." Tony and his bride, Princess Margaret. (United Press International)

31. *"A Ford was in her future."* Cristina and Henry Ford II returning
from European honeymoon. (*Wide World Photos*)

32. *"The wedding itself was a fantastic affair."* Jackie and Ari marry on
Onassis' private island, Skorpios. (*United Press International*)

town on the trousseau—for which, according to reports, Anna was paying—thirty-three dresses, seven mink stoles, three mink coats. As for the million-dollar trust fund, she was to get the principal in the event of Horace, Jr.'s death. However, if Gregg sought a divorce from him, the trust would be null and void. "I will never, never leave Horace," Gregg vowed fervently to her mother-in-law.

Anna came to dislike her son's fifth wife, who was not a hypocrite and refused to kowtow to her mother-in-law. Their fights were usually over the measly—for a multimillionairess—allowance she gave her son, and what this had done to his character. Anna, who clung to life until she was 102 years old, had her revenge by completely omitting Gregg from her will.

In November of 1953, the dream of every poor girl who marries a rich man came true. Gregg was pregnant. It's as good as millions of dollars in the bank. She was again separated from Horace, and living with her mother in Beloit. "And I'm staying here," she stated, "for the sake of my health and that of my unborn child, and because of Horace's drinking and the constant friction of our marriage." A month later, she was joined in Beloit by her husband, and all seemed well.

Gregg's son, John Francis Dodge, was born on March 18, 1954, in the Good Samaritan Hospital, West Palm Beach. He was named for his father's late uncle, John F. Dodge. The baby automatically received a $2 million trust fund, with his mother as executrix. At this time, the Dodge personal fortune was estimated at $200 million, all of which would be inherited by Gregg's baby. But the capital was still controlled by Mama, and the Horace Dodges were up to their necks in debt.

When Anna refused to pay for the jewels her son gave to his wife, Gregg had to return to the jeweler, Harry Winston, Inc., on Fifth Avenue, an $83,000 diamond necklace, an $82,000 pearl-shaped diamond ring, and a $5,800 ruby necklace. Mr. Winston is used to this, as so many rich men buy jewels from him for their ladies—and forget to pay. When Zsa Zsa Gabor squeezed that $150,000 engagement ring from Herbert Hutner, one of her husbands, she took it first of all on approval—it was the only way to make Hutner agree to the deal—and then clung to it during the marriage, and after. Hutner had to pay because he

cared about his reputation. Major Horace had long. since destroyed his.

The unhappy marriage lasted ten years, until Horace's sodden
death ended his money and drinking problems. Before and after
that day of release, the harassed Gregg was in and out of
trouble. In March, 1958, according to the newspaper reports,
she was fined fifty dollars in the Beloit municipal court for disorderly conduct. A police sergeant had charged that when she
was visiting her parents the previous December, she had been
speeding, and when he stopped her, she had kicked and slapped
him and threatened to knock hell out of him.

In August of 1959, Gregg was arrested in Hollywood at four-
thirty in the morning, charged with being drunk and disorderly.
The press reports had her in her Cadillac with a Chicago
columnist, shouting rude remarks at a passing police car. Two
police matrons swore in court that she kicked and spat at them
when they were putting her in a cell. Gregg was indignant at
the charges and hired the famed Jerry Giesler (Errol Flynn's
lawyer) to defend her on the charges of drunkenness and bat-
tery.

Gregg was found guilty on the drinking charge and fined
$100. Previously, in July, she and Horace were sued by Cartier's
for $69,800 for a diamond brooch and necklace taken on ap-
proval and never paid for by Horace or returned. In 1960,
a federal judge in Detroit ordered her to pay a fine of $16,600
for smuggling jewels from France—a gold and diamond wrist-
watch and a platinum and diamond ring, with earrings to match.
It would have been cheaper to have declared them to the
Customs men. In March, 1961, she paid $3,000 each to the two
police matrons of the 1959 arrest. They had sued for a total
of $170,000, but settled out of court.

In May, 1961, a gossip columnist printed that the Dodges were
going to spend $400,000 to buy an oceanside home in Palm
Beach and name it "Playa Riente"—"Laughing Shore," in Spanish—after her mother-in-law's Palm Beach home, which had
been burned to the ground two seasons before. Laughing Shore
would include two crystal chandeliers worth $200,000 from
their place in England, near Windsor Castle.

Four months later, Horace was suing her for divorce, charging Gregg had beat him up and returned to him in Grosse Pointe only to ask for more money. Gregg agreed that a divorce was likely, because of her husband's "continual drinking." With a winning smile, Gregg faced the court and demanded, "How could a helpless woman like me have been physically capable of assaulting such a big"—she paused, and did she almost say "ox," changing it to "man"?

In another divorce action in 1962, Gregg gave her age as forty, which would make her fifty-two today. During November of the same year, Horace brought Gregg before a court in Detroit to put limits on her spending. He charged she owed $300,000, although receiving $5,000 for monthly expenses from the usual source. In the settlement, Horace agreed, or rather his mother did, that Gregg would be paid $6,250 in cash every month *if* she would stop buying goods on credit. In return, Gregg dropped her petition for $15,000 a month temporary alimony, pending the outcome of his divorce suit.

When the great god of quarreling couples settled the matter with the death of Horace, Mama Dodge immediately totted up what she had lent her son and filed a $10,400,000 claim against his estate, which was in trust for his son, the then nine-year-old John Francis. Gregg received the interest on her widow's share of $2 million.

In March of the following year, with her tears of grief and frustration dried, Gregg filed the $11 million suit against her mother-in-law. The old lady couldn't take any more legal fights and grudgingly settled the case, which gave Gregg the $9 million—"tax free," added Gregg's lawyer. After Anna's death, the $20 million Dodge estate in Detroit, modeled after the Palace of Versailles, was sold. The auction of the valuable contents lasted a week.

Gregg was now reported in the company of Daniel D. Moran, the policeman from the Bronx, New York. Gregg may seem scatterbrained, but she was now rich in her own right. No more going to Anna and begging for bread, or rather cake. But she knew about girls and boys who married for money, and she waited sixteen months before marrying the handsome cop, on April 21, 1965.

She gave her age as forty-one, and her address as 13 East

63rd Street, New York City. Danny Desmond was twenty-nine. His address, 140 West 238th Street. Gregg had achieved the second ultimate wish of every woman who enjoys money. She was now rich enough to marry the poor man of her choice. *She* could now be paying, instead of taking, which she preferred. She was always a generous girl.

Gregg chose the Lady Chapel of Saint Patrick's Cathedral on Fifth Avenue in which to promise to love, honor, and obey husband number four. She was given away by her rich son, John Francis, now eleven years old. Monsignor J. P. O'Mahoney of the beautiful Saint Edward's Church in Palm Beach flew to New York to perform the ceremony.

Gregg bought her own wedding dress—a Mainbocher short beige gown and coat and matching veiling. The Lester Lanin trio played for dancing at the Regency Hotel reception. Of course, the first number requested by the happy Mrs. Moran was "Danny Boy." Her mother, Mrs. Helen Fjelstad, was, as usual, at her side. His mother was also there. She prayed that her darling Danny would be happy with the rich blond lady who was only ten years her junior.

Her prayers were answered. Danny *has* been happy, in spite of reports of battles between the good-looking pair. There was a story whispered loudly around Palm Beach last year—and as far as California and New York City—that, after the annual party Gregg gives her husband on Saint Patrick's Day, she had thrown a bottle at Dannyboy's head, which battered his handsome face and required hospitalization. It was printed as a blind item in Earl Wilson's Broadway column. He retracted a few days later, saying that Gregg had called him with the true version—to wit, that Danny had fallen over a flowerpot in the dark and banged his head on the sharp broken bits. Neither version is true—according to the victim.

Danny, quiet, serious, with only the faintest mark on his nose to remind him of the accident, assured me on my last visit to their home that this is what had happened, and I decided to believe him.

"I had been out to a late meeting" (he didn't say what). "I came home and was sitting with my dog just here where we are. The dog was asleep and I was looking through the window at the gathering storm outside. Suddenly, there was a loud clap of thunder, which startled my dog, who jumped up and bit me hard on the nose. Thank God, it wasn't higher up, he could have blinded me." He was in the hospital for ten days. In spite of my sophisticated life, I am still gullible.

The story that Danny had shot a man dead for trying to burgle their home is true. "We were living at 115 South Ocean Boulevard, our previous home," said Gregg. She had bought it from Brenda Frazier Kelly, the heiress who married the un-wealthy pro football player, Shipwreck Kelly, and divorced him some years later.

"We were having some alterations done," said Danny, "and there was scaffolding on the front of the house up to the third floor, where our bedroom was. I had dislocated a vertebra and my back was in a brace, which made it difficult for me to move quickly. I always sleep with a .45 under my pillow, which was lucky for us that night.

"I heard sounds of someone climbing up the scaffolding. I awakened Gregg and told her to go quietly to the side of the window and draw the drapes. I could see a man's head coming up the window. 'Stop,' I cried, 'or I'll shoot.'

"But he kept coming, so I fired a shot over his head. He must have been deaf or something, because he kept on coming. I could hear another man coming up below, so I pumped the first man full of lead, which dropped him to the ground. The other man scrambled down and ran away. He was never caught, but the first man was a mess, mashed to bits on the ground. Don't forget I was a policeman, trained to react quickly."

There was no inquest, and no arrest. In fact, the millionaire Palm Beachers who live in fear of robberies with murder wanted to give Danny a medal. A male friend of a woman socialite who dislikes Gregg circulated a story that the prowler had not come for money, but to visit the lady of the house. This obvious lie gives you an idea of the jungle known as Palm Beach.

My last visit to see Gregg was in my role of reporter. She was suing several people for $5 million! Previously I had lunched with the editor of a local magazine. He liked Gregg. "She's easy to be with, and you can talk to her like a man."

His version of the cause of the lawsuit was that an ex-actress who had married rich had inferred when talking to a magazine writer that Gregg had stuck to some of the money she had raised for her special charity, "Girls' Town." Because of these nasty rumors, Gregg, in January, 1967, turned the project over to the Catholic diocese of Miami and South Florida, who decided that Boca Raton, further south, would be the location for the home for delinquent girls. "I thought the slander about the cash for Girls' Town would die down, so I did nothing about it," Gregg told me. "Besides, I couldn't pin it on any particular person, although I was sure where it came from. But after the magazine story I talked to my lawyers and they advised me to bring a lawsuit. I will never settle. It's my reputation that's at stake.

"I founded the Heart Ball," Gregg continued. "Everyone came, from Jackie and Jack to Jack Dempsey. I mean real society, not little Mixmasters." Gregg then showed me the check for $25,000 she had written for Girls' Town. "If I was hard up enough to steal from my own charity, why would I give a check for $25,000?"

I read the article and shall not comment on it, except to wonder what Dora Fjelstad or her father, who was a janitor in the public school attended by Gregg in Beloit, would have thought of this $5 million suit, which includes Mary Sanford, one of the richest socialites in Palm Beach. In any case, the Fjelstads had been so poor that when Gregg was little, Papa had moonlighted, taking tickets in a movie house. When Dora won her beauty contest, she changed her first name to Gregg, from the shorthand system she was studying. She took Sherwood from the street on which she lived.

Like her father, Gregg was anxious to earn more money, and after the initial stint as a Powers model, she came home during a quiet modeling spell and took a job answering telephones for a taxi-cab company, and at nights worked in a wartime factory, welding and riveting. Her strong arms could do the job of a man.

Physically, I would say that Gregg is almost as powerful as her husband, Danny—who was born in Ireland, and came, with his parents, to the United States as a boy of fourteen in 1950.

Seven years later, he joined the New York City police force. How did he meet Gregg? One of those accidental things.

In 1960, Major Horace asked for a guard for a party he was giving and Moran was available, all six feet one inch and muscles all the way. He became a frequent bodyguard for Gregg, and also taught her swimming and improved her dancing.

In spite of, or because of, her stormy life, Gregg has her admirers of both sexes in Palm Beach. Top socialites such as Charles Munn and the Drexels have been photographed at her soirees. At one of her dinner parties I was seated between the sheriff of Palm Beach, Bill Heidtman, and George Matthews, whose grandfather, Henry Flagler, founded Palm Beach. They were both full of praise for Gregg. But mostly I remember the exquisite food—small shrimps floating in a mouth-watering sauce, followed by tender filet mignon, served with hot homemade loaves (you tore off the amount you wanted) and asparagus out of season. I've forgotten the dessert, because by that time I was too stuffed to eat it. I vaguely remember a delicious ice cake.

Gregg's close friends in Palm Beach are Betty McMahon and Mrs. Anne Spaulding, mother of actor George Hamilton and decorator Bill. Anne is proud of her face-lifts—as they say, the dimple on her chin is really her navel.

Where did Gregg learn to be a good hostess? The poor girls who marry rich men *always* learn. It's easy enough. You just hire good servants. Gregg has a butler, an internationally known chef, a gardener, a young man to park the cars, and several maids.

When she bought the beach house from Mrs. Jesse Donahue in 1969, she built on a terrace of rooms for the servants and a gymnasium for Danny. They had planned to build a big house for themselves, but found the two pavilions so comfortable, they never got around to it. "We will, one day," Danny promised earnestly. His opinion of Gregg, which seems to be unanimous (except with a certain group): "Gregg is a very honest person, kind and generous."

Some houses feature a cushion or framed plaque embroidered with "Home Sweet Home." Gregg has her cushion, but the words are different—"You can't be too thin. Or too rich."

15. "Cigarettes? Cigarettes?" — "Brownie" McLean

It is a long way from peddling cigarettes to her present position as Mrs. John (Jock) McLean, Palm Beach socialite, member of the exclusive Everglades Club, and chairman of the annual posh "April in Paris" Ball in New York. But Mildred Brown Schrafft McLean made it with a hop, skip, and a smile.

Mildred, nicknamed Brownie, came to New York from Hot Springs, Virginia, which at the time of her birth in 1918 had a population of 150. Brownie does not discuss her family, where she attended school, or what she was like as a girl. She was first noticed in New York City as a cigarette girl in the mid-40's at the popular Versailles and Copacabana nightclubs—a happy, blue-eyed blonde, rather stupid, they say, but I don't. No one is stupid who marries rich. In a milieu populated by wealthy men, Mildred Brown was pursued by them, including the candy and restaurant heir George Schrafft.

Brownie prefers to forget the early years, unlike her fellow Palm Beach hostess, Gregg Moran, but we do know more about her following her marriage to George Frederick Schrafft. The personable George was the darling of the debs and girls in nightclubs who check hats and sell cigarettes, wandering among the tables wearing the briefest of skirts and the most revealing blouses. In 1941 George, aged twenty-one, Harvard graduate, full of family money, surfaced as the water ace of Long Island, winner of every kind of race with sailing craft, motorboats, speedboats, and small yachts.

Mr. Schrafft is an optimist. No matter how many times he is disillusioned with matrimony, he comes up eager and ready for more. Two months before the attack on Pearl Harbor, he married Susan Stone Stephenson at Saint Bartholomew's Episcopal Church on Park Avenue. The bride was the daughter of the late James W. Stephenson and Mrs. Paul Forrester of New York City. Susan's sister Martha was at one time the wife of actor Victor Mature.

George started at the bottom of the family business and worked his way up. He and Susan lived in Brookline, Massachusetts, close to his job in the Schrafft shipping department in Boston. When George and Susan were divorced in Las Vegas in June, 1946, their daughter Candy was four years old. Sue received a whopping big settlement—in dollars, not sweets.

She went on to marry Carlos Guinle, the Brazilian millionaire, who lived in a thirty-five-room mansion in Rio de Janeiro. After one year, Susan sued husband number one, George, for failing to maintain his $400 a month support for their daughter. When Susan married Carlos on New Year's Day, 1947, George had already taken his second wife, "Brownie" Brown. Blond, blue-eyed Susan, a glamor girl of the previous decade, divorced her South American, stating that once you have been won by a South American Latin, he turns his wife into the old-fashioned woman of a century ago.

"It's hard for an American woman, used to freedom. I was losing my personality trying to become something that was false to me." And, escaping to New York: "It's just wonderful to be here breathing the free American air." This, of course, was before pollution.

Now, a warning. Susan then married another Brazilian millionaire, Anthony Veiga. Blond, blue-eyed girls are always going to Brazil to find them, but these South American millionaires are sometimes tight with money. Guinle often went dutch treat with his lady companions, except at the Copacabana, owned at that time by his family, when it was all free. Susan walked out on him one night at the club when he was playing the drums instead of paying attention to her.

Veiga, incidentally, had been married to Flor de Ora Trujillo, first wife of Porfirio Rubirosa. These girls will never learn. They marry playboys and expect them to spend the nights at home. There was some consolation for Susan in the fourteen-carat diamond engagement ring from Veiga, who was described at the marriage as "an industrialist and radio tycoon." "I get such a thrill out of it," she said in the early years of the marriage, "that at night I put it where I'll see it first thing when I wake up."

Back to Mildred (Brownie) and her second rich marriage, to John H. (Jock) McLean, whose mother, Evalyn Walsh McLean, owned the famous Hope diamond. Evalyn had bought the gem, reportedly wrenched from the forehead of an idol in India, in 1908. It had been sold to Louis XIV after its theft from the Hindu idol. It disappeared after Marie Antoinette and Louis XVI were guillotined. When the diamond reappeared in 1830, the stone had been cut down from the original sixty-six carats. It was said to bring bad luck to whoever touched it. Evelyn laughed at such nonsense, but hid it from her children. She had bought it for $40,000 and later refused an offer of $2 million. But shortly after her purchase, her daughter, Evalyn Jr., died of an overdose of sleeping pills and Mrs. McLean gave the forty-four-carat gem to the Smithsonian Institution.

Evalyn had another son, Ned, Jr., who first married the present Mrs. James Stewart and has now married again. His father Ned, Sr., died in 1941 of a heart attack in a Towson, Maryland, sanitarium.

As a young man, Jock worked as a reporter on the *Cincinnati Enquirer,* the newspaper established by his grandfather. His father also published *The Washington Post,* which has become more famous in recent years. The grandfather on Jock's maternal side was Tom Walsh, a successful gold miner in Colorado. Jock has been married three times. The first time around the marry-go-round was to Agnes Pyne, who married him in 1938. Agnes had previously divorced rich socialite Robert Ogden Bacon, Jr. Thirty minutes after the divorce from Bacon, Agnes married McLean. They both gave their ages as twenty-two. Agnes received custody of her daughter, Sandra.

It took five years for Agnes to divorce Jock on the grounds that his social pace was too much for her. Their son, John R. Jr., was three years old. Jock was reportedly eager to marry Mrs. Edward (Betty) Reeves, widow of the chain-store grocery heir, as soon as the divorce was final. Reeves had previously married Phyllis Haver, the Mack Sennett star bathing beauty whom I met with Eddie playing on the sands at a fashionable Long Island beach club.

In mid-February, 1944, Jock and Betty announced they had married on February 1. They would live in Dallas, where Jock owned and operated a plane factory during World War II. The society editor of the New York *Daily Mirror* reported that the factory had been financed by Agnes, his previous wife, who later sued Jock for the million dollars she had lent him. The court ordered Jock to pay back one fourth.

I'm beginning to wonder who was the Cinderella in the Brownie-Jock marriage! Brownie received a big bundle of dollars from George Schrafft when they divorced. At this time she may have been richer than McLean, whom she married in 1959. They went to Paris for the honeymoon. She had a Schrafft daughter, Victoria, who was left behind with George and his then wife.

You don't often see Brownie and Jock too much together these days, or in fact during the past few years. The popular Brownie is gregarious and attends most of the parties during the season in Palm Beach and New York, where the McLeans have a magnificent duplex apartment in the East Sixties. In Palm Beach during the season, Jock usually disappears after lunch, and cronies can find him either playing golf at the Seminole Club or at the bar in the Taboo Restaurant on Worth Avenue.

When Brownie becomes involved with her charity balls, Jock sometimes takes off for Palm Springs, where he has a house, or Beverly Hills, where he is loved by the A set, which includes his sister-in-law and her husband Jimmy Stewart.

The happy-go-lucky Brownie never lacks for an escort to the parties she loves. Her taste runs to attractive South American,

Mexican, or Spanish men, their dark coloring making her look even blonder than her perennial silvery long hair. Latins are great dancers, and Brownie adores dancing.

She is vague, seems to be in a sort of fog, and perhaps she is, because nothing seems to bother her—except *Ball*, the book written about her "April in Paris" charity affair. The author, William Wright, repeated a reporter's description of her as a fifty-three- (now fifty-five-) year-old frump, and that is not true—the frump part. Her clothes are spectacular, and while Brownie admits to being a bit overweight, the bubbly energy and fun-loving spirit seeps through the poundage.

Brownie is not at all calculating. Shrewd, but not clever. She succeeded in getting rich in spite of herself, although Jock is reportedly not as rich as he was. It might be Brownie who maintains the beautiful Spanish home, architectured more than a half century ago by Addison Mizener. His homes are the most beautiful and expensive in Palm Beach.

The McLean home is right by the ocean, with large rooms that are ample for lavish entertaining. She invites everybody to her parties, from socialite-radio-TV personality Maggie McNellis (Mrs. Clyde Newhouse) to film and TV star Hugh O'Brian, to any celebrity in town, to the swimming instructor from the Breakers Hotel. Plus, of course, her close friends, Mary Sanford, a doyenne of Palm Beach now that Mrs. Marjorie Post has passed away, and pretty Mrs. Loy Anderson, wife of the banker.

In spite of her husband's other interests, Brownie has managed to make a good life for herself. She is a happy person, always has been, from her early cigarette days to her present place in Palm Beach, Paris and New York society. A few years ago there was a rumor of divorce from Jock, but as of writing they are still together.

The fact that Brownie is not an intellectual—I have to be kidding—has helped to maintain her equilibrium in life where other more sensitive or brainy ladies might have collapsed. A well-known lady told me, "Brownie couldn't have been a cigarette girl because she cannot count and wouldn't have known how to make change." When she was suing Mr. Schrafft for child support, he had countered with "The only book Brownie ever read was *Black Beauty*."

If Brownie doesn't read much, she does know how to make friends and organize charity soirees. She was described recently as a leader in international society. She received this tag for her superb job in promoting the "April in Paris" balls in Paris as well as in New York. Brownie is so popular with all sorts of people in all gradations of society that the tickets to her various charity causes are always sold out, even though some of the more social buyers give the tickets to their chauffeurs.

I attended one "April in Paris" ball some years before Brownie took over the chairmanship, and while I found the scene exquisite, the affair with its parade of social ladies modeling the expensive gowns was stilted and boring. Everyone seemed to be looking for celebrities, even the celebrities.

Brownie works harder than a paid political organizer to make her balls a success. Each year she spends about $10,000 of her own money for the pre-parties, the traveling, the endless correspondence. It is a job only for the stout-hearted and socially ambitious.

With her silver tresses, dead-white makeup, heavily blacked eyes, Brownie has been described by an ungallant writer as looking like an albino raccoon. The effect *is* startling, but the first rule for Cinderellas who make it is to be one of a kind, to stand out from the crowd, to bring the second look, to be noticed by the rich men of their choice.

When some of them realize later that the man is a confirmed alcoholic and that some of the money can end with his death—those trust funds—they believe they are still better off than living in a small house in a small town with a poor man who might be a bore or drink as much as a rich man. They have fun today, for tomorrow they will die. They give parties for this and that —don't stop or you might realize the spiritual poverty of your rich life.

I am trying to imagine Mrs. Jock McLean in the year 2000. An old lady of eighty-two. Will she still be going to and giving parties? What else will there be for her to do?

16. "As Gregg Says, You Can't Be Too Rich" — Mrs. Frank McMahon

BETTY BETZ, JOURNALIST and cartoonist, was not exactly poor when she married Francis (Frank) McMahon, in April, 1956. Her pre-marriage income from her column, cartoons, teen-age photo albums, and lectures was estimated at somewhere around $100,000. Her studio apartment on Park Avenue was described as "luxurious and exquisitely decorated." But it was nothing compared to the multimillion-dollar fortune she would be sharing with her attractive Canadian husband.

Betty willingly retired from her comfortable career to become a super hostess in Palm Beach, New York, and various homes in Canada. She ranks with Brownie McLean and Gregg Dodge as a girl who made it onto the top rung of rich glamor hostesses in jet-set society.

Has Betty changed from the days when she took loads of bubble-gum and jelly beans to Istanbul for the adolescents she wanted to interview for her column? You bet she has. Betty is not as popular as Brownie. I have been told by some jealous Palm

Beachers that she does not waste time on people who are not important enough to be in her circle of friends.

I attended one of her pre-lunch Easter cocktail parties at "Concha Marina," their gracious oceanside home. The place was jammed with all sorts of people, from socialite Charlie Munn to eightyish Stanton Griffith, ex-U.S. ambassador to Spain —Stan recently married a poorish lady—and Jan Neff, millionaire sister of Walter Annenberg, our man at the Court of Saint James. Betty said she would like to give me a party—she had been a newspaperwoman herself. But when I explained I was leaving town the next day, her brown eyes took on the faraway look that Louella Parsons had when someone was bothering her in Hollywood.

Betty, five foot five, brunette, slender, and chic, dresses conservatively and is almost pretty. But she is also serious much of the time, and seems to be thinking of something else when she is talking to you.

I am told that in her teens she was an ugly duckling with mousy hair. She certainly isn't that now. There is a dignity about her that is in refreshing contrast to the overgregarious loudness of some of her group.

Mrs. McMahon is on her guard against people who want to do her favors. She believes they are after her money. For instance, a male acquaintance who was a regular at her parties drove to Concha Marina to give her a small present for Christmas. He hailed her when he saw her outside her front door. "What is it?" she snapped. "I've come to give you a present," he replied. "Well"—testily—"what is it, what is it?" And, raising her voice: "Everyone's trying to promote me because I married a rich man!" It had been a friendly gesture, a small painting as a thank-you for the good times he had had at her parties. True, he *was* in the picture gallery business, but he assured me he was not trying to sell her anything. I managed to keep a straight face.

Lately there have been rumors of trouble in her marriage. But they are still together, although nowadays they don't seem to have much in common. Frank has turned seventy, Betty is still in her fifties. She loves the social life—she could be a future

Queen of Palm Beach—and those interminable Palm Beach charity balls. Until three years ago, Frank was still energetically pursuing new avenues for making money. He still does, but without the same gusto.

The girls who marry super-millionaires in Palm Beach are usually energetic, worldly, and ambitious. It is hard for them to settle into the humdrum second spot to their powerful husbands. They want to be part of the scene, to be admired in their own right. So they give nonstop parties. How else can they work off the abundant energy?

The luncheons, dinners, and parties are always for the same group of friends and pluckable-for-charity acquaintances, but they too need the excuse to dress up, and it's like one big rich envious family. The piercing look that says, what has she got that I haven't? The women could be mere mannequins, draped in their husbands' affluence. And how they work on the treadmill of position! Refuse two invitations and you might as well be living on the moon. You are dropped with a thud that is heard in all the Palm Beach palaces. So, on with the dance, accept everything, especially the ghastly balls. You wash my back, I'll wash yours, come to my ball and I'll come to yours. But the balls give a *raison d'être* to life for the otherwise idle rich ladies—another chance to air the jewels, to kill time at the beauty parlor, shop for new gowns, and the smug satisfaction that they are giving employment to hundreds. And the residue of the money raised *does* go to worthwhile causes.

So they are not as silly and useless as they seem. Mrs. McMahon in particular has never seemed silly. In 1950, before she married Frank, she brought back film, maps, and researched material from a trip to Poland and Czechoslovakia to write a book revealing how the Iron Curtain countries enslaved young people.

Back in the United States, Betty's material mysteriously disappeared. "It is obvious," stated Betty, "that right here in America, the Russian secret police have stolen my material with the half-finished manuscript. But," she added, "I'm going right ahead with the book."

Betty reveals the same tenacity in her social life and is just as successful in it as she was in her former professional life.

But I wonder if she is as happy. Her husband is more likable than, let's say, Horace Dodge, and they spend more time together than Horace did with Gregg, but there is some sadness in Betty's bright brown eyes. But is anyone ever completely satisfied?

And is Frank McMahon happy? I don't think so. Frank was born in Moyie, British Columbia, in 1902. In 1956 it was reported that he was negotiating for a natural gas pipeline between the United States and Canada. He said it would be the fulfillment of a twenty-year dream. Also mentioned were his other interests in oil (the Pacific Petroleum Company), racehorses (the Alberta racing stable), golf, and Broadway plays.

The oil well in Alberta that had come in for Frank in 1948 had made him a rich man. The well was famous all over the world as Atlantic Number Three. Frank, with his brother and friends, had bought the property for $200,000. The gusher paid off in millions. His Westcoast Transmission pipeline, 650 miles from Peace River to Vancouver and the border of the United States, cost $190 million to build.

In 1965, money-making McMahon, as Chairman of Westcoast, had installed a new extension on his beloved pipeline, and with Max Bell, a Calgary multimillionaire, and Bing Crosby, whom he had known since their college days at Gonzala University in Spokane, cooperatively owned Meadow Court, the Irish Derby winner. He also bought a French Colonial home in Vancouver.

Everything Frank touched turned to money. He invested in the successful New York musical *Pajama Game*. He bought a stallion for $20,000 and the horse won the $250,000 Hollywood Gold Cup, after which he became a sought-after profitable stud. He was lucky for a long while—as marriages go today—in his marriage to Betty.

When Miss Betz said yes to her eligible millionaire in New York, the wedding party of seven flew in Frank's private plane to Branford, Connecticut, where the ceremony was performed by a justice of the peace. They flew back to Manhattan for the reception with thirty friends in the "21" Club's Blue Room. Guests included Millie Considine, wife of the columnist, who is close to both Brownie and Betty, the late Cobina Wright, and

Kathleen Winsor, who wrote *Forever Amber*, which is now considered a joke but was very daring at the time of publication.

At the age of fifty-five, Frank was described as having "graying brown hair, brown eyes, a round, genial, Irish face." The fight to install his pipeline had started in 1952 and was one of the most bitterly contested hearings held by the Federal Power Commission.

At this time, Frank was considered one of the top three Canadian industrialists. His oil and gas company was leasing 7,500,000 acres in Canada. What a world of wealth for Betty Betz to step into!

Frank and Betty were ecstatically happy, and almost ten months later, Francine Patricia was born. Frank had been married before and has three children from that marriage. He was not as rich then. It was the second marriage—to Betty—that spurred him on to making more and more money. If he could not lay the world at her feet, he would give her the riches concealed in its land and oceans.

Betty and Frank met Princess Margaret during her tour of Canada in 1958. According to a printed report at the time, the young bride wrote a friend, "We sure did entertain the Princess. Frank and I were her hosts in Fort St. John. She's real cute, gets bored with monuments, loves dancing, trapeze-style dresses [she still does]. She wore us out in the wide-open spaces, she walked all over, refused to ride in a limousine and asked Frank dozens of technical questions."

Back at Palm Beach, Betty was encountering some resistance from the Old Guard, who considered the McMahons social upstarts. But they reckoned without Mrs. McMahon's intelligence and persistence. Her first big chairmanship—the Heart Ball—was hugely successful. She sold tickets to everyone who had the price. The jealous old-timers closed ranks and said this was one ball too many.

Betty's friends (?) say she finally made it in 1959, when she was named number one in the Ten Best-Hatted Women of America list by Mr. John the hat-maker. He had nominated her in the millinery designers' annual poll. Women wore hats then, and, I'm glad to say, they are beginning to wear them again.

The following year, the McMahons bought a New York apartment on Fifth Avenue in the Sixties. In '61, they had a second daughter, Bettina. In '62, Betty was photographed as chairman of the Cancer Fund Benefit, looking genteel and trim, simply but fashionably dressed.

The following year, the McMahons bought the Palm Beach house, Concha Marina, from Isabel Dodge Sloane, who inherited both Dodge and Sloane fortunes.

Betty immediately grabbed Princess Margaret's butler, Cronin. He had left the Earl and Her Royal Highness's service after writing some stories about them for the national press in England. Very no-no. When Betty hired him, she adjured, "Now remember, Cronin, no memoirs." They might be more interesting than those he wrote about his time with Princess Margaret and Lord Snowdon.

In 1964 Betty was busy with the Flamingo Charity Ball, where she and her committee were presented with souvenir water glasses featuring hand-painted flamingoes—not much for all the work they had put in. At that year's "April in Paris" fandango, Betty held the limelight in her white ostrich floor-length Lanvin coat. Did she pay for it? Most of the gorgeous gowns you see at the charity balls are loaned by the fashionable couturiers. The more well known and rich the woman, the less she has to pay for her clothes, which are a walking advertisement for the dress designers.

At this time, Frank, with more gray hair, but not balding, was still a good-looking escort for his quietly elegant wife. Today he is not often in the photographs.

Still hustling at the age of sixty-three, Frank tried but at first failed to get a National Hockey League franchise in Vancouver. He succeeded later and donated $300,000 toward the $1 million McMahon Stadium, guaranteeing the bonds for the balance. Betty McMahon was thrilled when the conventioning Republican governors consented to be the guests of honor at the dinner dance she gave at Concha Marina in 1967. The party included two Rockefellers—Nelson of New York State and brother Winthrop, the late Arkansas governor.

At the party, Betty was photographed in pearls, bangs, little-girl headband, a strapless evening gown, with a big bow in front to flatter her brief bust, a floating stole to match the dress, and long white gloves. She looked stunning.

In recent years, Frank has been more interested in his horses than in Palm Beach society. He will appear for a short time when Betty has guests at the house, and then excuse himself to attend to his horsy affairs. With three other millionaires, he paid $4.5 million for the controlling interest in Churchill Downs in Kentucky, and had the satisfaction of seeing his horse Majestic Prince, for whom he had paid $250,000, win the Derby of 1969.

In October of the same year, Frank retired as chairman and chief executive officer of Westcoast Transmission, but he retained the courtesy title of director. His heart was with his horses, and in July, 1970, Frank set a world record, paying $510,000 for a full brother to Majestic Prince.

Will the rumors of a McMahon divorce come true? I am not as sure as some of Betty's Palm Beach cronies. A mature woman without a husband, anywhere, but more so in Palm Beach where status is so important, shrinks in stature in a way that is hard to describe. Unless she is living with a lover, there is an atmosphere of sterility in the mansion, a self-conscious coldness, an emptiness.

So I would be surprised if Betty is ever the plaintiff in a divorce. As Mrs. Frank McMahon, she can do as she pleases, live as she likes, and when the time comes for Frank to build his pipeline to heaven, she will get her widow's third of the estate. Then, if she wants to, Betty can marry again—a rich or a poor man.

17. *The Richest Rothschild — Baroness Edmund*

"MY FATHER was a policeman. My mother was—er—a house-wife." Baroness Edmond de Rothschild raised her arms to indicate the poor circumstances of her early life.

The petite wife of today's richest Rothschild and I were chatting in the garden of her Paris home on the Rue d'Elysée, opposite the Elysée Palace, the heavily guarded estate of the French presidents. It was three o'clock in the afternoon, and the sun on the upper-story windows had traveled farther west. A maid appeared on the eastern side of the mansion and turned the handle to roll back the shades. I had the impression that this ritual took place at the same sun-leaving moment every day in the summer while the Edmonds were in residence. They own some other town houses in the French capital, but this is where they live.

I had been a trifle early for our talk and the butler had taken me into the flowered garden and escorted me to one of the two white wrought-iron chairs with a matching table, under a large tree. I was grateful for the shade—it was a very hot day in Paris.

A few minutes later, he reappeared with a large glass of

orange juice. "Fresh from Israel," he proclaimed. It was delicious. I had almost finished it when the baroness appeared, apologizing for being five minutes late—"the luncheon . . ." she explained. I told her not to worry, that I have been kept waiting by experts during my years in Hollywood—Richard Burton, Elizabeth Taylor, and the top offender, Marilyn Monroe.

The baroness was wearing a simple, short-sleeved summer dress. "Dior," she said when I asked her. She told me that as Nadine Tailler she had played small roles in films and had been rehearsing for a more important part in a play, *Les Chansons de Bilitis,* based on a poem, when Baron Edmond had come into her life and changed it completely.

No more going the rounds of the agents, no more skimping to buy the pretty clothes she liked. It was lovely to be rich, she stated candidly. "My life now is so easy. I just have to ask for something and it is done." Her smile was truly happy.

There is no pretentiousness, no hidden secrets behind the eyes —I think they were blue or green—I didn't look too closely. I was more interested in what she was saying and writing it down at a fast pace. The hair is red, as is her husband's. Their son, a handsome boy, has brown hair.

"Was your hair always red?" I asked the baroness, because I had seen it described as brown. "Yes," she replied, without showing surprise that I would ask an intimate question. Perhaps it was the red hair that first attracted Baron Edmond. It runs in his branch of the Rothschilds, which goes back two hundred years to the founder of the family fortunes, Meyer Amschel Rothschild.

I am always eager to learn how the poor and the rich meet for matrimony. Nadine was happy to tell me; her face with the freckles that go with red hair was animated as she plunged into the eternal story that is always new.

"I met him at a dinner party in Paris. At the last minute I didn't want to go. I had been rehearsing all day and all I wanted was a warm bath and go to bed." She was living in a small apartment in the more Bohemian section of the city.

"I picked up the phone and dialed the number to say 'I cannot come.' My hostess had picked up the instrument at the same time to give me instructions on how to reach her home. After that I couldn't say 'I'm not coming.'

"At dinner I was placed next to Edmond." The baron had inherited something of his father Maurice's playboy way of life, and it was a thoughtful ploy to put him next to a pretty actress in her mid-twenties.

"No, it was not love at first sight," Nadine smiled, reliving the moment. "I knew he was married, and I would never get involved with a married man. I left early, telling my hostess, 'I'm sorry, but I'm working tomorrow.' Edmond went with me to the taxi, and after saying good-night, he said, most unexpectedly, 'I'm sure you're the love of my life.'

"I laughed when he continued, 'May I call on you?' To be polite I had to say, 'Yes.' The next day, he came to see me, and from that time we have never been apart. I go with him everywhere. In our fourteen years of marriage, I have never asked for him to take me with him. I go because he wants me to."

Nadine was twenty-nine when she married the baron. She is now forty-two and he is forty-seven. At the beginning of the romance, even their most devoted friends said it couldn't last. His family objected strongly. Nadine was a Gentile, as his first wife, Lina Georgina, was. Lina has been described as a model, a chorus girl, an usherette in a movie house—wrong: the latter, according to Nadine, was Yvette, who married James, one of the not-so-rich Rothschilds.

While a couple of the clan had married out of the faith, the huge family, especially Edmond's mother, wanted a nice Jewish girl for her new daughter-in-law. Lina, a Catholic from Bulgaria, had followed her own religion during the marriage, but had agreed that their sons would be brought up in the Jewish faith, while the daughters would be Catholic. Unfortunately for Lina's survival as a Rothschild, there were no children from the marriage, and for Edmond, the only son of an only son, it was essential to have a son. Remember, the Shah of Iran divorced Queen Soraya, to whom he had been devoted, for the same reason.

Nadine produced the heir and Mama Maurice accepted her, but Nadine is not resting lazily on her laurels. With fourteen servants in the Paris home, plus two secretaries and a butler, she is busy all day long and sometimes late into the evening.

You don't have to ask whether she is still in love with her husband—she adores him. It is one of the great love stories of our age. Perhaps you appreciate the happy ending more when the obstacles at the beginning seem insurmountable. Nadine had been divorced from Aristide Blanc, a French resistance leader in World War II, and the Rothschilds dislike divorces. There were rumors that Edmond could not find a rabbi to perform the ceremony in Europe. But the baron denies this. Nonetheless, he married Nadine in the United States, far from his family. It had taken four years to obtain the divorce, during which time the association was kept as secret as possible. The marriage, on November 26, 1959, was performed by Rabbi Joachim Prinz in a Reform Jewish service in Orange, New Jersey. Prinz was an old friend of the Rothschild family.

It was again decided that the sons would be Jewish, the daughters to follow the religion of their mother. But Nadine dug in her heels and said no, she thought it was wrong for half the family to be Jewish and half Christian. She did the sensible thing. She became Jewish. Not only that, but because she wanted to be completely involved with her husband's life, she became as zealous a Zionist as her husband is. She told me she was leaving in a few days for lunch at the Savoy Hotel in London to address a meeting for Hadassah International, of which she is the chairman.

The poem "How Do I Love Thee? Let Me Count the Ways," by Elizabeth Barrett Browning for her husband could just as well have been penned by Baroness Edmond. What is the true meaning of love? I asked her. She promptly replied, "Complete devotion to the man you love," which is almost the same as my own definition, giving without thought of receiving.

Nadine has received as much as she has given. She is the chatelaine of five magnificent houses. The house on the Rue d'Elysée was built in the eighteenth century during the extravagant reign of Louis XV. It was vandalized by the Nazis in World War II and all the precious paintings, furniture, and objets d'art were removed to Germany. Most of these, with the help of a Rothschild butler, were found in a cellar after the war and returned to Edmond.

The whole house, after fumigation, was restored to what it had been. Recently, the magnificent place was redecorated, with the addition of a large outdoor heated swimming pool—"I swim every day"—and a tropical garden with the right temperature maintained for the plants and exotic fish in the aquarium, and inside the house a projection room for the showing of films for the baron and baroness and their friends. "We like detective, crime, Westerns, and love stories." The façade of the house, as with all historical edifices in France, is the same as when it was first built.

"In the winter we go to our chalet in Megève in the French Alps." Edmond poured $5 million into what had been a small skiing resort to make it a major worldwide attraction.

"We also have a home in Austria, next to Saint Anton. We have a villa in the South of France, a house in Israel, and an estate in Geneva, which is only forty-five minutes by plane from Paris. We go there almost every weekend." They do not have a yacht or a private jet, preferring to use commercial planes and ships. The home in Geneva, "Pregny," is more of a castle than a house, and overlooks Lake Geneva. Edmond's father, Maurice, a great lover of art, bought Pregny and filled it with every kind of treasure. When the Nazis were desecrating the Paris mansion, Edmond was aesthetically comfortable in his castle. The country estate, le Château d'Armaivilliers, in Alsace, contains a huge artificial lake, a swimming pool, and woods for shooting. They are both good shots. In addition to the pheasants and woodcock, they are big-game hunters, and when visiting his gold and diamond mines in Africa, they side-trip to Kenya to stalk the big animals. The diminutive baroness is as brave as she is a good sportswoman. "I had a narrow escape in Kenya," she told me, "an elephant was charging toward me, but I shot him just in time."

Each home has its year-round butler and staff of servants—up to twenty when they are in residence. "We love to entertain," Nadine stated happily, "and it's never any trouble. At the last minute I can tell my secretary [they have a his and hers] we will be fifty for dinner, and that's all I have to do, everything is taken care of and is perfect." "Which is your favorite home?" I asked the baroness, to which she replied, "The Château de Pregny in Switzerland is a dream. There are always twenty servants there. I'm really very pleased"—the understatement of the decade. At one big party for Françoise Sagan, to celebrate the opening of her new play, the guests included seventy-four out of the seventy-five Rothschilds. Sam White, the Paris bureau chief for the London *Evening Standard*, wrote: "It was the greatest galaxy of Rothschilds since the Congress of Vienna."

"We have cinema parties, and these are smaller, about twenty people." They give or go to parties "all the time," as the baroness put it. At the "pink" soiree a year or so ago in Geneva, there were eighty for dinner, and another eighty for the supper dance. The ladies wore pink dresses, the gentlemen had pink buttonhole carnations.

In addition to the constant traveling to their six homes, they also fly to the baron's various business interests all over the world—stores, hotels, his Clubs de Mediterranée—small villas for tourists, price range from $20 to $150 a day—in the Caribbean, France, Corsica, Italy, and now expanding north at a total cost of $80 million, one tenth of his estimated fortune of $800 million. The clubs were started twenty-four years ago in Spain with 200 surplus U.S. Army tents and one wheezy outboard motorboat for the water skiers. His oil interests are in various parts of the world, gold and diamond mines in Africa, and his continual industrial expansion in Israel, where he financed the precious oil pipeline from Haifa in the north to Elath in the south—Emond's money is in every important industry and bank in the land of his forefathers.

The baron and baroness are both active in charitable projects. Edmond is president of the Ophthalmological Foundation in France. He gave $300,000 to the Alliance Israélite Universale to build a high school. The baroness is in demand as an organizer and speechmaker for fund-raising projects.

While sixty-four-year-old Guy de Rothschild is the eldest of the present crop of Rothschild brothers and is considered the head of the family, with the finest château, "Ferrières," Edmond is the richest. Not long ago, Guy was short of ready cash, and he sold some of his acreage and objets d'art. It was Edmond who bailed him out, and this was a triumph for the bespectacled baron, as until then he had been a rather neglected Rothschild. Edmond made it possible for Guy to hang on to his beloved Ferrières, where three years ago he gave the most talked-about party of the decade, with guests from all over the world, including the indefatigable and at that time inseparable Burtons, plus the rich cream of the crop of Rothschilds. Not all of the bona fide Rothschilds today are millionaires.

The twelve-year-old son of the house of Edmond had been lurking somewhere behind me, making bird noises. But with Nadine there and calling to him, he came out of the bushes to be introduced to me, after kissing his mother, whom he had not seen since he went off to school in the morning. "He goes to this school five mornings a week and twice a week in the afternoon. The other three afternoons he is tutored at home."

The home teaching is to make him thoroughly conversant with the Jewish faith. All the important Rothschilds are orthodox Jews, and the young, good-looking boy will be bar mitzvahed at the age of thirteen. He also studies economics, for the day when he is a partner with his father.

As I have mentioned, when Hitler moved into Paris, the Rothschilds, including Edmond, moved out, taking with them what they could of their possessions in the hasty flight. But in Vienna, Baron Louis de Rothschild decided to stay, and he calmly finished his lunch and made plans for the next day's menu while Nazi soldiers stood over him with guns. He was imprisoned for a year, and was then visited by Heinrich Himmler, Hitler's chief of the Gestapo, from whom he bought his freedom in return for all the family assets in Austria.

But all this seems like a million light years away. Looking at the glorious French paintings in the wide entrance hall and on the walls of the grand staircase—Fragonards, Corots, Watteaus, Ingres, Davids—I knew that Edmond de Rothschild had recovered completely from the Hitler nightmare, and with all his multiple activities in the modern world, he is increasing the fortune accumulated by Amschel and his five sons.

While the Baroness Edmond is a simple person, she enjoys dressing up for dinner parties and soirees. This lady, who was born in the north of France—"in St. Quentin, like the jail"—says of her present life, "It's like I'm still on the stage," where she began her acting career at the age of sixteen.

"I was glad to leave it," she confessed. "I am not the type to surround myself with a new generation of performers. My face and figure are not right for that. I would never succeed today. I don't miss the theater at all. We have so many attractions in and out of our homes." She is small and insists she is plump. "*Zaftig,*" says her husband.

"I like my life so much better now." Wherever the Edmonds go, they are entertained. "We stay with friends, especially in Africa, when we go for the shooting. Edmond is chairman of the de Beers gold and diamond mines there. I have the opportunity to meet the most fantastic, brilliant people in the world of politics, the arts, and the sciences, although I was not an educated girl." A mutual friend informed me that Edmond, before the marriage, brought in experts in various fields—dancing, speech, poise, education—to teach Nadine what she had not learned as a girl growing up, or while working for her living. By the time she was presented to society, she was the perfect lady outside, as well as she had always been inside. "My life is still essentially simple. After my marriage to Edmond, I wanted to do much for my family, but my father said, 'Just because you married a rich man, why should I change *my* way of life.' If I was unhappy, that would be another thing. But I have everything, a son, beautiful homes, a busy life, health, and a wonderful husband. Edmond is the most important for me, my wonderful husband, he has the heart like a mountain, it's never closed for anyone."

Her favorite hobby? "Shooting," adding, "and traveling. The world is a fantastic panorama for me—Mexico, Japan, Australia, France, Israel, Italy, North and South America."

Who could have imagined that all this could happen to a girl born poor in a small town, a girl not really beautiful, who, without much ambition started life as an extra in films?

"Actually, all I ever wanted was to be happy." I didn't have to ask, "Are you?" There had to be some flaw in this paradise, and I asked, "Do you feel lonely when your husband leaves in the morning for his office? I suppose he has an office?" "He has a bank," she corrected me, smiling.

Her contentment was catching. When I left the exquisite garden and the beautiful mansion, I was happy, as though *I* were living Nadine's glorious life. Thank heaven for little girls who get bigger and to whom it can happen.

18. The Compulsive Cleaner — Denise Minnelli Hale

"Wherever we go, Denise puts on rubber gloves, takes a can of Lysol, and cleans the whole place," said Prentis Cobb Hale, referring to his wife, the former Dancia Radosavltevic Gigante Minnelli and now Hale. Denise comes by her cleaning habits legitimately. She is basically a hausfrau. She slips into her chauffeur-driven limousine to go to market to buy fresh vegetables. She pinches the cantaloupe to make sure it is ripe.

Denise was born in Yugoslavia about forty-two years ago. Her father was an officer in the army. When the Germans took over, she fled to Italy, where she was promptly put into a concentration camp, complete with tattoo number on her wrist, which she later had removed via plastic surgery. She never saw either of her parents again.

Denise's journey from the camp to her present riches is a story of courage and ambition. Dad was a partisan in the patriotic underground army. A price was on his head. When he was arrested she knew she had to get out. To get to Rome from Yugoslavia was the first hurdle for the teen-age Miss

Radosavltevic. There is never any mention of Mama, so I assume she died before or after the great escape. Their young daughter, with another girl, got hold of a rowboat, and this is how they came across the Adriatic, only to land in a camp for political refugees.

Denise was a neat, clean girl, who was always scrubbing the quarters she shared with the other displaced persons. When the war was over she was still in the camp, her hair kept tidy in two pigtails, her dark eyes eagerly scanning the Americans who toured the camps wanting to help the hapless inmates.

The government had comandeered part of the Cinecittà Studios in Rome to house the stateless people. Cinecittà had been Mussolini's favorite film studio. A British film producer, John Shepridge, and his American friend, David Pelham, were making a film on one of the few sound stages that had been left for the moviemakers.

"We saw those poor people in the camp," David told me. "As the war was over and the Allies had won, visitors were allowed to take them out for a treat, to give them a meal or whatever. They had to be signed out and when you brought them back, signed in."

Because young people are better able to cope with discomfort than the old, it was mostly the aging inmates who received attention from the British and Americans. But one day, after David had noted the wistful expression on the face of Denise, he said to John, "Why don't we give the young ones a turn? Let's give them a taste of good living."

Denise still had the VO mark on her wrist, which meant she would be reserved for the German officers, four of them, V for *vier*—"four." She told the sympathetic film men that her father and mother had died in a concentration camp, and she didn't know where she came from (she knew, but it was a better story).

"We gave her a marvelous dinner in the best restaurant in Rome." Small wonder that after stuffing herself to the limit, little Denise refused to return to the camp. Even then she knew what she wanted, and especially what she did not want. If she didn't want to go back to the camp, and who could blame her, there was only one thing for the gentlemen to do. They took her back to their apartment until they could figure out where she could go.

"We had a maid who looked after us," David told me, "and Denise was terribly jealous of the maid. She was so grateful to us she wanted to do all the housework, to pay for her keep. She was always fluffing out our pillows, sewing on buttons, and staying up late for us to come home to make us coffee." The boys sometimes didn't return until 4 A.M. "She would tuck us into our respective beds and sing us Yugoslavian lullabies." It sounds like a fairy tale.

Only when the snoring told her that the men were asleep would she creep into her bed in the servant's room—the maid had left after screaming she would not put up with another helper who did more than was necessary, in her opinion, to keep the apartment clean.

Denise reveled in the housework. Soapsuds up to her elbows, she sang in time to the scrub, scrub, scrub. She learned to cook pasta and a few other Italian dishes—David, a good cook, taught her. It was a lovely arrangement for them all. Until the day when the boys came home for one of her pasta dinners and she was gone.

Great consternation. Denise was too young to be roaming around heaven knows where. The two men searched for her on the wide boulevards, and the narrow back streets of Rome, but they could not find her.

"I was in New York in 1951," David reminisced recently, "attending the Knickerbocker Ball in Whitelaw Reed's party [which included the Duke and Duchess of Windsor, Count Rudi and Countess Consuela Crespi—Mr. Reed owned the *New York Herald-Tribune*] and looking across the table I saw this beautiful girl, loaded with jewels, and exquisitely dressed. I was sure I knew her and stared, but she avoided my eyes. I leaned across the table, and said in Italian, '*Cometichiama*,' an intimate form of address that you use with children. It means, 'What is your name?' She looked down and said, 'Denise.' 'Oh, darling Denise,' I cried, 'Don't you remember me, David Pelham, of Cinecittà?' She looked me full in the face and said crisply, 'I don't remember anything before 1950' and turned to speak to her tablemate."

Two hours later, when David was outside getting a cab, he

felt two cool hands over his eyes. "I said, 'Who's that?' 'Denise,' she replied. 'Of course I remember you, darling.' " She told him she had shared an apartment with Betty Spiegel, who married film producer Sam Spiegel, while Denise became Countess José Gigante—he had made his money at the end of the war in China by the purchase of a rusty old freighter from the U.S. Navy that contained vast quantities of penicillin.

Whether it was the count or the British Eric Dudley (to whom she had been engaged) who lavished expensive jewelry on her, Denise never explained. But she had so much that when she was staying at the Savoy Hotel in London, they couldn't get it all into the hotel safe!

I remember meeting Denise when she first came to Hollywood. She was dripping with gems and gentleness, which like the jewels were on the outside. You would have to be tough to do as well as she has done, without any great beauty, but the necessary load of charm. Unlike Dru Mallory Heinz, who was in Hollywood before Denise, you could see the wheels going round in that sharp little head, although the sympathy in her eyes could win any woman, let alone the more simple man.

Her reason for being in Hollywood was that she had met Vincente Minnelli in Paris while he was there filming *Gigi*. Vincente, famous for his stage and film musical *An American in Paris*, was a friend of Eleanor Lambert, the New York fashion promoter, and he asked her to look after Denise, to round off the corners before she came to California. Vincente, who had previously been married to Judy Garland, was then at the height of his fame as a movie director. He found Denise restful after the turbulence of life with Judy. She seemed so sure of herself, compared to the insecurities of Miss Garland, with whom he had a daughter, Liza, who is now almost as famous as her more talented mother. He has another daughter, Christina Nina, by his first wife.

Vincente and Denise were married at the Palm Springs home of Laurence Harvey and Joan Cohn, the widow of the Columbia film studio tycoon, to whom he was then married. They settled into his expensive home in Beverly Hills. I sometimes visited Denise and Vincente there and usually found other columnists and reporters in the crowds of her acquaintances. Denise has always enjoyed publicity, and by making friends of the gossipists who reported her parties, she made sure of getting good publicity.

At the beginning it was all for Vincente, the parties, the people, and the publicity. But he had bad luck with his films. Television was taking over and a film had to be a blockbuster to do well at the box office.

The worse the reviews for Vincente's films, the more strenuously Denise tried to keep him in the forefront of attention. But the parties for sixty to one hundred in the upstairs room at the Bistro restaurant club in Beverly Hills were costly, and Vincente worried so much about the bills, he started to lose his touch, and his hair.

When he found it difficult to pay the mortgage on the big house, Denise came to the rescue and took over the payments. Vincente put the property into her name. If there is anything Denise detests in a man, or a woman, it is an obvious show of insecurity. "I only like secure men or women," she told me once, "I especially like attractive, secure women." She obviously likes herself, because that is how one would describe the ex-refugee.

Denise was now seen at parties without Vincente. She always asked him to accompany her but he said no—perhaps he felt too miserable about his failing fortunes and the mounting bills. It was now a question of time before the parting, and this occurred soon after Denise met multimillionaire Prentis Cobb Hale, at a dinner party given by the Jules Steins. Until his recent retirement, Jules was the powerful chairman of MCA, the colossal entertainment agency, which also included, until the law divided them, the Universal Film Studios.

Mr. Hale had asked his wife—they lived in San Francisco—to fly with him to the party, but she was tired and not in the mood to go to Los Angeles. The excuse of fatigue has often broken up what could have remained a happy marriage. If Prentis's wife had accompanied him to the Steins, he might never have fallen in love with Madame Minnelli.

Denise was seated next to Prentis, and she asked him intelligent questions about his various stores—Prentis at that time owned all the Broadway-Hale stores on the West coast, plus the fancy Neiman-Marcus store in Dallas. His gross income from his business brought him untold millions a year, plus the interest from his own private capital of $60 million.

It is more now. Prentis is not only super rich, but he is also handsome, the kind of man (like Jack Heinz) you would want to marry if he didn't have all that money. Between bites and even during mouthfuls, she asked his advice on this and that, poor little helpless girl—but above all she showed her admiration as a woman to a man.

It was a three-year waiting period, because neither her husband nor his wife would agree to a divorce. Vincente, who had been so generous and willing to please Denise, now unexpectedly dug his heels in and said, "No divorce." He loved her, had put his home in her name, and if they divorced, where would he go? He was adamant, even when the reigning Mrs. Prentis Hale committed suicide by jumping out of a high window in her home in San Francisco. There were several grown-up children from this marriage, and they were heartbroken. I am sure they had tried to make their father abandon Denise, until the tragedy decided the issue for him. He was free but Denise was not. She pleaded with dear, kind Vincente to give her the divorce she craved.

The question of the house arose. Would she deed it back to him? "Never." The "never" became less and less firm as some of the gossip in Beverly Hills and San Francisco boudoirs was channeled into her aching ear by some of her numerous acquaintances. To wit: "She will never marry Prentis."

Meanwhile, the lovebirds saw each other all the time, although some doors in San Francisco were closed to Denise. Wives always band together when an attractive intruder appears. Denise realized that if she were ever to sign her name Mrs. Prentis Hale she must give Vincente his home in Beverly Hills. So, before she married Prentis, she deeded the house back to her husband.

Vincente has the house and Denise is married to Mr. Hale. She had beaten those bitches in Beverly Hills and San Francisco who had laughed at her and said she could never pull it off. At the simple ceremony on September 9, 1971, Denise gave her age as forty. Prentis, a law graduate from Stanford University, was sixty-one.

"I arranged it all," crowed Denise, meaning the wedding. Her sycophants wanted her to have a stupendous ceremony and reception, but the wise lady said "No, when you get married the third time, simple is better." She still has that cute Yugoslavian accent.

There were parties galore, before and after the wedding, at which Denise wore a golden yellow chiffon gown and some of the diamonds given her by her various husbands. The huge diamond and sapphire ring from Prentis had been a family heirloom. Denise had it redesigned by Bulgari of Rome. Her wedding ring, from Cartier's, designed by Denise, is a circle of diamonds set in platinum.

There was no wedding cake at the reception, held at the fashionable Presidio Terrace in the home of Mr. and Mrs. William Orrick, in San Francisco. Denise had already had her cake and eaten it at the party she gave following the divorce from Vincente, who happily is again in demand as a director. Mr. Orrick was a childhood friend of Prentis and he was not going to be put off by a lot of faded dowagers who have still not accepted Denise.

There were not as many people at the reception as the society columnists had predicted. Denise explained this with an airy "Most of my friends are in the South of France at this time of the year." Gloria Vanderbilt Wyatt Cooper was matron of honor and she gave a party for the bride and groom. There was a wedding party before and after the day of the marriage. At the second soiree, Prentis was served with a summons in connection with the divorce of his son. The process server was in a dinner jacket and looked like a guest.

To judge by the write-ups in a certain New York society column, Denise has been giving nonstop parties ever since the marriage. Any good name will serve as an excuse. The Hales had seventy for the dinner-dance they gave in Beverly Hills for Princess Ghislaine de Polignac. They chartered three planes and flew with their guests to Los Angeles.

At the party, the hostess wore a black organza gown with a huge ruffled collar and hem. The low neckline was to display her diamond and sapphire necklace, the gift of the groom, which Denise wears once a year to dazzle her friends, earrings to match—and with the ring, Denise was a glittering sight. Among the guests were Truman Capote and the present Mrs. Henry Ford, who, as noted earlier, never missed a party if she could possibly help it.

When the Hales gave a cocktail party in their suite at the Waldorf Towers—it had been occupied by the late Cole Porter and also the Duke and Duchess of Windsor—Mrs. Elsie Woodward, the grande matriarch of Eastern society, came out of seclusion in the country to be the pièce de résistance for the Hales.

At one time, Denise staged a cross-country party. It started in New York, went on to Texas, and ended at the Bistro in Beverly Hills.

This time around, there are no frowns from a hubby when he receives the bills. This one can afford it all and more. In addition to his stores, Mr. Hale owns a large hunk of Syntex shares—he is president of the company—also a 10,000 acre ranch in Cloverdale, seventy miles north of San Francisco. On the cultural side, he has been president of the city's opera house.

While the couple honeymooned in Europe, the San Francisco home was redecorated to Denise's taste, and she has excellent taste—where did she learn it, certainly not in the refugee camp. But, as I cannot repeat often enough, these poor girls who marry rich men must be smart and able to learn along the way. Then they can fit into the rich man's life as though born to it.

Denise has learned to please her handsome husband. Mr. Hale did not like his wife in pigtails, which she had worn before the marriage, so no more pigtails. Mr. Hale loves roast pork. Denise learned how to cook it for him. She can now make French, American, as well as Italian dishes. Her specialty is chicken fricassee simmered in champagne. She used to get up at noon. Now she rises with Prentis at 7 A.M. Or rather she did in the first year of her marriage. Denise, like most people who enjoy staying up late, prefers to remain abed in the morning until it is time for lunch. Lately she has been backsliding a bit and getting up somewhere between seven and noon.

New York is her favorite city. His is San Francisco, but

Denise prefers Beverly Hills to the more sedate atmosphere of the Gold Coast. They compromise. She flies with her husband to New York on his business trips, even for a day or so. They fly a dozen times a year to Chicago on his store business. Denise dislikes flying, but she adores her husband, who gives her carte blanche in the area of shopping.

For her wardrobe she skips from Donald Brooks to Oscar de la Renta and Galanos. She can spend $12,000 on one dress—even with the discount at Bergdorf's and Neiman-Marcus. What a dream for a girl who loves clothes to have a husband who sells them!

Denise's hobby? Collecting jewelry, say her friends. Mr. Hale collects guns, of which she is femininely afraid. Denise prefers abstract art. Prentis collects French Impressionists, especially Berthe Morisot. They went to Czechoslovakia for the honeymoon—"to shoot pheasants," said Mr. Hale. But as Denise dislikes guns, they stopped first for one week in New York so that Denise could wallow in the luxury she loves.

"I don't like to rough it," she says frankly. She found the Czech chalet to be an uncomfortable place. That's when Denise went to work with the rubber gloves and the can of Lysol, so that the place would at least be spotless.

They consider honesty to be the number one virtue. Says Denise, "You can buy brains, but not honesty." From Prentis, "That is what I admire most in Denise, she's so honest, with great tenderness and understanding. I have complete happiness alone with Denise."

She: "Next to Prentis, I love my friends. I give a lot and expect a lot in return." She loves people, as most of the dollar winners do. People who like people are liked in return, which broadens the horizon for finding a suitable mate.

The secret of the happy Hale marriage, says Denise, is to do things on a fifty-fifty basis. She likes watching TV. He does not—except for football. She prefers to watch movies. So they have several His and Her sets. Prentis is a good swimmer. Denise learned to swim after the marriage. She cannot drive, and Mr. Hale is glad that she doesn't. She's afraid of cars—cars and planes have a masculine image, and Denise is nothing if not completely feminine.

And yet she is a strong woman. She has built up her ego to the point where she creates her own rules. In terms of glamor, she gives the best parties, with the possible exception of Mrs. William Paley, who has one advantage over Denise, she was born with great beauty. The fact that Denise was not gives her more credit for the position she has attained in life.

Denise loves a man with power. When they show weakness, she is not interested. "Powerful men are more interesting," she explains. She cannot bear to be bored, which she was at first at the big Cloverdale ranch, the pride of her husband. To please him, she forced herself to like it.

But while Denise is a compulsive cleaner, she dislikes the problems of a large home, and she wants her husband to sell the mansion in San Francisco. She would rather have small homes in several places. "A big house," she says, "is a waste of time." Dancia Radosavltevic Gigante Minnelli Hale has never wasted this precious heritage.

19. *The Billion-Dollar Siblings — Jo and Hunt*

FOR A WOMAN like Josephine Hartford Bryce it was not enough to have $500 million. The seventy-one-year-old heiress to The Great Atlantic and Pacific Tea Company—A & P—wanted all the benefits that such a fortune can bring. Mostly she wanted to be accepted in European society, which does not care how much money a woman has, it's her background and to whom she is married that counts. He must be a gentleman in the old meaning of the word, otherwise the doors of the aristocracy are closed.

Such a man is John (Ivar) Bryce, Etonian, and Christ Church, Oxford, graduate, suave, handsome, and a member of top society, as is apparent from his distinguished face. His family was never on the poverty line, but certainly not rich. In fact three decades ago they had to sell the family homestead in Essex, England.

Ivar's hair is gray now and I have not heard of much action on the sex front. When he became Josephine's fourth husband, on April, 1950, in Aikin, South Carolina, he was forty years old, brown-haired, six feet three, straight-backed—which he still is —a vigorous man, adored by most of the women who crossed his path. One of whom in describing his various attractions, stated, "Ivar was very well endowed." Meaning, he was a great lover. For Josephine, the bona fide English gentleman—his father was Major Charles Bryce of the Coldstream Guards, his mother the late Lady Phillimore—fitted the bill completely.

Jo is now plump and doesn't concern herself much with prevailing fashions. She washes her own hair and never has more than $1,000 in her current account. She can be cautious with her money but is at times impulsively generous. If you admire something she is wearing, don't be surprised if she gives it to you, as I discovered when dining with some friends and Jo at the Bistro in Beverly Hills a year ago. Not knowing of her propensity for giving, I patted her sable stole and said how pretty it was. She promptly removed it from her shoulders and gave it to me.

"Oh no!" I protested. "I didn't mean you to—" She interrupted my embarrassment and said in definite tones, "It's yours." "What can I give you in return?" I asked. "Here, take my coat." It was my best evening coat, and more than that, I looked thin in it. I was relieved when she refused my offer. I turned the stole into a one-piece necklet, which I have never worn, and into a halo-type hat, which I have only just begun to wear. And it was baum marten, not sable.

Josephine and her brother Huntington each inherited half a billion dollars when their father died. Most of her fortune is intact, but Hunt, who preferred to marry poor girls and invest in many losing ventures, today is credited with less than $30 million. Poor boy.

Ian Fleming, the creator of the James Bond novels, told me shortly before his death that Josephine's income was $15,000 a day. Her annual takings were around $5 million. How do you spend money like that? It boggles the mind.

Like Barbara Hutton and Doris Duke, the former Miss Hartford buys and builds luxurious homes and has also given a great deal to her husbands. The ranch on Long Island has an indoor swimming pool and tennis court. Josephine, who was very pretty and slim as a young woman, played tennis every day and hit a good ball. The New York town house is in the fashionable East Seventies. You have to dress for dinner at "Black Hole Farm," the South Vermont place. There is also a $100,000 home in Rhode Island. In the winter she divides her time between New York, Vermont, and the town house in Nassau. A beachfront home, "Xanadu," with the lake at the back and hundreds of flamingoes, is now the property of Mr. Bryce, from whom she separated almost a decade ago. When Jo goes to her different houses, she is accompanied by six staff members from the New York house—the butler, footman, cook and maids.

In 1956, some of the $300 million cash turnover from her A & P stock was spent renovating Ivar's former ancestral estate, Moyns Park in England. The estate is not as large as Blenheim Palace or Woburn Abbey, but it takes a lot of servants to run. "We're not doing too much," Ivar is quoted as saying at the time, "just putting in a few bathrooms, electricity, digging a well, redecorating and furnishing, building two new stables, and starting a stud farm. We want it for a couple of months each summer, when we're over from the States. It's small now, two hundred acres, but I grew up there as a boy and we managed to buy the house back in 1953." The Bryces built a bridge over the moat for the birds. A Chinese mission bell brought the guests in for meals and cocktails.

Jo and John—Ivar—were introduced during an Atlantic crossing on the old *Queen Elizabeth*. (Shipboard romances were then in full flower.) They spent the first part of the honeymoon returning to England on the same ship. "As you can see, I've not lost faith in marriage," Josephine assured the reporters, adding, "But it is a nuisance getting used to new names!" (This was her fourth marriage). About her wealth, she stated, "I've had lots of trouble because of my money. It hasn't brought me happiness, I don't like to talk about it."

We are all so sure that if we were rich *we* would be happy. The question is, would Josephine have been happier as a poor girl? Perhaps. These children of self-made tycoons often inherit the spunk that made the fortune possible. Mrs. Bryce is a clever businesswoman, and controls the Hartford Foundation, a charitable organization. She is the main voice in how the money is distributed. She manages her business interests with the expertise of a Wall Street wizard.

The gigantic A & P store complex with its five thousand supermarkets, its own canneries, bakeries, and fishing fleets, has not done as well in the past few years. The price of the shares has dropped—in 1950, the year she married Bryce, dividends paid out were $20 million. In one recent year there was a loss of $55 million. So instead of a $5 million income, Jo now receives a mere $1 million. How awful.

How do these rich women discuss the settlements with their comparatively poor husbands? Mr. Bryce is too much of a gentleman to talk about money matters. He would be more likely to direct the conversation so that *she* would make the offer. He told an intimate that he was prepared to give his wife her money's worth. He liked her very much and wanted the marriage to succeed. She adored him. Ah well, they had a good run for fifteen years, after which they parted, joining up sometimes in Nassau.

But, as Ivar had promised, he gave Jo full value. She was not only accepted by European society, she was introduced to British royalty when Ivar's niece Janet married the Marquess of Milford Haven, who was Prince Philip's best man for the marriage to Queen Elizabeth. He also drew her into the world of films, and together they went into horse racing on a big scale. She bought him his first racer, King of Troy, in 1951, less than a year after their marriage. In 1963 they won four races, including the British Derby with Doudance.

I attended a party several years ago at the Bryces' town house in London. It was to celebrate the premiere of Ivar's first film production, *The Boy on the Bridge*. His partner was Kevin McClory, who also did well, matrimonially speaking, by marrying British aviation heiress Bobo Sigrist. Bryce met Kevin when the latter bought the film rights of *Thunderball* from Ian Fleming, whose James Bond books until then had not been bought for films.

Ian, Kevin, and Ivar formed a company, backed by Josephine's money, to produce pictures. But *Thunderball* belonged to Kevin alone. Producers Harry Saltzman and Cubby Broccoli made Kevin a one-shot partner. *Thunderball* was a success: Kevin made millions. But *Boy on the Bridge* was a total disaster, and Josephine, a bad picker of husbands but shrewd where her fortune is concerned, said, "No more." As for Mr. Bryce, with the estate in England plus the racing stable and Xanadu in Nassau, it is safe to assume that he is now very well off. I doubt whether he will remarry. He is too happy as a free man.

Will Josephine remarry? It doesn't seem likely. She is past seventy, has had several husbands, several romances, and is rather disillusioned about love. During the past eight years there was a new man in her life whom she loved dearly, and when he died in 1973 in a snowmobile accident in Vermont she was inconsolable and cried, "My God, I was going to marry him!"

Before Jo married Ivar, she was in love with Lord Selby. In fact they were engaged for four years. 'Twas said at the time that she promised him a million dollars on the day the marriage would take place. She did not enjoy her position as a long-time engaged woman, she wanted to be a bride. When he continued to dilly-dally, she informed him that she could not go on like this, four years was too long to be in love with a man and not have a wedding ring from him. Soon after she married Mr. Bryce.

Ivar's two previous wives were the rich Mrs. Vera Sottamaior de Sa and Sheila Taylor Pease (the daughter of a leading Manhattan lawyer, and formerly married to Francis Taylor of Newport, New York, and San Francisco, and heir to one of America's oldest banking fortunes).

When Sheila divorced him at the beginning of 1950, his name was given as Ivar Bryce and not John, as he had been christened. The grounds for the divorce were "extreme cruelty." It was a messy business, with Sheila alleging his misconduct at the Hotel Vendôme in Paris the previous summer.

Josephine has two grown-up children, Columbus O'Donnell, and Mrs. Claiborne Pell, both from her first marriage. The elder O'Donnell was fairly well off, and from a good family, with homes in Newport, Rhode Island, Oyster Bay, Long Island, and Baltimore. The Long Island home was paid for by Jo, who was richer by a few hundred million dollars than her husband. At the time of their divorce in 1931, there was talk of "a generous settlement" on O'Donnell. They had been married eight years.

In the same year, one month after the divorce, Josephine

married thirty-nine-year-old Vladimir Makaroff, in a civil ceremony in Paris, followed by a Russian church wedding in Nice.
Vladimir was described as the son of a Russian admiral—aren't
they all?

Commander Makaroff had fled to the United States at the
start of the Russian Revolution. He returned to Russia in 1918
to fight the Bolsheviks in Siberia. After his group was routed,
he came back to America and became a successful inventor—
of a speed indicator used in antiaircraft fire control, a process
for freezing orange juice in paper containers, and a new type
of diamond drill in wildcat oil drilling. In New York he found
Makaroff and Co., Inc., an import business specializing in Russian caviar. Jo's third husband, Barclay Douglas, is known
mostly for having leased his Annandale Farm in Newport to
President John Kennedy as a summer White House.

Josephine's mother was Princess Guido Pignatelli, who gave
her prince a yacht, the *Joseph Conrad*. One day he received a
cable from the captain—"Have struck whale. Await instructions." Pignatelli flew to the ailing vessel, and shortly afterward
his princess divorced him. When she died she left an estate of
more than $5 million, from which her daughter received
$350,000, her son a lesser amount, the rest to the prince.

Before and after World War II, Ivar served with the British
Security Office in New York and later was attached to the
British embassy in Washington. He brought the same dedication
and diplomacy as he had to the women who loved him. I doubt
whether we will be hearing much more of Mr. Bryce. Marriage
to a rich woman brought him everything he desired. One can
only applaud him for going after and getting what he wanted
in life with such charming nonchalance.

No brother and sister are more different than Josephine and
George Huntington Hartford, named for his grandfather who
founded the family A & P fortune of tea and groceries in the
1850s. They don't even look alike—Josephine, brown-haired and
plump, Hunt, as his friends call him, slender, dark, and satur-
nine. But the chief difference between them is one of temperament. While Josephine is careful with her money—except where
husbands and lovers are concerned—Hunt rushes in and out of
projects like a sailor in a foreign port.

When Mr. Hartford isn't splashing millions around, he is making plans to do so. Most of his Great Ideas have failed. Just to make sure he would never starve, he was induced to put away $9 million in trust funds for himself, "So that I can't possibly spend it" and a million dollars for his three children. His three wives didn't do too badly either. The last one, Diane Brown, walked away with a $2.5 million settlement. His second wife, Marjorie Steele, received $350,000 in cash, a $2 million trust for their children, Cathy and John, plus $60,000 a year in alimony until she married again, which she did in 1961, to Dudley Sutton, a British actor with whom she had a son, Peter. She is now married to an English author.

Mr. Hartford was born in 1911, nine years after his sister. He was rich before his birth and by 1917 the A & P stores were worth $124 million. At the age of twenty-one, he inherited a $1 million trust, in addition to 10 percent of the A & P profits, which brought him the same annual $5 million as sister Jo. In his sophomore year at Harvard—he was twenty—he eloped with Mary Lee Epling, socialite daughter of a West Virginia surgeon.

They moved to Hollywood and it was a bad move for Hunt. Mary Lee was exposed to the charms of Hollywood's attractive actors, especially Douglas Fairbanks, Jr., whom she married after her divorce. She received a $1.5 million settlement from Hunt. The long-time Fairbanks marriage has been happy.

The disappointed food heir joined the navy and served as an ensign in the U.S. Greenland patrol during World War II. Transferred to the South Pacific, he saw combat as a lieutenant in the supply service. After his discharge in 1946, he started a Hollywood talent agency with Bill Deering, a former MGM executive whom he had met during the marriage with Mary Lee. He lived in a big house high up in the Hollywood Hills and gave big parties. The grounds were lit with lanterns, the trees bright with electric light flooding, a bar outside and inside, and the best food catered by Chasens, which is the most consistently good restaurant in Los Angeles.

I met Hunt at one of his parties, and he rather scared me. He was so unsmiling, with his brooding dark eyes. Surrounded by the famous personalities of Hollywood, he seemed a lonely figure. He was a busy patron of the nightclubs and I had the impression that he was trying to fill in the hours among people with whom he had nothing in common. It was at one of these night haunts, Ciro's on the Strip, that Hunt fell in love with pretty, blond cigarette girl, Marjorie Sue Steele.

You have seen as this book progressed that cigarette, hat-check, and chorus girls in nightclubs often marry rich men. They are in the front firing line where the rich men and play-boys go in search of pretty girls.

Marjorie, an electrician's daughter, was nineteen, Hunt almost twenty years older. She worked sometimes as a movie extra and had artistic aspirations. The cigarette job was only tem-porary, she wanted to be an actress and a painter. She was quiet, which suited Hunt. Like so many pretty but poor girls, her face was cast in an aristocratic mold. In San Francisco, where she was born, she had been interested in all forms of culture.

Hunt had found a pearl through the butts of the cigarettes she sold. They were married in Nevada in September, 1949. The honeymoon was in Portofino, Italy, where the adoring million-aire bought his bride everything a painter would need, and where she created her first work in oils.

The millionaire behaved rather like Orson Wells in *Citizen Kane*, who tried to transform the woman he loved into an opera singer by building her own theater. Hunt had better luck with Marjorie, who sold many of her paintings at the one-woman show he put on for her at the exclusive Wilderstein Art Gallery in New York. Marjorie and Hunt produced two children, Cathy, born in 1950, and John, three years later.

Whether it was his wife's influence or his own idea, Hunt founded an artists' colony on a fellowship basis at the 150-acre estate he bought at Pacific Palisades near Santa Monica. To promote Marjorie's acting career, he made a two-part film at RKO called *Face to Face*, with his wife starred in one of the segments, "The Bride Comes to Yellow Sky," for which he paid a large sum. The movie failed, but the bride had come to yellow (gold) sky. He then turned to authorship, and wrote two books, one of these titled *Has God Been Insulted Here?* The themes opposed obscenity in the arts.

Hunt was a busy man with a seeming built-in guilt about the

money he inherited, which is why, perhaps, he spread it around, giving it back to the people who made him so rich.

In 1953, he opened the Hartford Model Agency. It was the era when models had been brought to Hollywood to become film stars—Lauren Bacall, Suzy Parker, and so on. Hunt's idea was that his models would serve their time with his company, then go to Hollywood and become stars. But the film producers had stopped biting. Some of the models had proved to be bad actresses. Again he lost money. There is some mystery about an orphanage he acquired. But again, it cost him money by the time it closed.

Undaunted, Hunt bought the old Cecil B. de Mille Theatre on Vine Street, near Hollywood Boulevard. De Mille had built it in 1927. It was remodeled at a cost of $1,200,000. I was at the reopening of the now Huntington Hartford Theatre on September 27, 1954, with Helen Hayes starred in Barrie's *What Every Women Knows*. The elite of the film industry was there, the top producers, writers, directors, actors, and actresses.

"A smash!" proclaimed the Los Angeles critics the next day. But alas for Hartford's bank account, the movie people were not then fans of the legitimate theater. Hunt sold the theater seven years later and lost several million dollars on the project, which failed to draw except on the various opening nights, when it was important for the famous to be seen and photographed.

Would Mr. Hartford now call it quits in the theater? Not on your nelly, as Elizabeth Taylor would say. He spent another $250,000 on the Broadway production of Charlotte Bronte's *Jane Eyre*. Who was the playwright? Hunt himself. It was conceived as a present for Marjorie. But her last name was Steele, and in this matter she lived up to it. It would ruin her career, she told a friend after reading the play. And, more diplomatically, to her husband: "They would say it was just another rich man putting his wife in a play." She was right. *Jane Eyre* bombed, and closed soon after it opened with a half a million of Hunt's dollars down the drain.

Laurence Olivier, during lunch at the "21" Club, asked Hunt to put up $500,000 for the famed actor to star in a film version of *Macbeth*. "Oh gee," reportedly said the multimillionaire, "that's a lot of money. I could do another play for that." He might have made money on Olivier's *Macbeth*.

Hunt had always wanted to be a reporter, and he made sure of landing a job on a New York newspaper by investing $100,000 in the new paper *P.M.* But, after tremendous losses, *P.M.* went the way of so many of Mr. Hartford's ventures.

In June of 1959, Hunt bought a large (700 acres) piece of Hog Island off Nassau to be a vacation resort—cost for the land $11 million, and $14 million to develop it. He renamed it Paradise Island, but even this did not help. Paradise Island was sold in 1966 to the Mary Carter Paint Company for $5 million, with Hartford retaining a 25 percent interest. Nassau is not as popular as it was, and the investment is said to have cost the A & P heir close to $10 million.

I'm getting dizzy adding up the losses. But there were more to come, before and after the hell of Paradise. In June of '65, Hunt sold half of his A & P shares, leaving him with 900,000 shares valued at $40 million. The following year he sold another 750,000 shares, reducing the value of what he had left to $3,400,000.

Something had to give. The Gallery of Modern Art on Columbus Circle, New York, with several of Marjorie's paintings, had cost him $900,000 for the land and $4,500,000 to erect the building. In the first year of the gallery, Hartford admitted he had lost $300,000. The various reappearances and disappearances of his entertainment magazine *Show* lost him another fortune. He was minus $6 million from the first outing of *Show*. In the same year, 1964, Hartford was named head of a committee to save the Egyptian temples at Abu Simbel, which were threatened with flooding by the Aswan Dam. Naturally, he contributed to the project.

In his glorious $70 million spending spree, the generous philanthropist sometimes, once that I know of, paused before signing the check. A few years ago he was in New York with two chums. They were leaving his Beekman Place home when they stumbled over two almost frozen drunks, spreadeagled on the sidewalk. It was New Year's Eve, and the trio had with them three gorgeous girls in beautiful gowns and bedecked with jewels.

They were all in a convivial mood and sorry for the drunks,

although hysterical with laughter. They named one Willie and the other Joey. Hoisting them into the waiting Cadillac, they took them to the Bellevue Emergency Ward. It was like a battlefield, jammed with the early holiday revelers—drunks, car accident cases, and muggings. One doctor was sewing up a face, another extracting a knife from a back. Meanwhile, Willie and Joey had regained consciousness and were urinating on the floor.

Mr. Hartford, who was well known at the hospital because of his philanthropies, demanded immediate help for his protégés. He called a doctor from a minor case and said, "I'd like to have these two men processed." The doctor examined the men and told the millionaire, "Your friends are okay, just inebriated."

Hunt was now involved. He loved Willie and Joey, and they all, including the girls, went back to Beekman Place, where Hunt outfitted his "friends" from top to toe with new clothes from his own wardrobe, and gave them $50 each, "not to squander on drink." They left, winking grotesquely at their benefactor and leering at the girls.

At Bellevue, the generous Hartford had informed the doctor that he would start a foundation there, "tomorrow," for drunks, a special ward for them. He had borrowed the $100 for the boozy boys from one of his male companions—"I don't have any cash on me, lend me a hundred." "I never got it back", the man told me, "and the foundation was never started." They had all been very "happy" and Hunt must have forgotten the whole incident. But this was one of the few times that it didn't cost him anything.

In 1960 he had the brilliant idea of building an outdoor café in Central Park and put up a check for $862,500. But there was too much opposition from various organizations. The check remained for some time on deposit with the city controller. At the same time, he put his artists' colony in California up for sale.

Hunt has always been concerned about "the people." When the A & P employees were on strike for higher pay, he joined them in the picket line. This Don Quixote who was always tilting at windmills put up $100,000 to help save the old Metropolitan Opera House from demolition. He did not expect a profit from the Handwriting Institute that he established in New York. Hunt believes that you can tell the character of a person by his or her handwriting, and recently wrote a book on the subject. He obviously neglected to study the handwriting of his three wives.

There was *one* profitable venture, The Shale Oil Company—you can't be a loser with everything. This company financed by Mr. Hartford is worth in excess of $5 million. Later he resigned as chairman, claiming that the firm was being run incompetently. (He had made the same accusation against the A & P management.) But he retained his $5.4 million worth of Shale shares, as the largest private stockholder. They are worth much more today.

Mr. Hartford met his third wife, Diane Brown, at the home of mutual friends. She had come to New York for a New Year's Eve party and never went home. He promptly hired her to model for his Plaza Five Agency. Her family lived in a farming community in Pennsylvania. Mr. Hartford set about publicizing her. The first interview was for his *Show* magazine. The lady interviewer recently gave me a rundown of the scene: "I was supposed to write a piece on her love of the arts, to give a reason for the story. 'Are you interested in painting?' I asked her. 'No,' she replied. 'Are you interested in the movies?' 'No.' 'The theater?' 'No.' 'Are you interested in modeling?' 'Not really.' 'Well, what can you do?' 'I can milk a cow.' "

Hartford married Diane at Melody Farm, the Hartford family estate in New Jersey. At that time he still owned the house in Hollywood Hills with its 140 acres of land, the duplex on Beekman Place, and the place in New Jersey, with houses in Mayfair, London, Palm Beach, and Cannes. Also a home in Nassau.

Diane was entranced with her capture of this attractive man who was doing so much to help her. He had her speech fixed, also her teeth. But more marital trouble was in store for the in-love financier. The marriage to Diane might never have happened if his mother, Princess Pignatelli, had been alive. She had held a tight rein on her impetuous son, trying to quash his romances before they reached the altar. In fact, Mildred King, a Boston musician, claimed she won a cash settlement from the princess, who had hired her to be a platonic pal with Hunt and to keep him away from "unsuitable" women. The women *she* thought were unsuitable, that is.

After a brief bliss, Diane in 1965 brought a suit for separation from Mr. Hartford. The separation was short-lived. He had barely left when he was back again. In 1967, Hunt complained in a legal action against Diane that his wife was seeing too much of singer-actor Bobby Darin. Bobby insisted that the dates were platonic. It was Diane's turn and she sued her husband for divorce, three days after the New York State law had been changed on September 1 to include other reasons than adultery for divorce.

The ex-model stated through her lawyer that she would ask for alimony of $52,000 a year. The grounds for divorce would be "cruel and inhuman treatment," including his charges about Mr. Darin, whom she said she had been merely comforting because of his divorce from Sandra Dee, the young film star.

While charges and counter-charges were flying, Diane and Hunt were sharing the No. 1 Beekman Place residence again. At the same time, her divorce suit was slated for a Manhattan Supreme Court hearing for a reconciliation, as required by law.

On Pearl Harbor Day, December 7, Diane announced two important events—the reconciliation was official and she was pregnant! Her husband generously agreed to her request to settle a $1.5 million trust fund "to secure the future" of the expected child, a girl, Cynara Juliet, who was born the following July 4 in the Columbia Presbyterian Medical Center.

There was another separation, with Diane charging cruel and inhuman treatment and non-support. She claimed that Hunt, since their latest parting eight months previously, had not paid her the latest agreed allowance of $100,000.

American judges are usually kind to the ladies, and the law gave Diane temporary alimony of $2,500 a month, custody of Cynara Juliet, and separate lodging in his Beekman Place duplex, with the poor man (metaphorically speaking) paying all the expenses. Huntington may be gullible where women are concerned, but he has never quibbled over what they want from him. (If only I had met him when I was younger, with all that lovely alimony and expenses!)

In December, 1969, Diane was awarded $4,000 a month, of which $1,500 was for living expenses, with $2,500 to compensate her while the suit was in progress. In January of 1970, Diane and Hunt were suing each other for separation or divorce and both charging adultery. The harrowing matter was disposed of seven months later, when Diane received an uncontested divorce in Juarez, Mexico, on grounds of "incompatibility." Also the custody of their daughter, and a "substantial" sum in settlement.

If Diane had married Hunt for his money, she had succeeded. But there is no reason why she could not have married him for himself. He can be charming and when he's in love he will give you the moon. And when it's over, he hands you the sun and the stars. Who wouldn't want to marry him! He is still not too old, a young sixty-three, and I am sure he would like to marry again. To get him it will help to be pretty, with a good figure and the coolness that most girls have who marry rich men.

March, 1971, was a busy month for Mr. Hartford. He needed more money to fulfill his enormous obligations and auctioned several of his paintings at Parke-Bernet, including Dali's *Discovery of America by Christopher Columbus*, which he had commissioned for his gallery. Knoedlers bought it for $100,000. Altogether Hunt received about $500,000. "I need the cash," he explained. In March, the optimistic Mr. Hartford again revived his *Show* magazine. In April of '72 he opened a "Show Club" discothèque in Nassau. In October, he followed with a "Show Club" in Manhattan, inviting all the celebrities available, which received enormous publicity.

In conclusion, I must add that I have always admired Huntington Hartford in spite of or because of his failures. He really cares about the working people and actively helps them. No matter how much he loses in business and marriage, he comes up, not exactly smiling, but ready to do it all over again.

20. *The Stableman's Daughter — Mona Strader Schlesinger Bush Williams Bismarck Martini*

WHEN I MENTIONED the Cinderella theme of this book to my friends, a large number said, "You must do Princess Bismarck."

"Who is she?" I asked the first time. I was regarded with surprise.

"Don't you know? She's Mona Williams." Her father was a stableboy and she married, among others, some of the richest men in the world.

Of course I had heard of Mona. She was constantly in the news when I first went to America in the mid-thirties. She was to the twenties, thirties, and forties what Cristina Ford is to the seventies, and what Gloria Guinness was to the forties and fifties. More so.

Mona was on every best-dressed list in New York, London, and Paris, which was the first to give her the accolade. When it was printed in 1934 that Mrs. Williams was spending $50,000 a year on clothes, she retorted indignantly, "It is only $20,000 a year, and that is not too much for a lady who travels and entertains." In '34, this was the equivalent of about $70,000. Only Jackie Onassis spends more.

When Mr. Williams died in 1951, his wife's share of his hundred-million-dollar estate was $90 million. So it was not surprising that her next marriage was to a poor man, the grandson of Germany's famed Chancellor von Bismarck. Today's von Bismarck is so unrecognized that when an army of porters were unloading Mona's baggage from her yacht in Capri, and a bystander asked the name of the man with the lovely lady, he was told "Count Williams." Mona overheard and she laughed. Not so the count.

The seventy-six-year-old lady, now Mrs. Martini, has had her quota of husbands, all of them rich except the last two. With all those millions of dollars in the bank, she could afford to indulge her fancies. But as with all good Cinderella stories, we must start at the beginning. Not by the hearth this time, but in a stable.

Not much is known about Mona before her marriage in 1921 to James I. Bush, vice-president of the Equitable Trust Company. It was then learned that she had been married in 1917 at the age of nineteen to a rich Milwaukeean, H. J. Schlesinger. Schlesinger owned a stable of horses in Lexington, Kentucky. Mona's father, Mr. Strader, was hired to supervise the grooming of the horses.

Mona spent most of her free time in the rich man's stable, and as she blossomed into womanhood and a good equestrienne, the boss fell in love with the groom's daughter and married her. Harry Schlesinger was thirty-seven, almost twice as old as his bride.

Life with the staid Schlesingers in Milwaukee was heavy going for the young wife. The beautiful brunette was longing for excitement. In 1918, the monotony was somewhat lifted by the birth of a son, Robert. However, Mona was not the hausfrau, home-loving type. When she divorced Mr. Schlesinger in 1920, according to printed reports at the time, she agreed to give him custody of two-year-old Robert. In exchange, she received a settlement of $200,000. This would be a million today. She insisted that for the boy's sake she would spend some time in every year with him.

Her marriage had failed, she explained, because Harry's way of life was so different from hers that it was beginning to affect her health. I am sure she felt better after meeting James Irving Bush, a University of Wisconsin football star, who was nearer her own age. He was introduced to Mona after his wife died in 1920.

In October of the following year, Mona and the millionaire man-about-town Bush were married. One of the guests was Harrison Williams, a multi-multimillionaire. Weddings are always a good breeding ground for a future marriage. The bride is glowingly beautiful, even the homeliest one, and when Mona shed Mr. Bush in 1925, receiving a million-dollar settlement—multiply by five on today's marriage-divorce market—Mr. Williams, then a widower, and living with a spinster sister, came to call on Mona, whom he had learned to appreciate in the many times they had met socially during her marriage. They were married in the Williams Manhattan town house one year later. Three millionaires in thirteen years. Not bad.

It usually happens that once you marry a rich man, you marry another rich man, and another, à la marriage-maker Mrs. Rosemary Kanzler, who married four very rich men. The quality that attracted the first big fish will attract the next, and the next. What is that quality? It is usually an aloofness, springing from a coolness that starts in the brain, a calculation that will not allow passion to make a woman forget that she would like a wealthy man for a mate. Plus discipline, steel inside, charm outside—a serenity and unconcern.

This is one reason why so many models marry rich. They wear expensive clothes they do not own, which are bought by the women who are rich or who have rich husbands. They are as pretty or prettier than the women who attend the fashion shows. They have developed a cool, aristocratic manner that appeals to the men who are buying the clothes, and they look marvelous in them, often better than the wives who have become careless and shapeless.

Harrison Williams was born in Avon, Ohio. His business and social credits were imposing. He was a director and member of the executive committee of the American Gas and Electric Company; president of the Empire Corporation; treasurer and trustee of the Neurological Institute; president of the $600 million North American Company; and a former president of the Cleveland Electric Illuminating Company. His clubs included the Metropolitan Club in New York, Piping Rock on Long Island, Sons of the American Revolution, the New York Yacht Club, the Riding Club, the National Golf Club, and on and on. Williams had also financed William Beebe's expeditions to the Galapagos Islands and the Sargasso Sea and donated a ship for an expedition to Greenland for oceanic research.

The wedding was a complete surprise to society. This is another rule in the rich marriage game. Until you have the man securely in love with you, keep the romance as quiet as possible. You'd be amazed at how ruthless some of your best girl friends can be. And some of the men who are not secure in themselves tittle-tattle in places where it will do the most harm. Cristina Ford, for example, was able to realize her dream of marriage to the auto heir she loved because so few people knew about it.

Mona wore a navy and beige traveling ensemble with a black hat for the marriage ceremony. Only a few friends were present, and there were no attendants for the bride. The honeymoon was spent abroad on Harrison's luxurious yacht, the *Warrior*. As Bruce Forsyth, the British entertainer, would say, "Didn't she do well!"

Mona was very social. Mr. Williams was not. He did not have time for the frivolities of the rich. Mona was always in the gossip columns at this and that party for this and that charity event. When she gave parties in her own home, Harrison, a polite, serious man, would meet the guests, then retire to his suite of rooms in the house, and have his dinner served on a tray while perusing his business documents.

In 1933 Mrs. Williams was named one of the best-dressed women in the world by the World Fashion Court in Paris. Previously she was number one on the Ten Best-Dressed list of New York. Elsa Maxwell had named her "the smartest and best-dressed woman in New York." Now it was the world.

Talking of Elsa, she was homely, fat, poor, but top society danced to the tune she played on her fiddle-diddle. She did not have to marry a millionaire to live like one. The best hotels begged her to stay with them, free of course, and to give dinner parties in their restaurants. She didn't even have to tip. Her secret? She was her own woman, witty, outspoken, and she knew how to amuse the rich who—poor darlings—are often so bored once they have the money.

I doubt whether Mrs. Harrison Williams was bored. She was popular and always on the go-go. In 1933 she was described as having gray hair, wide-set gray-blue eyes, and skin as pearly as her favorite gems. She was thirty-five. Also, Mona realized that a rich woman has to be involved with something outside of herself. Now that she had enough money to spend "without adding it up," she turned to politics as an outlet for her considerable energy. Mrs. Williams was quoted widely when she stated that she was horrified at the general political apathy. She organized the new National Party in support of Franklin D. Roosevelt. The publicity releases for Mrs. Eleanor Roosevelt's Ball in 1934 to benefit her clubs for unemployed women described Mrs. Harrison as one of the twelve Most Beautiful Women in New York City. Her hair now had "heavy streaks of silver." She was sketched by Howard Chandler Christy wearing a pink and white gown, white hat, red slippers, and red handbag. It was noted that she preferred bright colors.

In November Mona started a new fashion in jewelry, wearing "that modernistic jewelry specially designed by young Madame Belperron—a pink tourmaline bracelet and clip, studded with rubies and a costume ensemble of pale blue semi-precious stones set with real sapphires." The story mentioned that Mr. Williams' fortune had dwindled from $100 million to $26 million. Some business deals had gone sour. Thank goodness they could still afford the house on Fifth Avenue, the estate in Bayville, Long Island, and the home in Palm Beach—the latter, the reporter noted, was decorated with Mona's "exquisite canons of taste, in Chinese porcelain, in which field she is an authority." When she had visited Palm Beach in the mid thirties, the society columns stated that she owned 129 square-cut sapphires, 144 square-cut emeralds, 762 small round diamonds, and 79 pearls. Mr. Williams joked about the jewels and said, "Sure I'm still rich, I have $700 million in newspaper dollars"—meaning he was credited with this sum by the press.

Another report in the same year revealed that Mrs. Williams was "near death" in the American hospital in Paris, after an emergency operation following an internal hemorrhage. Mr. Williams was in his home in New York, but Lady Mendl, the leader of the international set, was at her bedside. She had gone to Paris, it was said, to select new clothes. Apparently her new political involvements had not turned her against the fashion scene. The French couturiers were holding their fashion shows, and Mona recovered swiftly.

In November of '35 there was a printed story that she had decided to be patriotic and buy most of her clothes in the United States. Also that the Williamses were planning to buy a castle on Capri. They bought a villa built on the ruins of a palace built in the first century. She is still living in it, but with a different husband.

In January, 1936, Mr. and Mrs. Williams had three guests in their New York home: Prince Otto von Bismarck, his wife, and his brother, Count Albrecht Edward. Some of her friends were critical of the visit because of the Nazi situation in Germany. But it would be another three years before World War II and for Mona, 1936 was a good year.

She was again chosen as the world's best dressed woman in the Paris poll. A so-called friend remarked, "Harrison concentrates on making money, Mona on spending it." The same woman admired Mona's taste in clothes and decorating. "She has good taste, a studied simplicity."

Wallis Warfield Simpson's name was beginning to appear on the best-dressed women lists, and perhaps in competition with Wally, Mona bought four Schiaparelli cocktail jackets in royal blue, rose, pale green, and gold, all covered with bugle beads. They cost $750 each, a lot of money for a jacket in 1936.

Mona did not attend the marriage of her son, Robert H. Schlesinger, Jr., to Mary Porter Jones in Charlottesville, Virginia, in 1938. She was not on good terms with the Schlesingers. Mona was now spending most of the year in Capri, while Harrison toiled in New York to rebuild his fortunes.

The war in Europe brought the expatriates running home to the United States, Mona among them, bringing her dog, a mutt named Mick whom she had adopted in Capri. She soon became active in fund-raising for war charities.

The Duchess of Windsor appointed Mona president of the American branch of Les Colis de Trianon-Versailles, a charity to send comfort kits to soldiers. One of Mona's projects to raise money was to charge an entrance fee at a department store exhibit to show the favorite gowns of society women. Hers, of course, were included.

After the fall of France in 1940, Mona, with a group of Quakers, sponsored a Funds for France party to provide clothes and medical supplies for French women and children through the Vichy government. Her special guest at the ball was Gaston-Henri Haye, the Vichy government ambassador. He was an old friend and, in better days, the mayor of Versailles. There was some criticism, as many people believed the money, clothes, and medicine would fall into Nazi hands.

The social work did not prevent Mona being named with the best-dressed women of 1940. The poll now emanated from New York. The Duchess of Windsor, whom Mona feared might outpoint her in the fashion stakes, received only two of the fifty votes. In February, 1941, Mrs. Williams gave a party in Palm Beach for the Friends of Greece charity. She was again criticized, this time for charging $20 a plate. But the money was for a good cause.

A month before Pearl Harbor, the chic Mrs. Harrison Williams was profiled in a magazine. The writer commented on her high cheekbones, the fact that she was nearsighted, her ability to listen to others, that all her clothes were now made in the United States. (Was there any couturier activity in Paris during the Occupation?) That she seldom wore a hat—the start of another fashion—that she loved buying shoes, that she was a neat perfectionist and, O lucky woman, never had to diet to retain her slim figure.

With most of their young and middle-aged former servants now working in defense factories, the Williamses closed four of their five homes, reduced their help to ten from twenty-five, and put their eight cars into storage. They were living on only two floors of their thirty-room mansion on Fifth Avenue. They were being economical as well as patriotic.

Because of Harrison's financial problems, his yacht, the *Warrior*, had been sold in 1939 to Paul Getty. Mona, in an interview for *The World Telegram*, stated, "Harrison saw the handwriting on the wall. All we do is live from day to day. I admit our class led foolish and useless lives in the past. We did silly things, our values were wrong. But then"—brightening—"no period has been perfect." She added that she was no longer interested in clothes.

Nonetheless, after first dying her gray hair black, then brown, she was on the New York Dress Institute's best-dressed list in 1949. Earlier, Salvador Dali had painted her in rags and bare feet, but with every one of her then gray hairs in place, and wearing a jeweled necklace.

Harrison Williams died in January, 1954, and soon after she received her multimillion dollar inheritance from his estate. Mona was now rich enough in her own right to allow her hair to go back to gray and to marry her former guest, Count Albrecht Edward Bismarck, described as an interior decorator, the male equivalent of the female "model."

At the ceremony on January 5, 1955, before a judge in the municipal court at Edgewater, New Jersey, Mona gave her age as fifty-five, his fifty-one. She had fibbed by two years. They lived in her renovated ruin in Capri.

Elsa Maxwell's story in the spring of 1955 stated that the count had learned he had cancer, which accounted for the hasty marriage. When he returned to Germany, it was not to visit his family as reported, but to visit a specialist.

Nineteen fifty-five was a bad year for Mona. Her husband underwent an operation and he was never really well again. His long illness ended with his death on October 16, 1970, in the Capri villa. He was sixty-seven years old. Mona soon after married his physician, Dr. Umberto di Martini, a teacher of medicine at the University of Rome. The doctor was fifty, twenty-two years younger than his wealthy wife.

When I was in Paris last year, I was informed that the "princess," as she is called, lived there. There was no mention of Dr. Martini, but there has been no mention of a divorce, so I assume they still get together in Capri.

I wonder what Mona's memories are today as the old lady is driven around Paris or Capri by her chauffeur. Does she believe her life has been successful? Is she in touch with her son and his children? One question can be answered. She is still shopping for clothes and still interested in how she looks in them.

21. The Cool Chorus Girl from London - Lady Sylvia

How MANY YOUNG PEOPLE have heard of Lady Sylvia Ashley? And yet the seventy-year-old ex-chorus girl, Sylvia Louise Hawkes, was the most talked-of woman in her day. She was the classic example of a girl born poor who grew up to enter the highest echelons of society and money. She is a whole book in herself, and perhaps one day I will write it. Her family were in "service," which does not mean the armed forces. Her father was a footman in a grand house in England. Her mother was the second maid. Sylvia was born below stairs but, peeking upward, she learned at an early age how the rich lived. She liked what she saw and unconsciously the desire to be one of them was born.

The stage proved a sturdy stepping stone towards her dream. The blond, slim beauty landed a job as a chorus girl. Several girls in a London chorus had caught big matrimonial prizes, and Sylvia was to be no exception. She had the necessary qualities to attract the rich and aristocratic. She was cool and seemed unattainable. Randolph Churchill had been trying to make time with her, but she had no use for him. She was saving her assets for something more lasting and profitable. 'Twas Randolph who helped to spread the legend of her purity. If *he* couldn't have her, who could? He was only seventeen at the time, but egotistical, and a chaser of the ladies. Sylvia's first husband, in 1928, was Lord Anthony Ashley, heir to the Earl of Shaftesbury. The earl didn't care whether Miss Hawkes was pure or not, dammit, her parents were in service and he did his best to prevent the marriage, but nothing could stop the young lord.

For several years all went well. Lord Ashley himself instructed his young wife on the ways of the well-educated and the well-born. She learned to talk well and walk well, and the languid way of eating, not wolfing it down as she had sometimes seen in the kitchen where her mother worked.

What Lord Ashley did not realize was that he was making his wife more attractive for the next husband, the late Douglas Fairbanks, Sr., who was still married to Mary Pickford when Sylvia met him after the divorce from Ashley in 1934.

I first heard of the romance from Lord Beaverbrook, who was trying to help matters along for Sylvia, one of his friends. It seemed hopeless. Mary, America's Sweetheart, and the dashing Douglas were the King and Queen of Hollywood. It was forever—until Mr. Fairbanks met the cool Sylvia in London.

Lady Ashley had become bored with her lord. Mr. Fairbanks, still with the energy to climb straight walls and jump from tower to tower in his movies, needed something new to conquer. He found it in Lady Sylvia, a damsel who was not exactly in distress but shimmering somewhere out of his reach.

The shock of the Fairbanks's separation was felt around the world. When Mary came to New York from Hollywood alone in the mid-thirties, my first reporting assignment was to cover the story, with every other reporter in New York. I remember she was fairly cheerful but subdued. Perhaps she too had become bored with her aging but energetic husband. After the divorce, she married Buddy Rogers, a good-looking, gentle movie actor many years her junior.

Doug and Sylvia had three years of marriage before he died in 1939, leaving her several million dollars. Sylvia was now a rich widow and could marry a poor man if she chose to, but she saved that gesture for the last of her five husbands.

The Second World War had started in Europe when the blond lady returned to her native London. She shone like a beacon in the drab blackouts, and it was not long before Lord Edward Stanley, the sixth Baron Stanley of Alderney, left his calling card on the tray of her affections. His friends, especially Randolph Churchill, tried to turn him off. I remember the bitterness with which the now thirty-four-year-old army officer spoke about him. Randolph was gaining the weight that completely destroyed his good looks. But he still hoped to ensnare the beautiful woman of his adolescent dreams.

Sylvia married Lord Stanley in 1944. It was a disaster almost from the start. Her life with Fairbanks had been exciting, Hollywood had been fascinating, but London in the last years of the war was dull. The Allies now knew they were going to win, and while this knowledge was comforting, it caused a slowdown in the gaiety of the earlier years of the war—the live and laugh today because tomorrow you will die. People were now thinking soberly of the future. The marriage of the Stanleys outlived the war but in 1948 the noble peer divorced his wife, making sensational charges against Sylvia, who remained calm. Was it because she had already fallen in love with Clark Gable, the super screen lover for women all over the world?

With so many women ready to drop into his arms without being asked, Sylvia kept her head, and, as usual, this made the "Dear Mr. Gable" of Judy Garland's song determined to bed her, which meant he would marry her. Sylvia hesitated. "Under my so-called glamor," Sylvia explained to Clark, "is a very weak woman who is easily bruised. I don't want to be hurt." He swore he would not. Sylvia looked somewhat like Clark's previous wife, film star Carole Lombard, who had died in a plane crash while traveling on a War Bonds mission. Carole was witty and so was Lady Sylvia, but that is where the resemblance ended.

Clark and Carole had eloped in 1939, outwitting Louella Parsons, to whom Carole had promised the story before it happened. At least that is what Louella said. She was in San Francisco at the time on a studio junket. She was as angry as she ever allowed herself to be with a top star from whom she wanted future news. She forgave them magnanimously, hoping to get the story of the divorce when it came, as she believed it surely would.

Carole had enjoyed getting up at five in the morning for duck hunting with Clark. She had a great sense of humor and sent all sorts of weird presents to Clark on the set of his films. I remember a broken-down car, or was it a horse? Or both?

Sylvia is the complete indoor girl, and while she can make clever remarks, she does not have a boisterous sense of humor. There was the time when Clark brought her jewels from England to the United States without declaring them for Customs. I was in ignorance of this fact when Zsa Zsa Gabor told me that Sylvia's jewels had come with them to America.

"Which means she is going to stay here," said Miss Gabor, her eyes wistful at the thought of all that lovely stuff belonging to somone else.

The day before my story, Zsa Zsa invited me to lunch with Sylvia at Romanoff's. I had met her many times before, but this was to heal an early breach between Clark and me. Sylvia had promised to arrange a meeting with her husband. When my story of the jewels was printed, the enraged Mr. Gable shouted to his wife, "And I was just about to forgive her." Cross my heart, I did not know that the gems had been undeclared.

Clark, in spite of his glamor, was unsophisticated. Sylvia found him dull. According to reports in the Bel Aire boudoirs, the world's most famous lover-boy was not a good lover in real life. Perhaps he was trying to live up to his image, and that is always bad for sex. Clark began to detest the woman he had married, and his only wish was to be free of her. In 1952, he sued for divorce. Sylvia counter-sued.

It was all hush-hush, but on the morning of the day they were to appear in court at 3 P.M., I learned of the impending suits. I telephoned my local newspaper, the *Hollywood Citizen News*, with the story. But the owners were then ultraconservative, and the managing editor told me, "Let's wait until it appears in the other papers!" I telephoned the story to my New York City newspaper, the (morning) *Daily Mirror*, but Louella had her scoop after all. The *Los Angeles Examiner* was on the streets at 6 P.M. My story was in the 10 P.M. edition in New York.

Clark was not known for his generosity. His first wife, Josephine, who taught him to act, received nothing when they divorced. But Lady Sylvia's divorce settlement was ten percent of the gross of everything that Clark had saved in his Hollywood career. She returned to London with her jewels, much richer than when she had left.

Two years later, Lady Sylvia married a Georgian prince, Dmitri (Mito) Djordjadze, who earned his bread and jam as a hotel manager. She was now a princess. While number five lacked money, he had prestige.

They seemed happy in London, but when Mito landed a job with a top Texas oil company he announced, "The marriage is finished." Lady Sylvia prefers to remain in her beloved London with side trips to California, Palm Beach, Nassau (where she has a home), the South of France, and Paris. Her official residence is South Audley Street in Mayfair, and you hear little about her except when she is robbed, as happened a few years ago.

Her hobby is attending weddings, wearing dark glasses, and dressing as inconspicuously as possible. Perhaps Lady Sylvia is still yearning to be a bride again. At a recent church marriage she was heard to comment, "Isn't the bride beautiful?" Then, wistfully, "Every girl looks radiant on her wedding day."

22. How to Marry Howard Hughes

WHAT DO JEAN PETERS and Terry Moore have in common? They are both actresses, they were both married to Stuart Cramer III, and they were both in love with multimillionaire Howard Hughes. As you know, Jean married Mr. Hughes, but only after she had married Mr. Cramer. If she had not, I doubt whether she would now be the ex-Mrs. Howard Hughes and the wife of Stanley Hough.

Rich men like to think that what has been theirs is always theirs for as long as they want it. Especially girls. *They* do the throwing out, and when a woman has the audacity to leave before the rich man is tired of her, he usually puts up a big fight to get her back—even if he has to marry her.

I met Mr. Hughes when I came to this country from England, at a cocktail party at the former Park Lane Hotel on Park Avenue, hosted by Jack Duff, a rich young man about town. We were all young then, the rich men, the pretty girls, mostly models, myself, and Mr. Hughes. He looked like any normal young man then. He was well dressed and gregarious, and the deafness that afflicted his middle and older years was not notice-able. No sneakers, no long fingernails, no obsession for privacy.

I would love to have been there when he was informed of the fake autobiography of his life by Clifford Irving. I had a sus-picion the book was false when newspapers leaked the fact that in the book Howard was telling about the girls in his life. I had good reason to know that this was not true.

"Les Girls" were one thing he would never talk about, al-though their names were well known in Hollywood and in the gossip columns everywhere. When I arrived in Hollywood in 1936, he was in love with Katharine Hepburn, who liked him enough to invite him to the family home in Connecticut to meet her parents. They accepted him, and I'm not surprised. When Howard comes out from the iron curtain of his own making, he is quite pleasant, with a good sense of humor. And kind. Like sending a cable of congratulation to the seventy-one-year-old Gene Sarazen for the hole-in-one miracle during the Brit-ish Open Championship of 1973. And the care he took of the late restaurant owner Dave Chasen when he was recuperating from an illness. He had Dave and his wife flown to Las Vegas and put them up in a luxurious suite in one of the numerous hotels he owns. "No, we didn't see him," Dave said when I asked. He has loaned his planes to friends when they needed to get somewhere in a hurry. He has given money to people in trouble and pays enormous salaries to employees if he is sure they are loyal.

Before Miss Hepburn, there was Jean Harlow, whom he con-verted into a platinum-blond star. Ginger Rogers, Joan Fon-taine, Ava Gardner, Lana Turner, Mitzi Gaynor, Janet Leigh, Terry Moore, and Yvonne de Carlo are some of the girls who received his attentions. Most of them believed that Howard had marriage on his mind when he sent them flowers and invita-tions to dine. Several of them confided in me, and it always made a good story for my column. I can see the young Yvonne de Carlo lunching with me at the Universal Studios, her face flushed with happiness as she told me that Howard had asked her to marry him, "but he wants to wait awhile to be absolutely sure."

His first marriage, to Ella Rice of Houston in 1925, had

ended in divorce. She came from the wealthy family which founded the Rice Institute. At the time of the divorce, Howard's fortune was estimated at a billion dollars.

Howard was wary of another marriage, although I think he would have married the very young Elizabeth Taylor—she was about nineteen when he was in love with her in the early fifties. He flew Elizabeth and her mother to Nevada for a vacation. When Liz went to Europe to marry Michael Wilding, an employee of Hughes, Walter Kane, was on the same plane. To plead his cause? But Elizabeth only marries when she believes she is in love, and, to the young Elizabeth, Howard was an old man.

I have previously written of the half hour I spent with him at his bungalow on the grounds of the Beverly Hills Hotel. It was around midnight when he phoned and got me out of a sick-bed on the promise of a scoop, which he gave me personally from time to time. (He liked me but I was never one of his girl friends.)

Elizabeth was then in love with Stanley Donen, the film director, and Howard, carrying a torch for lovely Liz, was madly jealous. The "scoop" was a derogatory statement about Mr. Donen. I almost collapsed with annoyance and a temperature of 101 as I marched out while he was saying, "Hedda would give this a lead." "Then give it to her," I flung back. Really!

But this incident was not the cause of the diminishing of our friendship. I had promised to stop quoting his girls when they told me that Howard wanted to marry them but they must wait to be sure. In return, he would be available whenever I called and give me the scoop I was seeking. "But what if you really were going to marry one of them?" I queried. "I would *have* to write about that." "I will tell you," he assured me. "If I don't, you can crucify me." He complained my column items were hurting him in his business, which included the Hughes Tool Company, 70 percent of Trans World Airlines, and the RKO Studio, which he then owned.

It was a good bargain for me, and I readily accepted, especially as I was sure he would not marry again. But I disregarded our pact on the occasion of his sale of RKO. I had been calling him every day, trying to get the story from him. I was angry when it appeared in the rival *Hollywood Reporter*. I was then writing a column for *Daily Variety*, the other important trade paper.

I began my next column with "Terry Moore tells me she will marry Howard Hughes on May 18 [this was in 1952] but this is not what Howard is telling Mitzi Gaynor." It might have been Mitzi first and Terry second. All hell broke loose, with Howard calling me and threatening to "ruin" me. He did his best, but the good angels were on my side. He called Bill Hearst—several of the Hearst papers ran my column and I could have lost them all, but I apologized. We patched up the quarrel but it was never quite the same, and when he sold RKO and went to live in Las Vegas, he had no further use for me, or I for him.

To return to Jean Peters, she had lunched with me soon after she arrived in Hollywood in 1946, the winner of the Miss Ohio State newspaper beauty contest. The prize was $200 and a screen test. She was twenty years old, a sophomore at Ohio State University, and was planning to be a teacher, when 20th Century-Fox changed her life with a screen test that would eventually lead to marriage with Cramer, Hughes, and her present husband, Stanley Hough, 20th Century-Fox film executive with the title of vice-president and director of production operations.

Brunette, dark-eyed, and intelligent, she was not the usual type of starlet under contract to the various studios at that time. She told me she was determined she would never do the ridiculous things for publicity that starlets were eager to do. Because of her independent attitude, Jean was never a starlet. Her first film was the leading feminine role in *Captain from Castille*, opposite the studio's top glamor boy, Tyrone Power.

Mr. Hughes had discovered Jean even before I did. She gave me the familiar quote: "We are in love and Howard wants to marry me, but he wants us to wait until we are sure." I felt sorry for the pretty newcomer. I was sure it would never happen. Every year there was a new batch of hopeful faces, but the men who chased them remained the same, except that they were older.

While Jean was pretty, she was not particularly chic. She made her own clothes, and had no use for a Gillette or depilatory. Some of the studio personnel called her Miss Hairy-Legs, but not to her face. Jean was determined to remain as nature had made her.

She was completely honest, and this was her chief attraction for Hughes. She would *not* marry him for his money, he was sure. But while they were waiting, his close friend Stuart Cramer III was falling in love with Jean. She eloped with the young textile and oil millionaire, marrying him in a surprise ceremony in Washington, D.C., at the New York Avenue Presbyterian Church, known as Lincoln's church because President Lincoln had prayed there.

They had met in Rome the year before, when she was filming *Three Coins in the Fountain*. Only three members of the families were present—her mother, Mrs. Elizabeth Peters, and Stuart's parents. The bride was twenty-eight, the groom twenty-six. The officiating minister, the Reverend George M. Docherty, in a moment of whimsey, laid down a strip of golden carpet that had been used at the Westminster coronation of Queen Elizabeth II. The fifteen-minute ceremony was followed by a honeymoon in Bermuda.

I am sure Mr. Hughes was angry. Jean was *his* girl. How dare one of his best friends do the unforgivable and court her under his nose and then marry her? He must have now realized that he loved her.

Two months after Jean's marriage to Stuart, she separated from him. How much Mr. Hughes had to do with this I can only guess at. Jean had wanted to marry Howard. The elopement with Stuart was perhaps to prove her independence. Where she came from, if a couple were in love, they did not wait years to be sure, they got married. Jean divorced Stuart in California, where you had to wait a year for the divorce to be final. It is quicker now.

Howard replighted his troth to Jean in one of his Cadillacs in a lovers' lane on top of a Santa Monica mountain. This was for real. The marriage to Jean in March, 1957, took place secretly in Nevada. Howard kept the official document. In August, Jean was reported to be in the Montreal Neurological Institute for treatment of a back ailment. The institute denied it. And this reminds me of Dr. Verne Mason, perhaps the best pathologist in California, who saved Howard's life when he crashed with his plane in Beverly Hills on a Sunday, just before I was due to go on the air with my radio show. I had the scoop.

As a reward for saving his life, the grateful billionaire took our beloved Dr. Mason from us and set him up as head of a magnificent institute for research in Florida. He was my doctor, and saved my three-year-old son Robert's right leg by cutting away the plaster cast he had worn for six months on the prescription of a bone specialist, which was causing his leg to shrivel.

Dr. Mason was an honest doctor. When he didn't know, he would say so, and when I asked him, "How did Robert get polio?" he replied, "I don't know," and then, very quietly, "My son died of polio. Robert will be all right." Alas, a few years ago, Dr. Mason rejoined his son.

Jean had been gregarious and talkative when she first came to Hollywood, but after my interview with her appeared, Hughes, apparently annoyed, cautioned her never to discuss him again to the press or her friends, and from that day to this, she never has. After her marriage to Howard, it was as though she had been swallowed by an earthquake. No one in Hollywood saw her, although she sometimes came to town and had been studying anthropology at the University of Los Angeles. From being an active, normal woman, she became almost as much of a recluse as her husband.

Not long after the marriage, they lived in separate houses, with Jean making a once-a-week or monthly visit to her husband in a secret hideaway near his hotel empire in Las Vegas. If she would ever sit down with a tape recorder and tell the true story of her marriage, she could make a million dollars. But she never will, even though several publishers have made offers to Jean to write her story.

During the marriage, she occasionally saw her sister, nine years younger, and Arlene Stewart, her best friend at the university—Arlene had sent Jean's photograph for the Ohio State beauty contest—and also former quiz kid Vanessa Brown. People sometimes thought they glimpsed her at a drive-in movie with Mr. Hughes. She also made a once-a-week visit to the home of her friend at El Rancho Santa Fe, where Victor Mature has a place. I doubt whether Howard would have let her visit *him!*

On one occasion, Jean was spotted by a reporter at a performance of the Comédie-Française. He asked her why she had gone into hiding. "I haven't been ducking the press," she protested, "it's just that they aren't interested in an old married woman anymore." She said there would be no more movies for her unless it was a "dream role." She was wearing a big black mink coat. She disappeared into a black Cadillac limousine, sitting between two guards.

Jean had always been a fan of the Los Angeles Dodgers and attended several baseball games without being recognized. She was proud of her disguises, but not as proud as Mr. Hughes. The top disguise man in London recently reported that he had made several different masks and hairpieces for Howard so that he could come and go as he pleased from his top floor suite at the Inn on the Park, his home in London. Before, he had lived in a hotel in Nicaragua, and before that a hotel floor in Nassau, and there was his long hotel sojourn in Las Vegas. At last report he was back again in the Bahamas.

Why does he want to be a recluse? Is it the deafness that has grown worse in the past two decades? Is he afraid—as printed—of catching other people's germs? And yet the few people who have gained access to him report that he is perfectly normal and his brain is sharp—too sharp for some of the many lawyers working for his ex-employees and for the government.

In 1966 Howard's fortune was estimated at \$433,075,779.25. The money came mainly from the Hughes Tool Company, by whom Jane Russell was paid \$50,000 a year for twenty years, even when she was no longer in demand as a star—as Hughes predicted when she would not sign an overlapping contract.

The announcement of the Hughes-Peters divorce was almost as ambiguous as their marriage. It came from Howard's office in Las Vegas: "Jean Peters Hughes, wife of industrialist Howard Hughes, stated today that she and her husband have discussed a possible divorce [I love that 'possible'] and that she will seek to obtain one. This is not a decision reached in haste and it is only done with the greatest of regret." And, from Jean: "Our marriage has lasted thirteen years, which is long by present standards. Any property settlement will be resolved privately between us." Jean now owns houses in Beverly Hills, Bel Aire, and Hollywood.

When Jean and Stanley Hough applied for the license at the Santa Monica courthouse, she gave her occupation as "research interviewer," although whom she had researched—monkeys, perhaps, in her anthropology classes—or whom she had interviewed is not very clear.

The bride and groom had been married twice before. Mr. Hough revealed that Mr. Hughes had given them his blessing. I'm sure he did, as I am sure that if Jean and her new husband are ever in any kind of trouble, he will come to their assistance. His marriage to Jean had not ended with a bang, and not with a whimper. It had atrophied from boredom, on both sides.

Last year Jean decided to resume her career as an actress and gave her first interview—a press conference this time—since the marriage to Howard. It took place in a theater and was jammed with newsmen and photographers.

Jean was making her comeback at the age of forty-five in a television version of Sherwood Anderson's play *Winesburg, Ohio*. She has never been a fool, and she knew why the reporters were hanging eagerly on her every word. "I'm not so naïve," she smiled, "as to think that your being here is your interest in my career. But my life with Howard Hughes was and shall remain a matter on which I will have no comment." They managed to squeeze from her the fact that not only had she been able to get around in Hollywood and New York without being recognized, but so had Howard.

As Mrs. Stanley Hough, her life is the normal one of a Beverly Hills matron with a husband in the film industry. They attend movie previews, social functions, and are seen often at the Bistro, Trader Vic's, Chasens, and other restaurants. She is plumper than when she was married to Mr. Hughes, but seems happier in her less glamorous, more open life.

While the story of the serious girl from a small town in Ohio is not exactly the traditional rags-to-riches adventure—her first contract paid her $300 a week, and she might have become a highly paid star—it is still the tale of a modern Cinderella, who served her time with one of the richest men in the world.

23. "Did Mama Say Don't Marry a Millionaire?" The Cushing Girls

No. Mama must have said, "Marry a *multi*millionaire." All her daughters did. This could be a fantasy on the part of an imaginative reporter but it coincides with the history of the three beautiful Cushing sisters of Boston. Minnie (Mary) married Vincent Astor. Betsy is married to John Hay Whitney. Babe is Mrs. William Paley. Their father was Harvey V. Cushing, the famed brain surgeon. But mother was the brainy one in the family, which also included a son who is now a doctor in Boston.

The Cushings were comfortably well off, probably in the millionaire class, but when you divide one or two million dollars into five you can't live like a millionaire on the income. You can if you marry a man with a hundred million dollars to his credit. Mrs. Cushing, whether by design or not, made sure her daughters would be fit helpmates for the richest men in the land.

While her brilliant surgeon husband was stitching brains together in Boston, Mother Cushing took her girls to New York to visit museums, theaters, opera, and other cultural events. 'Twas said it was not only multimillionaires she wanted for her girls, she wanted *cultivated* multimillionaires. She raised her daughters to a plateau where they could converse easily on topics with the men to whom their beauty and intellect would be advantageous. No rich man likes a dummy for a wife. He might marry one, but it never lasts.

Minnie gave a good example to her sisters with her marriage to Vincent Astor, a magic name in multimillionaire circles. Vincent, perhaps the richest man of his time in the United States—he owned half of Manhattan—had one trait that he shared with Cary Grant, who is also a multimillionaire: he was afraid of being poor and he never had less than $1 million in his *checking* account. The money, which he could withdraw at any time, reassured him that he would never starve.

Nonetheless, knowing the alimony laws of our land, he gave Minnie and previous and subsequent wives $1 million each after the marriage ceremony. If *he* wanted the divorce, he would give an extra $150,000 in the settlement. If *she* wanted it, there would be a $50,000 deduction. Vincent would be sweet —and sour.

I personally found him charming when I was invited for the weekend to his fabulous estate in Rhinebeck, near Poughkeepsie, in New York State. I was in my "society" period, and calmly accepted the great luxuries—the indoor swimming pool, the outdoor pool, the squash rackets courts, the large stable. But I *was* impressed at dinner to see a footman behind every chair occupied by his guests.

I had fallen off one of his horses, galloping downhill with Prince Obolensky—a former high-ranking Cossack in the Czar of Russia's cavalry—and Captain Edward Head, a former polo-playing whiz in the Indian Army. I had been taught never to gallop downhill, but my horse had not attended my riding school and followed the two other expert riders. Lying on the grass, fighting for breath, I felt like a disgraced fool. Making a superhuman effort, I got to my feet and struggled back onto the horrible horse. We all went fairly slowly after that.

At dinner, I, being the stranger, a "society" girl from England, was seated on Vincent's right. "You were very brave to get back on that horse," he assured me. I beamed with pleasure. Why didn't I make a play for him? He was separated from his wife, but there was something about him that intimidated me, an impression of cruelty and the arrogance that often comes with an inherited fortune.

He was born rich and became richer when his father, John Jacob Astor IV, was drowned in the Titanic disaster of 1912 as was millionaire Reginald Vanderbilt, father of the attractive twins Gloria and Thelma (Lady Furness), who later introduced Wally Simpson to the Prince of Wales.

When Vincent died, his half brother John Jacob Astor V became the head of the family and promptly married a succession of non-rich beauties with the usual payoffs for the divorces. Minnie has for many years signed her name Mrs. James Fosburgh—James has a fine reputation as a painter. He is also rich.

Babe—Barbara, born in 1917—was formerly married to the very rich, very social Stanley G. Mortimer, Jr. They had two children, Tony and Amanda, and divorced in 1946. The following year, she married William Paley, the multimillionaire chairman of the Columbia Broadcasting System. There were two marriage ceremonies, one in a synagogue, where all the men, gentiles as well as Jews, wore the yarmulke, the Jewish cap for prayer, the other in an Episcopalian church of Babe's faith. Their two children, Bill, Jr., and Kate, have been raised as Episcopalians.

Mr. Paley, sixteen years older than his wife, was born in Chicago and started his working life in his father's Congress Cigar Company in Philadelphia. He might have become a cigar tycoon, but for the fact of putting a cigar commercial on a local radio station. He was amazed by the response. In 1928, he bought the small—nineteen stations—United Independent Broadcasters, Inc. He had to find $400,000 for the purchase, and this was an enormous gamble because commercial radio was only two years old. The following year he changed the name of the company to the Columbia Broadcasting System, with the promise to give "quality programming." Thirty years later, Paley's company owned 201 radio stations and 232 television affiliates.

Mr. Paley was responsible for the importance of world news on radio. He brought in expert reporters such as Edward R. Murrow, William Shirer, Eric Sevareid, and Howard K. Smith. He "lifted" stars such as Bing Crosby, Edgar Bergen, Amos 'n Andy, and Jack Benny, whom he resembles, from NBC, the rival network. CBS, at Paley's suggestion, backed the Broadway musical *My Fair Lady*, with Rex Harrison and Julie Andrews. The film rights brought more millions to the CBS stockholders.

As a young man, Paley had stated that he would retire at the age of thirty-five. Recently he was reminded of this. The seventy-three-year-old six-foot suntanned billionaire smiled and said, "I just don't talk about it anymore."

Beautiful Babe is usually on the New York Dress Institute's annual Best-Dressed List. There is nothing flimsy, whimsey, or clumsy about this gracious woman. She would not care for the party-go-round of Palm Beach, which is why the Paleys do not own a house there. There is no reason to. They have three of the best-run and most elegant homes in the United States and Jamaica. Most weekends are spent at Kiluna Farm, Manhasset, the home on Long Island. For longer visits there is the estate at Lake Winnipesaukee, near the Bald Peak Colony Club—very chic—in New Hampshire. Their mansion on the edge of the ocean at Round Hill, the exclusive area in Jamaica, is a proud showpiece.

Babe is always dressed properly for the occasion. When she arrives at the ballroom for charity events to arrange the flowers, and so on, she usually wears jodhpurs and a silk shirt. Before her first marriage, when she worked as an editor for a top fashion magazine, she came to the office wearing plain suits or unfrilled dresses. She also worked as a model and was in great demand, receiving top fees. She was unique, with her chiseled features, eggshell complexion, elegantly coiffured dark hair, her slim figure and graceful movements.

Mrs. Paley is often asked for her opinion on the fashions of the day. At one time she cautioned, "Lots of women go overboard on clothes. It's terrible on style and pretty bad on men's pocketbooks too. Once you get where you are going, you forget what you have on, so why fuss all the time about a lot of clothes?"

The former Babe Cushing is so secure within herself that she does not fuss about anything, and what a blessing this must be for her busy executive husband. She is a great companion for him—a mixture of cool dignity, charm, and wit. Her mother, who is now educating the angels in heaven, had reason to be proud of her Babe, who absorbed her teaching so well.

Betsy Cushing married James Roosevelt in 1930, two years before his father was elected President of the United States. The marriage, which lasted ten years, produced two children who romped around the White House with the other FDR grandchildren. James was not rich but had his share of Grandma Sara Delano Roosevelt's fortune, a few million dollars, not much to divide by today's multimillionaire standards. Betsy, distinguished-looking but not as beautiful as Babe, was in love with James, who is a great charmer, and believed her future with him would be happy. It was, in the early years. She and James, who was his father's campaign manager, were active campaigners during the 1932 presidential elections.

James sounded like his father, and a great political future was predicted for him. It never quite came off, although he won a congressional seat in 1954 and was reelected by large margins in '56 and '58. If James had a hobby, it was to make money. He had been an undistinguished student at Groton, the traditional Roosevelt school, and at Harvard University. Even in 1931, when he was working to get his father elected, he was involved in the insurance business.

It was hard for James to be the son of his father, whose enemies tried to discredit him to prove that if FDR could not control his own family, then how could he run the United States? James was forced to release photostatic copies of his income from the insurance company to prove his business was legitimate. He became discouraged with the business world, and worked as film tycoon Sam Goldwyn's vice-president of production at a salary of $25,000 a year. James admitted his name had something to do with the post after he was accused of using his father's name to get the job, "but," he added, "Sam Goldwyn is too good a businessman to hire me for my name alone."

The Second World War gave Jimmy a chance to prove his

mettle. Even his enemies conceded that although his last name was perhaps responsible for his captaincy and further promotion, he had done well as a soldier. Years later, when General Eisenhower was running for the presidency, Jimmy switched sides and campaigned for him.

In 1941 he married Romelle Schneider, a nurse, with whom he had three children. Romelle named a half-dozen corespondents to obtain her divorce in 1955. The following year, he married his secretary, Gladys Irene Owens. She was a good secretary but apparently failed to make him happy as a wife. Their battles were always reported luridly, and heaven knows where Gladys is now, but she is not with Jimmy Roosevelt.

In 1942, Betsy Cushing Roosevelt made her mother happy, I am sure, with her marriage to John (Jock) Hay Whitney, the multimillionaire. They were married in Mama's New York apartment. Jock quietly adopted Betsy's two daughters and made them his heirs. Sara was then ten years old, and Kate, six.

In the spring of 1942, Jock, long an aviation enthusiast, was commissioned a captain in the U.S. Army Air Force. He then became a staff officer for Lieutenant-General Ira C. Eaker, who was commanding the Allied Air Forces in the Mediterranean. In 1944—he was now Colonel Whitney—he, with four other officers, were captured by the Germans in the South of France, where he had once courted the pretty ladies on the beach. They were locked into a railroad box car. One of the captured men succeeded in breaking the lock, and while the train was passing a forest, Jock and the others jumped out. They were hidden by the French villagers and there they waited until the American Army arrived.

I had known Jock in Hollywood when he and his cousin "Sonny" Whitney were financing David O. Selznick's production of *Gone With the Wind*, the greatest moneymaker of all films. Jock had a good return on his investment, but he sold his percentage too soon to MGM, while Sonny held on and made more millions.

Jock sometimes took me to the Selznicks for dinner—we had met at the Santa Anna race track, and on the set of *Becky Sharp*, the film version of Thackeray's *Vanity Fair*. It was the first full-length feature film in color. Whitney money was financing it.

I was fascinated by the way he tilted his head back and squeezed drops into his eyes from a little bottle he always carried. He would do this in the middle of dinner, or a conversation, or during a race.

In 1943 I was in London to write stories about the war for my newspaper syndicate, and I called on Jock at 20 Grosvenor Square, where he was functioning as an aide to General Eisenhower. I wanted an interview with his former boss, General Eaker, and thought he could help me. Jock was pleased to see me but suggested a lesser general for my story. We discussed the years in Hollywood and the big party he had given for Marlene Dietrich. It was the most glamorous event of the year. Even his wife, Liz Altemus of Philadelphia, left her beloved horses to attend the party, although Liz and Jock were estranged at the time.

I was the only press member invited, but I had to plead for the invitation. "You'll write about it," Jock protested. "Of course I will," I replied. "Why do you think I want to come?" The evening was translated into a beautiful column.

For his war services, the millionaire received the Legion of Merit, the Bronze Star, and the Order of Commander of the British Empire. He remained close to the general after the war and campaigned for him vigorously and financially—he was finance chairman of Citizens for Eisenhower–Nixon during the successful fight in 1952 for the presidency. He was equally generous later for President Nixon's campaigns. He was given important political jobs, and in February of 1957 Eisenhower gave him the U.S. ambassadorship to the Court of Saint James. When I next see Jock, I must ask him what he thought about Watergate.

Betsy was of enormous help to him. This quiet, dignified lady was an excellent hostess at the various functions inherent in the position of ambassador. Jock could afford to give big receptions and dinner parties—he spent about a quarter of a million dollars of his own money for the political entertaining that is a part of the job. They were both very popular with the British, from the royals to the man and his wife in the street.

The mass of British people have always been fascinated by

wealth, long for it themselves, and get a vicarious thrill when someone else has it. The first question visiting celebrities are asked by the press on arrival is "Are you rich?" Jock and Betsy are rich enough to satisfy a continent.

During his tenure as ambassador, Mr. Whitney bought the *New York Herald-Tribune*. After a valiant struggle to make the failing newspaper a success, he was forced by strikes and rising costs to close it down. He has an interest in the combination *Tribune-Times-Post*, still published in Paris.

The Whitney interests are too numerous to mention, except to say that they cover every field: the arts—he is chairman of The Museum of Modern Art in New York—magazines by the score, industry, aviation, and the theater.

When he considered backing the play *Life with Father*, he asked his close friend Robert Benchley, critic for *The New Yorker* magazine, whether he thought it would be a good investment. Bob told me the story. "I advised him against the play, but he went ahead and made another fortune."

When Benchley borrowed money from Jock, he insisted on paying five percent interest, to which Whitney finally agreed, as much for Bob's pride as the fact that he is a good businessman who wants a return on his money. Except from the charities, which add up to almost the hundred million dollars he inherited. He is a great philanthropist. In 1970 he donated $15 million to Yale University, which had become coeducational, to provide more lodging for the students. He has given a great deal to his Alma Mater.

Apart from the charities and horses—the "Greentree" stables, which he owns with his sister, Mrs. Joan Payson, have produced many winners; if not, he would surely have sold them —he is careful with his money. He obviously has remembered his father's advice: "Don't be wasteful just because you're rich."

A man making a deal for some Whitney land tried to get it cheaply by claiming that as a young man starting in life he had pulled a pushcart. "You tell him," Mr. Whitney replied, "that your uncle Jock may not have started off with a pushcart, but he has no intention of ending up with one either!"

While rich and social, neither Betsy nor Jock have cared about the attention that is afforded their class. When the New

York *Social Register* asked them for verification of residences, etc., Jock asked to have their names dropped, explaining, "Betsy and the kids and I felt it was anti the American scene."

The "kids," Sara and Kate, have long since married, with children of their own. Heiress Sara was married in 1953 to Anthony di Bonaventura, the musician son of a New York Italian barber. The older Bonaventura had come to New York from Italy as a young man of twenty-two. All his children were musical. Tony's sister, Anna, was a music teacher. Sara was a frequent visitor at their home and enjoyed the music and the Italian home cooking.

Tony had just graduated from the Curtis Institute of Music in Philadelphia when Betsy announced the engagement to her daughter. It was stated that he was the son of Mr. and Mrs. Fred di Bonaventura of 349 East Seventeenth Street, a poor section of New York City. Dad ran the three-chair barber shop across the street from the apartment. Betsy and Jock attended the ceremony in a small Catholic church in Lower Manhattan. Afterward, they all went to the senior Bonaventuras' apartment on the East Side and stuffed to the hilt with delicious pasta, the creation of Tony's mother. Jock provided the champagne. He also gave the young couple a house on his Greentree estate in Manhasset, Long Island.

Tony had met "Loi," as her friends call her, while she was a student at Bryn Mawr and he was studying music in Philadelphia. They saw each other at various parties and began going around together. He was asked when he had first learned that she would inherit a fortune. "It was common knowledge," he replied. "I didn't think one way or another about it. She never mentioned it to me, and I never asked."

When they tied the knot at the Mary Help of Christians Church on East Twelfth Street, the block was closed off and the street was jammed with people, some of whom threw bits of newspaper at them in lieu of confetti. Tony was twenty-three, Sara twenty-one.

While he was in the army, Sara, on June 10, 1954, gave birth to their first child, a son. Tony has made good in his career as a pianist. He has played at Carnegie Hall and Town Hall, and at one time they spent four years touring Europe while he performed at concerts.

I wish I could write that Sara and Tony lived happily ever after. Alas, they were divorced in December, 1972, in a hearing that lasted less than five minutes.

Sister Kate was luckier. When she married William Haddad in October of 1959, he was working as a reporter for the *New York Post*, where he won two awards for his stories exposing slum conditions and municipal graft. Kate had refused to make a formal entrance into society, explaining, "We don't care for debuts."

Mr. Haddad has made a name as a crusader to improve conditions for the poor. In 1964 he tried for the Democratic congressional nomination on a reform platform, but he was defeated by the incumbent Democrat, Leonard Farbstein, who described Haddad as a rich man's son, "when in fact," Bill told the voters, "my family was on welfare when I was a boy." But the accusation stuck. After all, his wife's stepfather was John Hay Whitney, the multimillionaire. They have three children, all girls. Camilla (called Scrumpy), Laura (Tweaky), and Andrea (Bebo).

In 1971 William became executive chairman of the Committee for Public Education and Religious Liberty. He was an associate director of the Peace Corps, and at one time tried to start a newspaper, *The Manhattan Tribune*, "to bridge the gap between angry, frustrated blacks, and frightened whites." But the money men were not interested and he would not go to his wife's stepfather, whose family has been true-blue Republican since his maternal great-great-grandfather, John Hay, was private secretary to President Lincoln, ambassador to England, and Secretary of State under Presidents William McKinley and that fierce Republican, Theodore Roosevelt.

But Mr. Whitney's own immediate family are Democrats—including Betsy, who went over to FDR when she married James Roosevelt. Did she change again when she married Jock? If she did, she kept it quiet like the tactful lady she is.

What a pity Mama Cushing is not alive to see the present happiness of her three daughters, Minnie, Betsy, and Babe, who I am sure delighted her by each marrying a multimillionaire, men who looked for charm and intelligence in their respective wives.

24. *Rich As Rockefeller*

BARBARA (BOBO) Eva Paul Jievute Paulekiute Sears Rockefeller is fifty-six years old. She lives in Switzerland. Her marriage in 1948 to Winthrop Rockefeller, grandson of the billionaire oil tycoon John D., was the Cinderella story of the decade. The nuptials in Palm Beach on Valentine's Day, at the home of Mr. and Mrs. Winston Guest, were attended by the Duke and Duchess of Windsor, the Marquess of Blandford, "Prince" Mike Romanoff, and heiress Brenda Frazier.

There was almost as much publicity as for the Watergate hearings. The marriage of the poor girl, daughter of a Lithuanian-born miner, to the most eligible man of the day brought forth bushels of adjectives from excited society and news reporters. It was even more than Rita Hayworth received when she married Aly Khan.

Barbara had been married before—to Richard Sears, Jr., a moderately well off, socially prominent Bostonian. Winthrop's marriage to Barbara Sears—whom he nicknamed Bobo—was his first. When they divorced, he was the only one of John D.

the Second's five sons ever to leave a wife. Later, brother Nelson would shed his mate of thirty years to marry the lady known as Happy Murphy.

I knew Bobo in Hollywood when she was trying to make it as a movie actress. Honey-haired, blue-eyed, and pretty, she had won a Lithuanian beauty contest at the Century of Progress Exposition in the Chicago 1933 World's Fair. "It opened up a whole new life for me," she said later. "When I said I was thirsty, someone rushed to bring me a glass of water. It was the first time in my life that I had been pampered." She used some of the money she earned with the title to attend Northwestern University for a short while—studying drama— then worked as a model in Chicago and New York. In New York she had lived with her sister in a cheap walkup apartment on Third Avenue with the clatter of the El railroad rattling the dishes and disturbing their sleep.

As I have pointed out, modeling is the fast route to Hollywood (and/or marriage to a rich man). Barbara's career as an actress was not too successful. Her two marriages, to the Harvard-educated Mr. Sears and Winthrop Rockefeller, did not last long either.

As a starlet at 20th Century-Fox, Bobo played bit roles in Western movies, earning $75 a week. In Hollywood, home was an old, small apartment house near the studio. Her best friend was another poor girl, Lucy Cochrane, also a starlet under contract to the same studio. Lucy's family were socially prominent in Boston, although her mother had been a small-time actress. At one time they shared an apartment together in Hollywood. Lucy, like Bobo, went on to marry a multimillionaire, Winston Guest. It gave her pleasure to serve as Bobo's matron of honor.

Cee Zee Guest, as Lucy is called, is one of the top society hostesses in New York, Long Island, and Palm Beach. Her polo-playing husband is not quite as rich as he was, but there are still many millions to maintain their social position and the three homes they own. Lucy has been smarter than Bobo. She has made a success of her marriage. She is not as warm and friendly as Bobo, but she's a powerful woman who knew what she wanted and how to keep it. From her style of living since the marriage to Winston, you would think she had always lived richly.

It is hard to believe that when Cee Zee Guest first came to Hollywood to try for fame and fortune she was a beefy lass who weighed slightly more than 150 pounds. As you know from the thousands of newspaper and magazine photographs, the blond, beautiful Mrs. Guest is as svelte as it is possible to be without cracking.

Her old pal Bobo has gained a bit of weight, but it does not worry her. She enjoys her present life, taking it easy at her house in Switzerland and in an apartment near the Champs Elysées in Paris, with many visits to New York City to see her chums. In Palm Beach she usually stays with another girl in this book who made good, Betty McMahon.

Bobo was on view recently in the United States when her son, Winthrop Paul Rockefeller, aged twenty-two, and Deborah Cluett Sage, twenty, were married. They had met at Oxford, before Winthrop dropped out. His mother and father attended the church ceremony at Williamsburg, Virginia. Bobo was described as still good-looking and sparkly.

When Bobo decided to divorce Winthrop, Sr., reams of stuff were given to the newspapers by Bobo, who, according to printed stories at the time, believed her husband's lawyers were trying to nullify her just demands as a Rockefeller wife.

No one knows how much money is in the control of this family, and I wouldn't hazard a guess, but I am sure it is more than a billion dollars. While the case dragged on, Bobo changed lawyers five or six times. She complained in court that her husband had left her penniless and that she was living a hand-to-mouth existence with nowhere to lay her weary head. One night, according to press reports, she managed to get into Winthrop's fifteen-room terraced apartment on Park Avenue with their small son. It took a year to dislodge her.

The other Rockefellers were aghast. The conservative family had never experienced this sort of publicity, and they wanted it to end. Which is why Winthrop finally agreed to a settlement for Bobo of $5.5 million, and a $3 million trust fund for their son. Bobo retained custody of the boy, but his father was granted visiting rights.

When she moved out of the penthouse into a hotel, the $30,000 engagement ring from her rich husband had disappeared. "And I had only just taken it out of pawn," she wailed. "It's the only valuable piece of jewelry I had and it kept me going these past two years."

I could have wept for her, remembering the fairy-tale wonderful wedding. Poor Cinderella, returned to the hearth. But strong women always come out ahead, especially if their husbands hate scandalous publicity. When Bobo obtained the divorce in Reno in 1954, it was on the grounds that she and the oil millionaire had been separated for five years, which gave them little more than a year of wedded bliss.

Bobo is a Virgo. She was born on September 16, 1917, in a small mining town in Pennsylvania, where many Lithuanian immigrants worked in the coal mines. She was six years old when her parents divorced, and her mother took her to Chicago, where they lived near the odorous stockyards. Bobo did not see her father for thirty-one years, not until the spring of 1954. He was in a hospital with a heart condition when she visited him shortly before she obtained her divorce. Perhaps Bobo's own troubles had made her more sympathetic, but it is hard for a child of six to forgive and forget such parental desertion. Ingrid Bergman's daughter, Pia, was twice that age when the star ran to Roberto Rossellini in Rome, but it took many years for the reconciliation with her mother.

Bobo's father was known as Jieuve Paulekiute when he immigrated to the United States. He Americanized his name to Julius. But it was still too foreign-sounding for his honey-haired daughter, Jievute, who Anglicized and shortened her name to Eva Paul. Under this name she appeared in road companies in *School for Brides*, and *You Can't Take It with You*, the small roles that led to her meeting Richard Sears in Boston, where she was playing Pearl, the slatternly girl in *Tobacco Road*.

During the estrangement from Winthrop, she stated airily, "I was surprised to find that the Rockefellers were included in the *Social Register*. The Sears family considered them merchants." She used to refer to herself as Mrs. Rockingpuss, and when asked about her social position, replied, "It's easier to go from the bottom to the top and skip the whole middle class.

My mother was a strict old-fashioned European. She wasn't much different from the correct Bostonians I hobnobbed with during my first marriage."

While she was fighting for the settlement with Winthrop, Bobo read many books on trusts, tax laws, and personal estate planning. "If you're going to have any money at all," she explained, "you might as well know how to handle it intelligently." She has increased the record settlement from Mr. Rockefeller with good investments and the buying and selling of antiques. She has been a good and strict mother and has raised her son to know the value of money. He is the only Rockefeller extant who can speak Lithuanian as well as English.

Before deciding to live in Switzerland, Bobo's residence in Manhattan was a four-story white stone house in the fashionable East sixties. She converted the rooftop into a baseball court for her son.

Unlike her friend Cee Zee, Bobo has a sense of humor. The year after the divorce from Winthrop, her Christmas card was of Rockefeller Plaza. Her temperament has a high boiling point. When a maid accidentally dropped a lighted match on the dining-room carpet, burning part of it, Bobo shrugged and said, "It doesn't matter, it's only a rug." She is a good cook and specializes in Lithuanian dishes.

Bobo has changed in recent years. She now wants to help the world. She was in a Palm Beach garden having a few beers—beer is her tipple—when she suddenly stood up and exclaimed, "I'm violently in geopolitics." She made a bid to buy a local society magazine to change it into a political magazine—"to straddle the globe." You can see what money can do to a once-poor peasant girl!

Winthrop, who served many years as Governor of Arkansas, after the divorce from Bobo, died of cancer last year in Palm Springs, California. He had married again, but that too ended in divorce. Winthrop, Jr., and his wife are living happily ever after, we hope, on Papa's farm in Arkansas.

So, in a small way, you could call this a happy ending to Bobo's story. She has money, and as the queen mother, her son and his wife make her welcome at the rich Rockefeller home.

Steven and Anne Marie

When Mrs. Nelson Rockefeller wrote a reference for her maid, Anne Marie Rasmussen, dated November 14, 1957, she stated, "She has shown herself to be absolutely honest, sober and reliable. She has a very pleasant personality, is most willing, and is very clean and neat. Everybody in the house, including the children, was very fond of her. We are sorry to lose her, and wish her all success."

Mary Todhunter Clark Rockefeller was a powerful wisher. Eighteen months later, Governor Nelson Rockefeller and his wife officially announced the engagement of their son Steven to their former housemaid, Anne Marie.

The governor did not sound overpleased about the match, but accepted the fact gracefully, and stated that he considered her "a very attractive and intelligent young lady. I have a very high regard for this girl. It is their life and their decision and I am in back of them. They are the ones who are concerned and it is their decision."

If his speech was not as enthusiastic as it would have been for a pretty young lady in the *Social Register*, the news was received joyfully in Anne Marie's native Norway. It took precedence over a news event concerning King Olav. Norway's defense minister, Nils Handal, exclaimed happily, "I feel as if millions of dollars are streaming in at this moment."

With all that money in the Rockefeller bank vault, Steven has never been impressed by the wealth of his family. He is the third of the five children of Nelson and his first wife: Rodman, Ann (Mrs. Robert L. Pierson), Steven, and the twins, Michael and Mary. Michael drowned on an expedition to find primitive art in Borneo.

Steven was twenty-three when he married his mother's twenty-one-year-old ex-maid. Young, but his father had married at the age of twenty-one. Steven graduated from Princeton in 1958 and helped his father's campaign for governor. In January, 1959, he enlisted in the army under the reserve training program for six months' active service, which left him free to marry later in the year without the interruption of the draft. He immediately flew to Oslo, then to Sogne, where Anne Marie's father, a former fisherman, was operating a general store.

Anne Marie was born on June 10, 1938. Her father's name was then Kristianson. He changed it to his wife's name of Rasmussen. Miss Rasmussen had come to New York in 1956 to learn English. By day she had worked as a maid in the Rockefeller home at 810 Fifth Avenue. In the evenings she attended night school. When her English was more or less understood, she said good-bye to scrubbing floors, making beds, and polishing silver, and took a job as a clerk in Bloomingdale's store, then landed in the same capacity at the Mutual Insurance Company of New York.

Having fulfilled her objective—to learn English—and knowing that she could now get a very good job back home, she returned to Norway. It is traditional among Scandinavians to work in a foreign country, learn the language, and come home for a better position or to marry a local boy or girl and settle there.

Anne Marie had been unofficially engaged to a young Norwegian, twenty-two-year-old Tor Frysaa, a carpenter's assistant, before she left for New York, where she had lived with relatives in the Bronx, afterward renting a room from Mrs. Karl Mattson, a cabinetmaker's widow. This lady, interviewed after the engagement to Steven, remembered he had often called to take the blue-eyed Miss Rasmussen to the movies, or on long walks, "or they would just sit and talk for hours."

In Mrs. Mattson's opinion, Steven was "wonderful, he is so nice I could listen to him all night. He is no snob. He is tall, dark, and handsome, she's tall and blonde, just as nice as they could be. I don't think you could find a more wonderful couple." When father Rasmussen was asked his opinion about his future son-in-law, he said, "He's not how one sometimes thinks of a millionaire's son—he is a pleasant, quiet boy."

Back in Norway, Anne Marie, before the official announcement, was already wearing her diamond engagement ring. It was so small that Steven smiled and said, when reporters questioned him later, "Yes, it could have been larger." But he had paid for it from his mini-allowance. Steven bought a motorbike in Norway, and Anne Marie was often seen riding with him, her arms tightly around his waist.

A Scandinavian girl who met Steven at this time was disappointed in him. She sniffed, "You certainly wouldn't think he was a millionaire when you look at his clothes. His shoes especially. They are awful—old and dirty tennis shoes."

Two other girls who had formerly dated Steven described him as quiet, artistic, sensitive, intellectual, a young man who doesn't flash his money, who liked long walks, not much of a drinker, and lots of fun. One was a showgirl at the Latin Quarter nightclub, the other an actress-model. I wonder what had made Steven so insecure that he did not date girls of his own plateau and upbringing.

The marriage took place in the bride's hometown. Steven would have preferred the small sixteenth-century wooden church in Sogne. He said it was more primitive and beautiful. But Anne Marie wanted the seventeenth-century steepled "new" church. I am sure she chose it because it was large, so that all the people she knew could see her in all her glory, the fisherman's daughter who had captured the son of one of the richest men in the world. The governor in a way *did* give money to Norway. Instead of "the millions rolling in," the Rockefeller Foundation gave a grant of $9,900 to the Institute of Social Research in Oslo.

Anne Marie's Uncle Svendsen—a policeman—and aunt, who lived in the Bronx, came home for the wedding. The church doors, at the back and on the side, were boarded up, and a policeman was stationed at the front entrance to keep out the crashers. It seemed that everyone in the town wanted to attend and claimed friendship or relationship.

A Rockefeller family member and a Rasmussen relative double-checked the names of the guests. All of Sogne's policemen were drafted to keep order among the five thousand people milling outside the church in spite of the rain, and outside the reception hall. As the town had only three policemen, and forty were required, surrounding communities loaned their men. There is a Norwegian proverb that rain on the wedding day means that the bride would be rich.

Anne Marie's former boyfriend, Tor, boycotted the marriage.

Reporters tried to get a statement from him, but he refused to talk. It was an official holiday for the whole town of Sogne, and the entire military guard of twenty-nine were brought in to help the police in keeping order.

A news service estimated Steven's personal fortune at $50 million, which was double that of the richest man in Norway. Some of the townspeople expressed shock at the cost of the wedding—$1,500—which normally the bride's father would have to pay. It was as much as his annual retirement income, so you know who paid.

Steve's wedding present to Anne Marie was a $27 instrument, a cross between a harp and a zither, which the bride had learned to play as a young girl. This would go with them to America. Two of his brothers, Michael and Rodman, were among the six ushers. The other four were Princeton buddies of Steven, all of whom had been staying in the Rasmussen home. Because of the Norwegian tradition that bride and groom must separate before the marriage, Steven had moved into a hotel with his family. Another tradition of the country is that the ceremony omits rings. Steven insisted on a platinum ring for his bride. But there was no kiss after they were pronounced man and wife. It simply is not done in the cold northern regions.

The bride wore a floor-length white brocade duchesse satin and tulle gown. The veil was short, and her vows did not include the word "obey." Fruit punch instead of champagne was served—the Rasmussens are teetotalers—at the reception at the nearby town of Kristiansand, where Anne Marie's forbears on her father's side had lived for the past four hundred years. Some newspapers made a point of this, criticizing the hullabaloo and what was this Cinderella thing—nearly everyone in the world was poor compared to a Rockefeller. There is no dancing at Norwegian weddings—maybe for the same reason as no kissing. But Steven danced with his wife, and felt foolish because no other couples followed suit.

The governor attended at a big press reception during which Mr. Rasmussen was jostled out. Rockefeller pulled him back in, embraced him, and said, "You're a darn good sport. You're a true Norwegian," and mentioned that his oldest son, Rodman, who was then twenty-seven, had also married a lady of Scandinavian descent.

The bride and groom dodged newspapermen by going off in a large limousine, but came back to spend the wedding night at the Rasmussen home. Another Norwegian tradition? The next day they flew to New York with the Rockefeller family and their guests. The couple lived quietly in their New York apartment. Their son, Steven, Jr., was born on July 21, 1960. Baby Ingrid Rockefeller arrived three years later. Jennifer had been added to the family by the time their surprise separation was announced in 1969. What happened? No one was talking.

They had been living in a house on the Rockefeller estate in Pocantico Hills in New York State. Anne Marie still lives there. Her nickname of Mia was revealed at the time of the separation. Sadly she divorced her multimillionaire husband in Juarez, Mexico. Steven agreed that she should have custody of the children. The settlement was described as "generous."

What a pity that such a beautiful love story, of the poor servant girl and the rich nice son of her employer, had to end in divorce. If this had been a fairy tale, they would have lived happily ever after.

25. I'd Rather Scrub Floors?

I SOMETIMES WONDER why I have never wanted to marry a rich man. Is it because so many are not likable, that the money they make or inherit turns them into smug, arrogant ogres? Or is it that I do not believe I could cope with a rich man as most of the ladies in this book have done?

Could I handle a Henry Ford? Could I be as good a hostess as Dru Mallory Heinz? I doubt it. I could never be as elegant and cultured a mate for William Paley as his wife, the former "Babe" Cushing. Or as interested in the power that comes with money as Jacqueline Bouvier Kennedy Onassis has been.

Could I have been comfortable as the wife of Jock Whitney during his tenure as U.S. Ambassador to the Court of Saint James? Or as generous with inherited money as Huntington Hartford? Or as happy as ballerina Doreen Wells with her Marquess of Londonderry? I'll never know. And yet I too was a dancer, and I too have learned along the way, from orphanage to factory, to servant girl, to the chorus, to society lady, to Hollywood columnist, Palm Beach party goer, and writer of books.

My first husband, Major John Graham Gillam, D.S.O., taught me manners and had me presented to the King and Queen of

England in the same year as Mrs. Wallis Warfield Simpson, who never had to work for her living, while I am still at it. My beginnings were as good as, if not better than, the British actress whose father was a barber and who lived with her married, titled lover for years, and had children with him and finally married him after the new divorce laws made it possible. Or the American nightclub floosie who married into a rich social family and who later figured in a messy scandal. Or the former manicurist who married a multimillionaire business tycoon with homes all over the world. Or the expensive "call girls" who are now among the richest society queens. Or the jet set girl who lived by her wits, as the saying goes, and married one of the richest dukes in Britain. Or to go all the way back to Theodora, a strip-teaser who married Justinian, the Roman Emperor.

The fact is I am uncomfortable with rich men, not as uptight with rich women, although I was never really at ease with Josephine Bryce, or Barbara Hutton, or Nancy Oakes. I could never be quite natural with them. As Scott Fitzgerald noted, the rich *are* different from the rest of us. They seem superior, although some are not. They have an aura of "we can have everything."

We make allowances for the rich, we speak of them in awed tones, we are nicer to them. They have people running around for them, relieving the day-to-day problems that plague other mortals. They do not have to add up the cost.

Of course, the rich have sorrows too—Miss Hutton losing her son, an only child; multimillionairess Dina Merrill recently mourning her son and her mother, Mrs. Marjorie Post, within the same week; wealthy Mrs. Clare Luce also lost her daughter, an only child, in an accident in Europe. All the money in the world cannot compensate for the loss of one beloved life. But these tragedies happen to poor people as well, and for them there is no cruise or visit to another place or collapse into a private suite in a hospital.

I have come to the conclusion, rather late in life, it is better to be rich. In my youthful arrogance I used to say "I'd rather scrub floors than be married to a rich man I did not love." I'm not sure I would say that today. When you are older you don't have to love a man to be happy with him. Liking can last longer than loving. Was Mrs. Luce right when a character in her play *The Women* said, "It's being together at the end that counts"? I don't altogether agree, but if you are alone and getting on a bit, a large wad of dollars can provide a comfortable cushion for aching memories—and bones.

I, foolish girl, decided at an early age to make good in life through a career. Without realizing it, I have been a Woman's Libber all my life. I have always worked, always detested housework. I still cannot cook, except for the simplest dishes. I have paid the rent during two of my marriages. I have never enjoyed taking, I have always given. I have been uncomfortable when I had to ask for a favor. But lately I have decided it is just as blessed to receive as to give.

It occurred to me recently that I have robbed potential givers of the pleasure *I* receive in helping others, either with time or money. The rich men and women who marry poor girls and boys have, in most cases, great satisfaction that they can do so much for the people they like or love. I realize now that I have been stupid to have turned down some millionaires chiefly because of their money. I didn't give myself a chance to learn to love them; while I have usually had confidence in my work, I have lacked the inner ego possessed by the characters in *How to Marry Super Rich*.

Today I would like to be the wife of a rich man, to be pampered, to have the easy life he could give me. I would like to be driven in a chauffeured limousine. Although I quite like driving my own car, it's the finding a parking space that is exhausting. I'd like to have an internationally famous chef, as Gregg Moran has, and a live-in staff of servants. With the prices you pay for help today, only the multimillionaires can afford this. I'd like to have someone pay all the monthly bills, so that I could lavish what I earn by writing—without the harassing deadline—on my three grandchildren, whom I adore. I might even give my critics pleasure by not writing at all!

In brief, I want to marry rich. Perhaps it is too late. In any case, I don't want to marry a rich *young* man and I doubt whether he would want to marry me, and the *old* rich men seem to have eyes only for the pretty chicks. But, to reiterate my creed in life, you can get what you want if you really want it. So . . .